Mometrix

TEST PREPARATION

M000275317

TExES

Core Subjects EC-6 (391)

Secrets Study Guide

Part 3 of 3

DEAR FUTURE EXAM SUCCESS STORY

First of all, **THANK YOU** for purchasing Mometrix study materials!

Second, congratulations! You are one of the few determined test-takers who are committed to doing whatever it takes to excel on your exam. **You have come to the right place.** We developed these study materials with one goal in mind: to deliver you the information you need in a format that's concise and easy to use.

In addition to optimizing your guide for the content of the test, we've outlined our recommended steps for breaking down the preparation process into small, attainable goals so you can make sure you stay on track.

We've also analyzed the entire test-taking process, identifying the most common pitfalls and showing how you can overcome them and be ready for any curveball the test throws you.

Standardized testing is one of the biggest obstacles on your road to success, which only increases the importance of doing well in the high-pressure, high-stakes environment of test day. Your results on this test could have a significant impact on your future, and this guide provides the information and practical advice to help you achieve your full potential on test day.

Your success is our success

We would love to hear from you! If you would like to share the story of your exam success or if you have any questions or comments in regard to our products, please contact us at **800-673-8175** or **support@mometrix.com**.

Thanks again for your business and we wish you continued success!

Sincerely,
The Mometrix Test Preparation Team

Need more help? Check out our flashcards at:
http://mometrixflashcards.com/TExES

Written and edited by the Mometrix Exam Secrets Test Prep Team
Printed in the United States of America

TABLE OF CONTENTS

Social Studies

Government and Citizenship

Principles of the Constitution

The six basic principles of the Constitution are:

1. **Popular Sovereignty** – The people establish government and give power to it; the government can function only with the consent of the people.
2. **Limited Government** – The Constitution specifies limits on government authority, and no official or entity is above the law.
3. **Separation of Powers** – Power is divided among three government branches: the legislative (Congress), the executive (President), and the judicial (federal courts).
4. **Checks and Balances** – This is a system that enforces the separation of powers and ensures that each branch has the authority and ability to restrain the powers of the other two branches, thus preventing tyranny.
5. **Judicial Review** – Judges in the federal courts ensure that no act of government is in violation of the Constitution. If an act is unconstitutional, the judicial branch has the power to nullify it.
6. **Federalism** – This is the division of power between the central government and local governments, which limits the power of the federal government and allows states to deal with local problems.

Classic Forms of Government

Forms of government that have appeared throughout history include:

- **Feudalism** – This is based on the rule of local lords who are loyal to the king and control the lives and production of those who work on their land.
- **Classical republic** – This form is a representative democracy. Small groups of elected leaders represent the interests of the electorate.
- **Absolute monarchy** – A king or queen has complete control of the military and government.
- **Authoritarianism** – An individual or group has unlimited authority. There is no system in place to restrain the power of the government.
- **Dictatorship** – Those in power are not held responsible to the people.
- **Autocracy** – This is rule by one person (despot), not necessarily a monarch, who uses power tyrannically.
- **Oligarchy** – A small, usually self-appointed elite rules a region.
- **Liberal democracy** – This is a government based on the consent of the people that protects individual rights and freedoms from any intolerance by the majority.
- **Totalitarianism** – All facets of the citizens' lives are controlled by the government.

Influences of Philosophers on Political Study

Ancient Greek philosophers **Aristotle** and **Plato** believed political science would lead to order in political matters, and that this scientifically organized order would create stable, just societies.

Thomas Aquinas adapted the ideas of Aristotle to a Christian perspective. His ideas stated that individuals have certain rights, but also certain duties, and that these rights and duties should determine the type and extent of government rule. In stating that laws should limit the role of government, he laid the groundwork for ideas that would eventually become modern constitutionalism.

Niccolò Machiavelli, author of *The Prince*, was a proponent of politics based solely on power.

Parliamentary and Democratic Systems of Government

In a **parliamentary system**, government involves a legislature and a variety of political parties. The head of government, usually a Prime Minister, is typically the head of the dominant party. A head of state can be elected, or this position can be taken by a monarch, such as in Great Britain's constitutional monarchy system.

In a **democratic system** of government, the people elect their government representatives. The term democracy is a Greek term that means "for the rule of the people." There are two forms of democracy—direct and indirect. In a direct democracy, each issue or election is decided by a vote where each individual is counted separately. An indirect democracy employs a legislature that votes on issues that affect large number of people whom the legislative members represent. Democracy can exist as a Parliamentary system or a Presidential system. The US is a presidential, indirect democracy.

Bill of Rights

The **United States Bill of Rights** was based on principles established by the **Magna Carta** in 1215, the 1688 **English Bill of Rights**, and the 1776 **Virginia Bill of Rights**. In 1791, the federal government added 10 amendments to the United States Constitution that provided the following **protections**:

- Freedom of speech, religion, peaceful assembly, petition of the government, and petition of the press
- The right to keep and bear arms
- No quartering of soldiers on private property without the consent of the owner
- Regulations on government search and seizure
- Provisions concerning prosecution
- The right to a speedy, public trial and the calling of witnesses
- The right to trial by jury
- Freedom from excessive bail or cruel punishment
- These rights are not necessarily the only rights
- Powers not prohibited by the Constitution are reserved to the states

Review Video: Bill of Rights
Visit mometrix.com/academy and enter code: 585149

Making a Formal Amendment to the Constitution

So far, there have been only **27 amendments** to the federal Constitution. There are four different ways to change the constitution: two methods for proposal and two methods for ratification:

1. An amendment is proposed by a two-thirds vote in each house of Congress and ratified by three-fourths of the state legislatures.
2. An amendment is proposed by a two-thirds vote in each house of Congress and ratified by three-fourths of the states in special conventions called for that purpose.

3. An amendment is proposed by a national convention that is called by Congress at the request of two-thirds of the state legislatures and ratified by three-fourths of the state legislatures.
4. An amendment is proposed by a national convention that is called by Congress at the request of two-thirds of the state legislatures and ratified by three-fourths of the states in special conventions called for that purpose.

Division of Powers

The **division of powers** in the federal government system is as follows:

- **National** – This level can coin money, regulate interstate and foreign trade, raise and maintain armed forces, declare war, govern United States territories and admit new states, and conduct foreign relations.
- **Concurrent** – This level can levy and collect taxes, borrow money, establish courts, define crimes and set punishments, and claim private property for public use.
- **State** – This level can regulate trade and business within the state, establish public schools, pass license requirements for professionals, regulate alcoholic beverages, conduct elections, and establish local governments.

There are three types of **delegated powers** granted by the Constitution:

1. **Expressed or enumerated powers** – These are specifically spelled out in the Constitution.
2. **Implied** – These are not expressly stated, but are reasonably suggested by the expressed powers.
3. **Inherent** – These are powers not expressed by the Constitution but ones that national governments have historically possessed, such as granting diplomatic recognition.

Powers can also be classified as reserved or exclusive. **Reserved powers** are not granted to the national government, but not denied to the states. **Exclusive powers** are those reserved to the national government, including concurrent powers.

Stages of Extending Suffrage in the U.S.

Originally, the Constitution of 1789 provided the right to vote only to white male property owners. Through the years, suffrage was extended through the following five stages.

1. In the early 1800s, states began to eliminate **property ownership** and **tax payment qualifications**.
2. By 1810, there were no more **religious tests** for voting. In the late 1800s, the 15th Amendment protected citizens from being denied the right to vote because of **race or color**.
3. In 1920, the 19th Amendment prohibited the denial of the right to vote because of **gender**, and women were given the right to vote.
4. Passed in 1961 and ratified in 1964, the 23rd Amendment added the voters of the **District of Columbia** to the presidential electorate and eliminated the poll tax as a condition for voting in federal elections. The **Voting Rights Act of 1965** prohibited disenfranchisement through literacy tests and various other means of discrimination.
5. In 1971, the 26th Amendment set the minimum voting age at **18 years of age**.

Major Supreme Court Cases

Out of the many Supreme Court rulings, several have had critical historical importance. These include:

- **Marbury v. Madison** (1803) – This ruling established judicial review as a power of the Supreme Court.
- **Dred Scott v. Sandford** (1857) – This decision upheld property rights over human rights in the case of a slave who had been transported to a free state by his master, but was still considered a slave.
- **Brown v. Board of Education** (1954) – The Court ruled that segregation was a violation of the Equal Protection Clause and that the "separate but equal" practice in education was unconstitutional. This decision overturned the 1896 Plessy v. Ferguson ruling that permitted segregation if facilities were equal.
- **Miranda v. Arizona** (1966) – This ruling compelled the reading of Miranda rights to those arrested for crimes the law. It ensured that confessions could not be illegally obtained and that citizen rights to fair trials and protection under the law would be upheld.

Review Video: Marbury v. Madison
Visit mometrix.com/academy and enter code: 573964

Review Video: What was the Dred Scott Decision?
Visit mometrix.com/academy and enter code: 364838

Famous Speeches in U.S. History that Defined Government Policy, Foreign Relations, and American Spirit

Among the best-known speeches and famous lines known to modern Americans are the following:

- The **Gettysburg Address** – Made by Abraham Lincoln on November 19, 1863, it dedicated the Gettysburg battleground's cemetery.
- The **Fourteen Points** – Made by Woodrow Wilson on January 18, 1918, this outlined Wilson's plans for peace and the League of Nations.
- **Address to Congress** – Made by Franklin Roosevelt on December 8, 1941, it declared war on Japan and described the attack on Pearl Harbor as "a day which will live in infamy."
- **Inaugural Address** – Made by John F. Kennedy on January 20, 1961, it contained the famous line: "Ask not what your country can do for you, ask what you can do for your country."
- **Berlin Address** – Made by John F. Kennedy on June 26, 1963, it contained the famous line "Ich bin ein Berliner," which expressed empathy for West Berliners in their conflict with the Soviet Union.
- "**I Have a Dream**" and "**I See the Promised Land**" – Made by Martin Luther King, Jr. on August 28, 1963 and April 3, 1968, respectively, these speeches were hallmarks of the Civil Rights Movement.
- **Brandenburg Gate speech** – Made by Ronald Reagan on June 12, 1987, this speech was about the Berlin Wall and the end of the Cold War. It contained the famous line "Tear down this wall."

Closed and Open Primaries in a Direct Primary System

The **direct primary system** is a means for members of a political party to participate in the selection of a candidate from their party to compete against the other party's candidate in a general election. A **closed primary** is a party nominating election in which only declared party members can vote. Party membership is usually established by registration. Currently, 26 states and the District of Columbia use this system. An **open primary** is a party nominating election in which any qualified voter can take part. The voter makes a public choice at the polling place about which primary to participate in, and the choice does not depend on any registration or previous choices. A **blanket primary**, which allowed voters to vote in the primaries of both parties, was used at various times by three states. The Supreme Court ruled against this practice in 2000.

Important Documents in United States History and Government

The following are among the greatest **American documents** because of their impact on foreign and domestic policy:

- Declaration of Independence (1776)
- The Articles of Confederation (1777)
- The Constitution (1787) and the Bill of Rights (1791)
- The Northwest Ordinance (1787)
- The Federalist Papers (1787-88)
- George Washington's Inaugural Address (1789) and Farewell Address (1796)
- The Alien and Sedition Act (1798)
- The Louisiana Purchase Treaty (1803)
- The Monroe Doctrine (1823); The Missouri Compromise (1830)
- The Compromise of 1850
- The Kansas-Nebraska Act (1854)
- The Homestead Act (1862)
- The Emancipation Proclamation (1863)
- The agreement to purchase Alaska (1866)
- The Sherman Anti-Trust Act (1890)
- Theodore Roosevelt's Corollary to the Monroe Doctrine (1905)
- The Social Security Act (1935) and other acts of the New Deal in the 1930s; The Truman Doctrine (1947); The Marshall Plan (1948)
- The Civil Rights Act (1964)

Federal Taxes

The four types of **federal taxes** are:

- **Income taxes on individuals** – This is a complex system because of demands for various exemptions and rates. Further, the schedule of rates can be lowered or raised according to economic conditions in order to stimulate or restrain economic activity. For example, a tax cut can provide an economic stimulus, while a tax increase can slow down the rate of inflation. Personal income tax generates about five times as much as corporate taxes. Rates are based on an individual's income, and range from 10 to 35 percent.
- **Income taxes on corporations** – The same complexity of exemptions and rates exists for corporations as individuals. Taxes can be raised or lowered according to the need to stimulate or restrain the economy.
- **Excise taxes** – These are taxes on specific goods such as tobacco, liquor, automobiles, gasoline, air travel, and luxury items, or on activities such as highway usage by trucks.
- **Customs duties** – These are taxes imposed on imported goods. They serve to regulate trade between the United States and other countries.

United States Currency System

The Constitution of 1787 gave the United States Congress the central authority to **print or coin money** and to **regulate its value**. Before this time, states were permitted to maintain separate currencies. The currency system is based on a **modified gold standard**. There is an enormous store of gold to back up United States currency housed at Fort Knox, Kentucky. Paper money is actually **Federal Reserve notes** and coins. It is the job of the Bureau of Engraving and Printing in the Treasury Department to design plates, special types of paper, and other security measures for bills and bonds. This money is put into general circulation by the Treasury and Federal Reserve Banks, and is taken out of circulation when worn out. Coins are made at the Bureau of the Mint in Philadelphia, Denver, and San Francisco.

Employment Act of 1946

The **Employment Act of 1946** established the following entities to combat unemployment:

- The **Council of Economic Advisers** (CEA) – Composed of a chair and two other members appointed by the President and approved by the Senate, this council assists the President with the development and implementation of U.S. economic policy. The Council members and their staff, located in the Executive Office, are professionals in economics and statistics who forecast economic trends and provide analysis based on evidence-based research.
- The **Economic Report of the President** – This is presented every January by the President to Congress. Based on the work of the Council, the report recommends a program for maximizing employment, and may also recommend legislation.
- **Joint Economic Committee** (JEC) – This is a committee composed of 10 members of the House and 10 members of the Senate that makes a report early each year on its continuous study of the economy. Study is conducted through hearings and research, and the report is made in response to the president's recommendations.

Qualifications of a U.S. Citizen

Anyone born in the US, born abroad to a US citizen, or who has gone through a process of **naturalization** to become a citizen, is considered a **citizen** of the United States. It is possible to lose US citizenship as a result of conviction of certain crimes such as treason. Citizenship may also be lost if a citizen pledges an oath to another country or serves in the military of a country engaged in hostilities with the US. A US citizen can also choose to hold dual citizenship, work as an expatriate in another country without losing US citizenship, or even renounce citizenship if he or she so chooses.

Rights, Duties, and Responsibilities Granted to or Expected from US Citizens

Citizens are granted certain rights under the US government. The most important of these are defined in the **Bill of Rights**, and include freedom of speech, religion, assembly, and a variety of other rights the government is not allowed to remove.

Duties of a U.S. citizen include:

- Paying taxes
- Loyalty to the government, though the US does not prosecute those who criticize or seek to change the government
- Support and defend the Constitution
- Serve in the Armed Forces as required by law
- Obeying laws as set forth by the various levels of government.

Responsibilities of a U.S. citizen include:

- Voting in elections
- Respecting one another's rights and not infringing upon them
- Staying informed about various political and national issues
- Respecting one another's beliefs

Representative Democracy

In a system of government characterized as a representative democracy, voters elect **representatives** to act in their interests. Typically, a representative is elected by and responsible to a specific subset of the total population of eligible voters; this subset of the electorate is referred to as a representative's constituency. A **representative democracy** may foster a more powerful legislature than other forms of government systems; to compensate for a strong legislature, most constitutions stipulate that measures must be taken to balance the powers within government, such as the creation of a separate judicial branch. Representative democracy became popular in post-industrial nations where increasing numbers of people expressed an interest in politics, but where technology and census counts remained incompatible with systems of direct democracy. Today, the majority of the world's population resides in representative democracies, including constitutional monarchies that possess a strong representative branch.

Democracy

Democracy, or rule by the people, is a form of government in which power is vested in the people and in which policy decisions are made by the majority in a decision-making process such as an election that is open to all or most citizens. Definitions of democracy have become more generalized and include aspects of society and political culture in democratic societies that do not necessarily represent a form of government. What defines a democracy varies, but some of the characteristics of a democracy could include the presence of a middle class, the presence of a civil society, a free market, political pluralism, universal suffrage, and specific rights and freedoms. In practice however, democracies do have limits on specific freedoms, which are justified as being necessary to maintain democracy and ensure democratic freedoms. For example, freedom of association is limited in democracies for individuals and groups that pose a threat to government or to society.

Presidential/Congressional System

In a **presidential system**, also referred to as a **congressional system**, the legislative branch and the executive branches are elected separately from one another. The features of a presidential system include a *president* who serves as both the head of state and the head of the government, who has no formal relationship with the legislative branch, who is not a voting member, who cannot introduce bills, and who has a fixed term of office. *Elections* are held at scheduled times. The president's *cabinet* carries out the policies of the executive branch and the legislative branch.

Political Parties

A **political party** is an organization that advocates a particular ideology and seeks to gain power within government. The tendency of members of political parties to support their party's policies and interests relative to those of other parties is referred to as partisanship. Often, a political party is comprised of members whose positions, interests and perspectives on policies vary, despite having shared interests in the general ideology of the party. As such, many political parties will have divisions within them that have differing opinions on policy. Political parties are often placed on a political spectrum, with one end of the spectrum representing conservative, traditional values and policies and the other end of the spectrum representing radical, progressive value and policies.

Types of Party Systems

There is a variety of **party systems**, including single-party systems, dominant-party systems, and dual-party systems. In a **single-party system**, only one political party may hold power. In this type of system, minor parties may be permitted, but they must accept the leadership of the dominant party. **Dominant-party systems** allow for multiple parties in opposition of one another, however the dominant party is the only party considered to have power. A **two-party system**, such as in the United States, is one in which there are two dominant political parties. In such a system, it is very difficult for any other parties to win an election. In most two-party systems, there is typically one right wing party and one left wing party.

Democratic Party

The **Democratic Party** was founded in 1792. In the United States, it is one of the two dominant political parties, along with the Republican Party. The Democratic Party is to the left of the Republican Party. The Democratic Party began as a conservative party in the mid-1800s, shifting to the left during the 1900s. There are many factions within the Democratic Party in the United States. The **Democratic National Committee (DNC)** is the official organization of the Democratic Party, and it develops and promotes the party's platform and coordinates fundraising and election strategies. There are Democratic committees in every U.S. state and most U.S. counties. The official symbol of the Democratic Party is the donkey.

Republican Party

The **Republican Party** is often referred to as the **GOP**, which stands for *Grand Old Party*. The Republican Party is considered socially conservative and economically neoliberal relative to the Democratic Party. Like the Democratic Party, there are factions within the Republic Party that agree with the party's overall ideology, but disagree with the party's positions on specific issues. The official symbol of the Republican Party is the elephant. The **Republican National Committee (RNC)** is the official organization of the Republican Party, and it develops and promotes the party's platform and coordinates fundraising and election strategies. There are Republican committees in every U.S. state and most U.S. counties.

Political Campaigns

A **political campaign** is an organized attempt to influence the decisions of a particular group of people. Examples of campaigns could include elections or efforts to influence policy changes. One of the first steps in a campaign is to develop a **campaign message**. The message must then be delivered to the individuals and groups that the campaign is trying to reach and influence through a campaign plan. There are various ways for a campaign to communicate its message to the intended audience, including public media; paid media such as television, radio and newspaper ads, billboards and the internet; public events such as protests and rallies; meetings with speakers; mailings; canvassing; fliers; and websites. Through these efforts, the campaign attempts to attract additional support and, ultimately, to reach the goal of the campaign.

> **Review Video: Political Campaigns**
> Visit mometrix.com/academy and enter code: 838608

Voting

Voting is a method of decision making that allows people to express their opinion or preference for a candidate or for a proposed resolution of an issue. In a democratic system, voting typically takes place as part of an **election**. An individual participates in the voting process by casting a vote, or a **ballot**; ballots are produced by states A *secret ballot* can be used at polls to protect voters' privacy. Individuals can also vote via *absentee ballot*. In some states voters can write-in a name to cast a vote for a candidate that is not on the ballot. Some states also use *straight ticket voting*, allowing the voter to vote for one party for all the elected positions on the ballot.

U.S. Elections

In the United States, **officials** are elected at the federal, state and local levels. The first two articles of the Constitution, as well as various amendments, establish how **federal elections** are to be held. The **President** is elected indirectly, by electors of an electoral college. Members of the electoral college nearly always vote along the lines of the popular vote of their respective states. Members of **Congress** are directly elected. At the state level, state law establishes most aspects of how elections are held. There are many elected offices at the state level, including a governor and state legislature. There are also elected offices at the local level.

Voter Eligibility

The United States Constitution establishes that individual people are permitted to **vote** in elections if they are citizens of the United States and are at least eighteen years old. The **fifteenth** and **nineteenth amendments** of the United States Constitution stipulate that the right to vote cannot be denied to any United States citizen based on race or sex, respectively. States regulate voter eligibility beyond the minimum qualifications stipulated by the United States Constitution. Depending on the regulations of individual states, individuals may be denied the right to vote if they are convicted criminals.

Advantages and Disadvantages to Two-Party System

Advocates of the **two-party system** argue that its advantages are that they are stable because they enable policies and government to change slowly rather than rapidly due to the relative lack of influence from small parties representing unconventional ideologies. In addition, they seem to drive voters toward a middle ground and are less susceptible to revolutions, coups, or civil wars. Among the critiques of the two-party system is the claim that stability in and of itself is not necessarily desirable, as it often comes at the expense of democracy. Critics also argue that the two-party system promotes negative political campaigns, in which candidates and their respective parties only take positions on issues that will differentiate themselves from their opponents, rather than focusing on policy issues that are of significance to citizens. Another concern is that if one of the two major parties becomes weak, a dominant-party system may develop.

Campaign Message

Political campaigns consist of three main elements, which are the campaign message, the money that is necessary to run the campaign, and the "machine," or the capital that is necessary to run the campaign. A campaign message is a succinct statement expressing why voters should support the campaign and the individual or policy associated with that campaign. The message is one of the most significant aspects of a political campaign, and a considerable amount of time, money and effort is invested in devising a successful campaign message, as it will be repeated throughout the campaign and will be one of the most identifying factors of the campaign.

Modern Election Campaigns in the U.S.

Political campaigns in the U.S. have changed and continue to change as advances in technology permit varied campaign methods. Campaigns represent a civic practice, and today they are a high profit industry. The U.S. has an abundance of professional political consultants that employ highly sophisticated campaign management strategies and tools. The election process varies widely between the federal, state and local levels. Campaigns are typically controlled by individual candidates, rather than by the parties that they are associated with. Larger campaigns utilize a vast array of media to reach their targeted audiences, while smaller campaigns are typically limited to direct contact with voters, direct mailings and other forms of low-cost advertising to reach their audiences. In addition to fundraising and spending done by individual candidates, party committees and political action committees also raise money and spend it in ways that will advance the cause of the particular campaign they are associated with.

Voter Registration

Individuals have the responsibility of **registering to vote**. Every state except North Dakota requires citizens to register to vote. In an effort to increase voter turnout, Congress passed the **National Voter Registration Act** in 1993. This Act is also known as "Motor Voter," because it required states to make the voter registration process easier by providing registration services through drivers' license registration centers, as well as through disability centers, schools, libraries, and mail-in registration. Some states are exempt because they permit same-day voter registration, which enables voters to register to vote on the day of the election.

Presidential Elections

The President of the United States is elected **indirectly**, by members of an **electoral college**. Members of the electoral college nearly always vote along the lines of the popular vote of their respective states. The winner of a presidential election is the candidate with at least 270 electoral college votes. It is possible for a candidate to win the electoral vote, and lose the popular vote. Incumbent Presidents and challengers typically prefer a balanced ticket, where the President and Vice President are elected together and generally balance one another with regard to geography, ideology, or experience working in government. The nominated Vice Presidential candidate is referred to as the President's *running mate*.

Electoral College

Electoral college votes are cast by state by a group of electors; each elector casts one electoral college vote. State law regulates how states cast their electoral college votes. In all states except Maine and Nebraska, the candidate winning the most votes receives all the state's electoral college votes. In Maine and Nebraska two electoral votes are awarded based on the winner of the statewide election, and the rest go to the highest vote-winner in each of the state's congressional districts. Critics of the electoral college argue that it is undemocratic because the President is elected indirectly as opposed to directly, and that it creates inequality between voters in different states because candidates focus attention on voters in swing states who could influence election results. Critics argue that the electoral college provides more representation for voters in small states than large states, where more voters are represented by a single electoral than in small states and discriminates against candidates that do not have support concentrated in a given state.

Congressional Elections

Congressional elections are every two years. Members of the **House of Representatives** are elected for a two year term and elections occur every two years on the first Tuesday after November 1st in even years. A Representative is elected from each of the 435 House districts in the U.S. House elections usually occur in the same year as Presidential elections. Members of the **Senate** are elected to six year terms; one-third of the Senate is elected every two years. Per the Seventeenth Amendment to the Constitution, which was passed in 1913, Senators are elected by the electorate of states. The country is divided into **Congressional districts**. Critics argue that this division eliminates voter choice, sometimes creating areas in which Congressional races are uncontested. Every ten years **redistricting** of Congressional districts occurs. However, redistricting is often partisan and therefore reduces the number of competitive districts. The division of voting districts resulting in an unfair advantage to one party in elections is known as gerrymandering. Gerrymandering has been criticized as being undemocratic.

State and Local Elections

State elections are regulated by state laws and constitutions. In keeping with the ideal of separation of powers, the legislature and the executive are elected separately at the state level, as they are at the federal level. In each state, a **Governor** and a **Lieutenant Governor** are elected. In some states, the Governor and Lieutenant Governor are elected on a joint ticket, while in other states they are elected separately from one another. In some states, executive positions such as Attorney General and Secretary of State are also elected offices. All members of state legislatures are elected, including state senators and state representatives. Depending on the state, members of the state supreme court and other members of the state judiciary may be chosen in elections. Local government can include the governments of counties and cities. At this level, nearly all government offices are filled through an election process. Elected local offices may include sheriffs, county school boards, and city mayors.

Campaign Finance and Independent Expenditures

An individual or group is legally permitted to make unlimited **independent expenditures** in association with federal elections. An independent expenditure is an expenditure that is made to pay for a form of communication that supports the election or defeat of a candidate; the expenditure must be made independently from the candidate's own campaign. To be considered independent, the communication may not be made with the cooperation or consultation with, or at the request or suggestion of, any candidate, any committees or political party associated with the candidate, or any agent that acts on behalf of the candidate. There are no restrictions on the amount that anyone may spend on an independent expenditure, however, any individual making an independent expenditure must report it and disclose the source of the funds they used.

Campaign Finance and Activities of Political Parties

Political parties participate in federal elections at the local, state and national levels. Most **party committees** must register with the **Federal Election Committee** and file reports disclosing federal campaign activities. While party committees may contribute funds directly to federal candidates, the amounts that they contribute are restricted by the campaign finance contribution limits. National and state party committees are permitted to make additional **coordinated expenditures**, within limits, to assist their nominees in general elections. However, national party committees are not permitted to make unlimited **independent expenditures**, also known as soft money, to support or oppose federal candidates. State and local party committees are also not permitted to use soft money for the purpose of supporting or opposing federal candidates, but they are allowed to spend soft money, up to a limit of $10,000 per source, on voter registration and on efforts aimed at increasing voter participation. All party committees are required to register themselves and file disclosure reports with the Federal Election Committee once their federal election activities exceed specified monetary limits.

Public Opinion

Public opinion represents the collective attitudes of individual members of the adult population in the United States of America. There are many varied forces that may influence public opinion. These forces include *public relations efforts* on the part of political campaigns and political parties. Another force affecting political opinion is the *political media* and the *mass media*. Public opinion is very important during elections, particularly Presidential elections, as it is an indicator of how candidates are perceived by the public and of how well candidates are doing during their election campaigns. Public opinion is often measured and evaluated using survey sampling.

Mass Media and Public Opinion

The **mass media** is critical in developing public opinion. In the short term people generally evaluate information they receive relative to their own beliefs; in the long term the media may have a considerable impact on people's beliefs. Due to the impact of the media on an individual's beliefs, some experts consider the effects of the media on an individual's independence and autonomy to be negative. Others view the impact of the media on individuals as a positive one, because the media provides information that expands worldviews and enriches lives, and fosters the development of opinions that are informed by many sources of information. A critical aspect of the relationship between the media and public opinion is who is in control of the knowledge and information that is disseminated through the media. Whoever controls the media can propagate their own agenda. The extent to which an individual interprets and evaluates information received through the media can influence behaviors such as voting patterns, consumer behavior, and social attitudes.

Municipalities in Texas

Large

Larger cities (those exceeding 225,000) have a unique authority: that of "**limited annexation**," whereby an adjoining area may be annexed for purposes of imposing city ordinances related to safety and building codes. The residents can vote for mayor and council races but cannot vote in bond elections (and, consequently, the city cannot collect city sales tax from businesses or city property tax from owners). The purpose of limited annexation is to allow the city to control development in an area that it eventually will fully annex; it must do so within three years (though it can arrange "non-annexation agreements" with local property owners). During each of the three years, the city must develop a land use plan, identify needed capital improvements, and identify the financing for such improvements as well as to provide essential services. Municipal elections in Texas are **nonpartisan** in the sense that candidates do not appear on the ballot on party lines, and do not run as party tickets. However, a candidate's party affiliation is usually known or can be discerned with minimal effort (as the candidate most likely has supported other candidates on partisan tickets). In some instances, an informal citizen's group will support a slate of candidates that it desires to see elected. However, each candidate must be voted on individually.

Small

Texas does not have townships; areas within a county are either incorporated or unincorporated. **Incorporated areas** are part of a city, though the city may contract with the county for needed services. **Unincorporated areas** are not part of a city; in these areas the county has authority for law enforcement and road maintenance. Cities are classified as either "general law" or "home rule." A city may elect **home rule status** once it exceeds 5,000 population and the voters agree to home rule. Otherwise, it is classified as **general law** and has very limited powers. One example of the difference in the two structures regards annexation. General law cities cannot annex adjacent unincorporated areas without the property owner's consent; home rule cities may annex without consent but must provide essential services within a specified period of time (generally within three years) or the property owner may file suit to be deannexed. Once a city adopts home rule it may continue to keep this status even if the population later falls below 5,000.

Founders of Republic of Texas

The following are some of the founders of the Republic of Texas and their contributions:

- Stephen F. Austin (1793–1836), "Father of Texas"
- Edward Burleson (1798–1851), Texas soldier, general, and statesman
- David G. Burnet (1788–1870), interim President of the Republic of Texas
- Lorenzo de Zavala (1788–1836), first vice-president of the Republic of Texas and signer of the Texas Declaration of Independence
- Sam Houston (1793–1863), first President of Republic of Texas, later U.S. Senator from Texas and Governor of Texas
- Anson Jones (1798–1858), last President of the Republic of Texas, called the "Architect of Annexation"
- Mirabeau B. Lamar (1798–1859), second President of Republic of Texas
- Jose Antonio Navarro (1795–1871), Texas statesman, revolutionary and politician
- Thomas Jefferson Rusk (1803–1857), Secretary of War between Texas and Mexico, chief justice of the Supreme Court of Texas and Senator from Texas after admission to the Union.
- Edwin Waller (1800–1881), judge, signer of the Texas Declaration of Independence

Important People from Texas During Civil War

The following are some important people from Texas during the Civil War and their contributions:

- Dick Dowling (1838–1867), commander at Sabine Pass and famous Houstonian
- John "Rip" Ford (1815–1897), Texas Rangers legend and commander at the Battle of Palmito Ranch
- John Bell Hood (1831–1879), commander of Hood's Texas Brigade and Confederate General
- Albert Sidney Johnston (1803–1862), Confederate General and commander of the Confederate western forces
- John B. Magruder (1807–1871), Confederate General at the Battle of Galveston
- Pleasant Tackitt (1803–1886), Confederate Officer and county official at Fort Belknap, Texas. One of the founders of Parker County, Texas.
- Charles S. West (1829–1885), Confederate officer and judge advocate general for the Trans-Mississippi Department
- Louis T. Wigfall (1816–1874), Confederate General and Senator from Texas, secured the surrender of Fort Sumter

Important People from the Texas Revolution

The following are some important people from the Texas Revolution and their contributions:

- Jim Bowie (1796–1836), frontiersman, died at the Battle of the Alamo
- Davy Crockett (1786–1836), frontiersman and U.S. Congressman, died at the Alamo
- James Fannin (1804? –1836), key figure during the Texas Revolution
- Benjamin McCulloch (1811–1862), soldier in the Texas Revolution, Texas Ranger, U.S. Marshal and brigadier general in the army of the Confederate States during the American Civil War
- Henry Eustace McCulloch (1816–1895), soldier in the Texas Revolution, Texas Ranger, and brigadier general in the army of the Confederate States during the American Civil War
- Juan Seguin (1806–1890), Tejano hero during the Texas Revolution
- William B. Travis (1809–1836), commander of Texas forces at the Alamo
- Logan Vandeveer (1815–1855), Hero of San Jacinto

Internal Politics of the Republic

Internal politics of the Republic were based on the conflict between two factions. The **nationalist faction**, led by **Mirabeau B. Lamar** advocated the continued independence of Texas, the expulsion of the Native Americans, and the expansion of Texas to the Pacific Ocean. Their opponents, led by **Sam Houston**, advocated the annexation of Texas to the United States and peaceful coexistence with Native Americans. The first flag of the republic was the "Burnet Flag" (a gold star on an azure field), followed shortly thereafter by official adoption of the Lone Star Flag. The Republic received diplomatic recognition from the United States, France, the United Kingdom, the Netherlands, and the Republic of Yucatán.

Important Texans in Science and Medicine

The following are some important people in the fields of science and medicine who are from Texas:

- Denton Cooley (b. 1920), pioneering heart surgeon
- Michael E. DeBakey (b. 1908), pioneering heart surgeon
- Chu Ching-wu, physicist
- Robert Dennard (b. 1932), computer scientist.
- Bryce DeWitt, physicist, co-developed Wheeler-DeWitt equation ("wave function of the Universe")
- Leonard Eugene Dickson, mathematician
- G.B. Halsted, mathematician
- M. King Hubbert (1903–1989), geophysicist
- Jack Kilby, electrical engineer
- Hermann Joseph Muller, geneticist, Nobel Laureate in Physiology or Medicine
- Ilya Prigogine, physicist and chemist, Nobel Laureate in Chemistry
- John Tate, mathematician, Wolf Prize in Mathematics
- Beatrice Tinsley, astronomer
- Karen Uhlenbeck, mathematician, National Medal of Science
- Harry Vandiver, mathematician
- Steven Weinberg, Nobel Laureate in Physics
- Spencer Wells, geneticist and anthropologist
- John A. Wheeler, physicist, Wolf Prize in Physics, coined the term 'black hole'

Statehood of Texas

On February 28, 1845, the U.S. Congress passed a bill that would authorize the United States to **annex** the Republic of Texas and on March 1 U.S. President **John Tyler** signed the bill. The legislation set the date for annexation for December 29 of the same year. On October 13 of the same year, a majority of voters in the Republic approved a proposed constitution that specifically endorsed slavery and the slave trade. This constitution was later accepted by the U.S. Congress, making Texas a U.S. state on the same day annexation took effect (therefore bypassing a territorial phase). One of the primary motivations for annexation was that the Texas government had incurred huge debts which the United States agreed to assume upon annexation. In the **Compromise of 1850**, in return for this assumption of $10 million of debt, a large portion of Texas-claimed territory, now parts of Colorado, Kansas, Oklahoma, New Mexico, and Wyoming, was ceded to the Federal government.

Spindletop

Anthony F. Lucas, an experienced mining engineer, drilled the first major oil well at **Spindletop** on the morning of January 10, 1901 on the little hill south of Beaumont, Texas. The **East Texas Oil**

Field, discovered on October 5, 1930 is located in east central part of the state, and is the largest and most prolific oil reservoir in the contiguous United States. Other oil fields were later discovered in West Texas and under the Gulf of Mexico. The resulting "Oil Boom" permanently transformed the economy of Texas, and led to the first significant economic expansion after the Civil War.

Texas Secession from United States During Civil War

Texas **seceded** from the United States on February 1, 1861, and joined the **Confederate States of America** on March 2, 1861. Texas was mainly a "supply state" for the Confederate forces until mid 1863, when the Union capture of the Mississippi River made large movements of men, horses or cattle impossible. Texas regiments fought in every major battle throughout the war. The last battle of the Civil War, the **Battle of Palmito Ranch**, was fought in Texas on May 12, 1865.

Capital of Texas

Austin is the capital of Texas. The State Capitol resembles the federal Capitol Building in Washington, D.C., but is faced in Texas pink granite and is topped by a statue of the "Goddess of Liberty" holding aloft a five-point Texas star. The capitol is also notable for facing south toward Mexico City and for purposefully being built seven feet taller than the U.S. national capitol.

Texas Constitution

The Texas Constitution, adopted in 1876, is the second oldest state constitution still in effect. As with many state constitutions, it explicitly provides for the **separation of powers** and incorporates its **bill of rights** directly into the text of the constitution (as Article I). The bill of rights is considerably lengthier and more detailed than the federal Bill of Rights, and includes some provisions unique to Texas.

Offices of U.S. Government in Texas

Texas has a **Governor**, elects two U.S. **Senators** and 32 U.S. **Representatives**.

Legislature of Texas

The Legislature of Texas, like the legislature of every other state except Nebraska, is **bicameral** (that is, it has two chambers). The **House of Representatives** has 150 members, while the **Senate** has 31. The speaker of the house leads the House, and the lieutenant governor leads the state Senate. The Legislature meets in regular session only once every two years. The Legislature cannot call itself into special session; only the governor may call a special session, and may call as many sessions as often as desired.

Executive Branch of Government in Texas

The executive branch consists of the Governor, Lieutenant Governor, Comptroller of Public Accounts, Land Commissioner, Attorney General, Agriculture Commissioner, the three-member Texas Railroad Commission, the State Board of Education, and the Secretary of State. The comptroller decides whether expected state income is sufficient to cover the proposed state budget. Except for the secretary of state—who is appointed by the governor with the advice and consent of the Senate—each of these officials is **elected** (the three Railroad Commission members are voted at-large; the State Board of Education members are voted in single-member districts). There are also many state agencies and numerous boards and commissions. Partly because of many elected officials, the governor's powers are quite **limited** in comparison to other state governors or the U.S. President. In popular lore and belief the lieutenant governor, who heads the Senate and appoints its committees, has more power than the governor. The governor commands the state militia and can veto bills passed by the Legislature and call special sessions of the Legislature (this power is exclusive to the governor and can be exercised as often as desired). The governor also appoints members of various executive boards and fills judicial vacancies between elections.

County Government in Texas

Texas has a total of 254 **counties**, by far the most counties of any state. Each county is run by a **commissioners court** consisting of four elected **commissioners** (one from each of four precincts drawn based on population) and a **county judge** elected from all the voters of the county. The county judge does not have the authority to veto a decision of the commissioners court; the judge votes along with the commissioners. In smaller counties, the county judge actually does perform judicial duties, but in larger counties the judge's role is limited to serving on the commissioners court. Certain officials, such as the sheriff and tax collector, are elected separately by the voters, but the commissioners court determines their office budgets and sets overall county policy. All county elections are partisan. Counties also have much less legal power than municipalities. For instance, counties in Texas do not have zoning power. However, counties do have eminent domain power. Counties do not have "home rule" authority; whatever powers are not specifically granted by the state are not permitted. Unlike other states, Texas does not allow for consolidated city-county governments. Cities and counties are permitted to enter "interlocal agreements" to share services.

Judicial Branch

The judicial system of Texas has a reputation as one of the most complex in the United States, with many layers and many overlapping jurisdictions. Texas has two courts of last resort: the **Texas Supreme Court**, which hears civil cases, and the **Texas Court of Criminal Appeals**. Except in the case of some municipal benches, partisan elections choose all of the judges at all levels of the judiciary; the governor fills vacancies by appointment.

Science

Scientific Inquiry and Lab Safety

Components of Scientific Experimentation

- A **hypothesis** is a tentative supposition about a phenomenon (or a fact or set of facts) made in order to examine and test its logical or empirical consequences through investigation or methodological experimentation.
- A **theory** is a scientifically proven, general principle offered to explain phenomena. A theory is derived from a hypothesis and verified by experimentation and research.
- A **scientific law** is a generally accepted conclusion about a body of observations to which no exceptions have been found. Scientific laws explain things, but do not describe them.
- A **control** is a normal, unchanged situation used for comparison against experimental data.
- **Constants** are factors in an experiment that remain the same.
- **Independent variables** are factors, traits, or conditions that are changed in an experiment. A good experiment has only one independent variable so that the scientist can track one thing at a time. The independent variable changes from experiment to experiment.
- **Dependent variables** are changes that result from variations in the independent variable.

Science as a Series of Processes

Science is not just the steps of experimentation. While the process of posing a question, forming a hypothesis, testing the hypothesis, recording data, and drawing a conclusion is at the heart of **scientific inquiry**, there are other processes that are important as well. Once the scientist has completed the testing of a hypothesis and possibly come up with a theory, the scientist should then go through the process of getting feedback from colleagues, publishing an article about the work in a peer-reviewed journal, or otherwise reporting the results to the scientific community, replicating the experiment for verification of results (by the original scientist or others), and developing new questions. Science is not just a means of satisfying curiosity, but is also a process for developing technology, addressing social issues, building knowledge, and solving everyday problems.

Drawing Conclusions After Experiments

Conclusions are based on data analysis and background research. The scientist has to take a hard look at the results of an experiment and check the accuracy of the data to draw preliminary conclusions. These should be compared to the background research to find out if the preliminary conclusion can be supported by previous research experiments. If the results do not support the hypothesis, or if they are contrary to what the background research predicted, then further research is needed. The focus should be on finding a reason for the different results. Finally, the scientist provides a discussion of findings that includes a summary of the results of the experiment, a statement as to whether the hypothesis was proven or disproven, a statement of the relationship between the independent and dependent variable, a summary and evaluation of the procedures of the experiment (including comments about successes and effectiveness), and suggestions for changes/modifications in procedures for further studies.

Steps of the Scientific Method

The steps of the **scientific method** are as follows:

1. The scientific method begins with, and absolutely depends upon, the **observation** of objective, unbiased data. Any prejudice or bias in the observed data nullifies its validity. Thus the basic input from the observations must be rigorously screened to ensure objectivity.
2. The development of a **theory or hypothesis** based on objective data is the next step in the scientific method. These theories or hypotheses pose logical expectations that the experiment may yield.
3. Construction of a rigorous and valid **experimental method** designed to test the theories is the next phase of the scientific method. This experimental method must be carefully constructed to give objective, unbiased conclusions based on the hypotheses posited.
4. Careful and statistically correct **analysis and evaluation** of the experimental results make up the next stage.
5. **Modification and replication** of the experiment must then follow to provide a statistically accurate demonstration of the validity of the hypothesis. Equivalent results must be shown from a number of repetitions of the experiment.

Review Video: The Scientific Method
Visit mometrix.com/academy and enter code: 191386

Steps of the Scientific Inquiry

Scientific inquiry is the impetus and catalyst for all scientific research and experimentation. It grows from questions about the observed world and gives us a template with which to apply the scientific method. Steps in scientific inquiry include the following principles:

- Determination of the content and scope of the questions to be investigated is the first step. These may range from simple to extremely complex questions to be explored by scientists.
- The design, strategy, and method of the inquiry are then carefully considered, and a model for the inquiry is constructed.
- The formulation of theories and models based on the careful observation of objective, unbiased data then follows. This formulation is derived from the scope of the scientific inquiry and the questions to be investigated.
- Analysis of possible alternative conclusions drawn from the models and results of experimentation follows.
- Postulating a theory or constructing a scientific statement based on conclusions is the next logical step.
- Defending the scientific statement against alternative hypotheses is a critical function of scientific inquiry.
- Defense of the theory or conclusion against critical analysis is the final step in the process.

Science

Science is a method of acquiring and obtaining knowledge. It is the process of gaining reliable information about the real world, including the explanation of phenomena. It is the development of a body of knowledge about observable phenomena, using the best capabilities humans have at their disposal. The process of organizing and classifying knowledge, through objective observation and evaluation, is a major goal of science. Science can be considered *reliable*, but it is not *infallible*. The limits of human knowledge are constantly growing, often making yesterday's science obsolete and simplistic. Science is thus never fixed; it is always subject to change as new information is gained and synthesized with existing knowledge. Ultimately, science is the sum total of knowledge in any period of time, based on the current abilities of man to understand the world of phenomena, verifiable by observable data.

Limitations of Science

There are clear **limits** on what science can explain. The demand for objectivity both strengthens knowledge we gain from scientific experiments and limits what we can explore. Beyond the realm of scientific inquiry are such questions as "Why does anything exist?" or "What is the meaning of life?" These are subjective questions that do not lend themselves easily to scientific inquiry. These questions, and others like them, come from within, and their conclusions, not validated by science, shape the very fabric of a society. They attempt to give meaning to what may be viewed as chaos.

Periodically, science will impact these **subjective conclusions** with new evidence. For example, the theory of evolution is regarded as blasphemy by many religious fundamentalists. These conflicts may cause great upheavals in society, leaving many to wonder how science and religious belief can be reconciled. Ultimately, observation of the external world must stand as the true test of science.

Hypothetico-Deductive Process

The **hypothetico-deductive process** states that to have an idea and then formulate a hypothesis are essentially creative processes, driven by eons of human experience. Statements about reality are the logical conclusions of observed experience. Such creative propositions are the basis for scientific inquiry. Empirical evidence must then validate these hypotheses. Creative inspiration and scientific validation are interdependent aspects of scientific inquiry. New observations often are the catalyst for creative new theories. Science thus proceeds through creative thinking and scientific validation. There are criticisms of the hypothetico-deductive process: The problem of deduction points out that the original hypothesis may be proved wrong in the future, thus invalidating all subsequent conclusions. The problem of induction, building a theory from generalizations, is that any generalization may be proved wrong by future objective observations. The hypothetico-deductive process, and its problems, is a fascinating subject to philosophers of science.

Hypothesis

It is important to form a **hypothesis** in order to make a tentative explanation that accounts for an unbiased observation. To be scientific, the hypothesis must be testable through experimentation. Careful construction of the experiment provides that predictions derived from the hypothesis are valid. The hypothesis must be formulated in a manner designed to provide a framework for evaluating the results of an experiment. In many scientific experiments, a hypothesis is posited in negative terms because scientists may accept logically plausible ideas until they are proven false. It is more difficult to prove that a hypothesis is true because its validity must be proven in all possible situations under endless variable conditions. Scientists tend to construct hypotheses for testing by creating experiments that might prove them false. If they succeed in proving it false, the hypothesis must be modified or discarded.

Basic Science and Applied Science

Basic science and applied science share many attributes but are generally motivated by different influences:

- **Basic science** is spurred on by scientific inquiry, the human need to explain the observed physical world. It may have no specific goal, but is mankind's response to questions that arise from human curiosity and interest. It is usually an attempt to explain the laws of nature by using the scientific method.
- **Applied science** has a specific practical goal or application: It is designed to solve a problem. Industry and government are institutions that use applied science regularly.

Thus, basic and applied science share many qualities, including scientific inquiry and the scientific method. The goals of each can be very different. It should be pointed out that basic science very often provides results that have uses in applied science.

Benefits of Basic Science

Although **basic science** may have no stated goal or target, it provides many benefits to society:

- Basic science contributes greatly to human understanding and culture, enriching society in many ways.
- Basic science has been responsible for major breakthroughs that have great social and economic impact.
- Basic science provides derivative solutions that can be used in applied science. For example, basic science was critical to the development of the space program, from which countless valuable applications have been derived.
- Basic science contributes to education and research across the broad spectrum of society.

Measuring, Organizing, and Classifying Data

Measuring data is a crucial part of the scientific process. Measurements are most useful if they are quantified—expressed in numbers. Measuring is the process of determining variables such as time, space, and temperature of objects and processes in precise numbers. The metric system is the universal standard of measurement in science. Data must be **organized** in a practical, useful manner to be valuable. Scientists use graphs, charts, tables, and other organizational tools to make data more useful. Data must then be **classified**—grouped into organizational schemes for easy access and use. These schemes attempt to organize the maximum amount of useful data in a format that scientists can use. Although these steps may be less glamorous than other areas of science, they are essential.

Review Video: Terminology for Tables and Graphs
Visit mometrix.com/academy and enter code: 355505

Review Video: Understanding Charts and Tables
Visit mometrix.com/academy and enter code: 882112

Scientific Laws

Scientific principles must meet a high standard to be classified as laws; scientific laws are identified as follows:

- **Scientific laws** must be true, not just probable. A highly probable principle may still be proven false.
- Laws are statements of patterns found in nature.
- Laws may have a universal form but be stated conditionally. For example, the statement "All living human beings breathe," may be restated "If a thing is a living human being it must breathe."
- Laws refer to a general, not a particular, class.
- Laws have purely qualitative predicates.
- Laws must have a formal language of expression to be fully understood. Such a language does not exist now.
- Laws may be probabilistic. For example, a law may state "Eight percent of all dogs are terriers."

Common Criticisms of the Deductive Model

The **deductive model** of the scientific method has the following criticisms:

- The deductive model fails to make logical distinctions among explanations, predictions, and descriptions of things to be explained.
- The deductive model is restrictive: It excludes most scientific examples.
- The deductive model is too inclusive: It admits data that cannot be explained.
- The deductive model requires an account of cause, law, and probability, which are basically unsound.
- The deductive model leaves out the elements of context, judgment, and understanding.

Prediction

These are the two widely accepted definitions of **scientific prediction**:

1. In the language of science, prediction is stating in advance the outcome from testing a theory or hypothesis in a controlled experiment. Based on objective observation of data, scientists move from observation of facts to a general explanation, or hypothesis, which must be confirmed by testing through experimentation.
2. Another definition of prediction favored by scientific philosophers is the ability of a hypothesis to lead to deductions of scientific statements that could not be anticipated when the hypothesis was posited. In this sense, prediction means what the scientist can verify from what he or she has deduced from the hypothesis.

Laboratory Safety

The following basic rules should be supplemented by standards appropriate to individual laboratories:

- Hazardous areas must be identified and warnings posted regarding risks.
- A hazard containment plan must be in effect and readily available.
- Safe control of airflow must be maintained at all times.
- Safe work practices must be taught to all who work in the lab.
- Proper maintenance of laboratory equipment must be enforced.
- Safe storage of hazardous material must be implemented.

- Procedures for safe disposal of hazardous wastes must be followed at all times.
- An updated emergency procedure manual must be available.
- A complete emergency first aid kit should be accessible at all times.
- Regular education on the basics of lab safety should be implemented.

Verification and Confirmation of Data in Valid Science

A critical distinction should be made between confirmation and verification of scientific data. **Verification** establishes once and for all the truth of the statement. **Confirmation** is the testing of claims to see how true they are. For a claim to be testable, an experiment must be devised to ensure the validity of the results. A claim can only be confirmed when we know the conditions for verification. A claim confirmation is always relative to the testing procedures. Test results must always be objective and observable. Actually, no factual claim can ever be verified because there is always the possibility of new evidence appearing that proves the claim false. A scientific law must also be confirmed by making predictions based on unbiased, observable data.

Scientific Measurement and Unit Systems

The basis of quantitative measurement is the **unit system**. In order to properly describe how large, how heavy, or how hot something is, it is necessary to have some reference unit. The most commonly used unit system in the world is the **SI**, short for the Systeme International d'Unites, although the English system is still in popular use in the United States. In SI, there are base units and derived units. Derived units may be stated as some combination of the base units. The SI base units for length, mass, time, temperature, and electric current are meter (m), kilogram (kg), second (s), kelvin (K), and ampere (A), respectively. Some common derived units are newtons (kg m/s^2) and pascals (kg/(m s^2)). Most SI units can be scaled up or down by adding a prefix. To alter a unit by 10^3, 10^6, or 10^9, add a prefix of kilo (k), mega (M), or giga (G). For instance, a kilometer (km) is 10^3 meters. To change the unit by a factor of 10^{-3}, 10^{-6}, or 10^{-9}, add a prefix of milli (m), micro (μ), or nano (n). For instance, a microsecond (μs) is 10^{-6} seconds. It is important to note that the SI base unit kilogram has already employed a prefix to scale up the smaller unit, gram (g). *Order of magnitude* is a concept that deals with the comparison between two values. If one value differs from the other by a factor of 10^n, it may be said that it differs by n orders of magnitude. Other SI base units include the mole and the candela. Some lesser used prefixes include: hecto (h), 10^2; deca (da), 10^1; deci (d), 10^{-1}; and centi (c), 10^{-2}.

Data Collection and Analysis

In order to take **data measurements** from their experimental setups, scientists will often use measurement devices wired to a computer running data-acquisition software. This allows them to take numerous readings per second if necessary. Once the data is collected, it will often be organized using a spreadsheet, such as Microsoft Excel. This multipurpose program contains several options for displaying the data in graphs or charts, as well as tools for performing statistical analyses or linear regressions. Linear regression is a technique used to determine whether gathered data fits a particular trend or equation. It attempts to fit a common line or curve equation to the data set. A very important concept to understand when taking data is that of **significant figures**. Significant figures, or significant digits, indicate how precisely a quantity is known. Each non-zero digit is always significant. A zero is significant if either: 1) it is to the right of both a non-zero digit and the decimal point; or 2) it is between two other significant digits. For instance, 1.0230 has five significant figures while 0.0230 has only three because the trailing zero is the only zero to the right of both a non-zero and the decimal. When multiplying (or dividing), the product (quotient) has as many significant figures as the factor (dividend or divisor) with the fewest. When adding (or subtracting), the sum (difference) should be rounded to the highest final decimal place of the involved terms. For example, $3.4 + 56.78 = 60.18$ rounded to three significant figures is 60.2.

Interpretation and Drawing of Conclusions from Data Presented in Tables, Charts, and Graphs

One of the reasons data are so often plotted on graphs is that this format makes it much easier to see **trends** and draw **conclusions**. For instance, on a simple position vs. time graph, the slope of the curve indicates the object's velocity at each point in time. If the curve becomes level, this means the object is not moving. In a simple velocity vs. time graph, the slope of the curve indicates the object's acceleration at each point in time. Additionally, the area contained under the curve indicates the total distance traveled. For instance, if the object is traveling at a constant 5 m/s for 10 s, the velocity vs. time graph will be a straight line at $y = 5$ between $x = 0$ and $x = 10$. The area under this curve is $(5\text{ m/s})(10\text{ s}) = 50\text{ m}$. Thus, the object traveled 50 meters. Nearly any type of quantity may be graphed, so it is important to always check the axis labels to ensure that you know what the graph represents and what units are being used.

Data Errors and Error Analysis

No measurements are ever 100% accurate. There is always some amount of **error** regardless of how careful the observer or how good the equipment. The important thing for the scientist to know is how much error is present in a given measurement. Two commonly misunderstood terms regarding error are accuracy and precision. **Accuracy** is a measure of how close a measurement is to the true value. **Precision** is a measure of how close repeated measurements are to one another. Error is usually quantified using a confidence interval and an uncertainty value. For instance, if the quantity is measured as 100 ± 2 on a 95% confidence interval, this means that there is a 95% chance that the actual value falls between 98 and 102. When looking for the uncertainty in a derived quantity such as density, the errors in the constituent quantities, mass and volume in this case, are propagated to the derived quantity. The percent uncertainty in the density, U_ρ/ρ, can be found by the equation:

$$\frac{U_\rho}{\rho} = \sqrt{\left(\frac{U_m}{m}\right)^2 + \left(\frac{U_V}{V}\right)^2}$$

Science, Technology, and Society

Debate over Science and Ethics

Debates over issues paramount to **science and ethics** are rarely resolved unambiguously. Ethical conclusions should be based on reason, logic, and accepted principles that represent a consensus of current thinking on a question. Education and debate are important in clarifying issues and allowing intelligent participation in a democratic process. Deciding issues of science and society usually requires an examination of individual cases. Generalizations in these areas tend to lead to extreme positions that exclude mainstream opinions. There are no blanket solutions to most problems involving science, technology, and societal ethics.

Major Effects of Improvements in Scientific and Technological Knowledge on Human and Other Life

Since the Industrial Revolution, **technological improvements** to agricultural production have made agriculture productive on an industrial scale, while advances in medical knowledge have brought about the cures for many diseases. People in many parts of the world live longer and enjoy a higher standard of living than ever before. However, this progress does not come without a price. The effects on the **environment** of industrialization are almost exclusively negative. Monoculture farming practices resulting from industrialization mean that farming no longer exists as a closed ecosystem; the chemical fertilizers that create record crop yields have changed the nutrient environment, and the waste products of industrial agriculture pollute the water rather than fertilizing the soil. Increased travel creates dangerous carbon dioxide emissions and depletes the earth's limited store of fossil fuels. Water pollution means limited access to potable water, and deforestation has begun to change the makeup of ecosystems and cause the extinction of many species. Through the increased contact made available by improved technology, however, humans are also collaborating on solutions to these new problems.

Review Video: Industrialization
Visit mometrix.com/academy and enter code: 893924

Major Energy Issues

Since the Industrial Revolution, **energy** for industrialized human needs has come from fossil fuels, particularly coal and petroleum, but increased use means that this source of fuel is quickly being depleted, in addition to causing pollution. The search for **alternative, safe sources** of energy for an increasingly industrialized world population is therefore increasingly important to scientists. An ideal source of energy would be efficient, renewable, and sustainable. Various sources of alternative energy have been proposed, including wind, water, solar, nuclear, geothermal, and biomass, but thus far none have been made practically available on a large scale. Some, such as wind and water, blight the landscape, while the conversion methods for other sources, such as solar and biomass, are still relatively inefficient. The scientific community is still unclear on the best way to harness the power of photosynthesis and biomass for energy needs in a way that would allow a large-scale energy industry to use it. Scientists remain at work studying the long-term solutions to an increasingly urgent problem for humanity.

Controversies Surrounding Use of Nuclear Power

Nuclear fission power, while sustainable, has a host of attendant controversial problems. Among them is the incredibly dangerous transportation and long-term storage of its radioactive waste products, for which there is still no safe long-term solution. The effects on those environments and creatures that come in contact with nuclear waste are still largely unknown. In addition, nuclear materials can be used in weaponry, and accidents at nuclear power plants like the one at Chernobyl can be devastating for thousands of years. Scientists continue their study of the process of **nuclear fusion**, hoping that if humans can learn to harness the energy produced by smashing atoms rather than splitting them, the attendant problems of nuclear waste storage will be minimized.

Review Video: Nuclear Fusion
Visit mometrix.com/academy and enter code: 381782

Effects of Increased Production of Consumer Goods After Industrial Revolution

Electric-based, industrial production of **manufactured goods** has led to an increase in the standard of living for many, especially those in the industrialized world. Consumer goods are produced more cheaply than ever before, since the means of production is not as dependent on the physical abilities of human beings. Scientific advancements have led to a huge number of new synthetic materials from which goods can be made, including plastics and nylon. However, this increased production damages the **environment**. Waste products are now created of which humans can make no use, a new phenomenon. Trash created from these new products is buried in landfills, where it has no access to the air, water, and sunlight that are a necessary part of biodegradation; trash made from some synthetic materials does not biodegrade at all. While some waste products can be recycled, many byproducts of industrial manufacturing are hazardous, with no safe way to dispose of them. The long-term sustainability of the environment as a result of massively increased consumer production is an issue of increasing urgency for scientists.

Issues Concerning Management of Renewable Resources

Natural resources can be divided into two types, renewable and non-renewable. **Renewable resources** include plants and animals, along with water, air, and soil. A pre-industrial earth was a self-sustaining system, maintaining a natural balance among plants, animals, and non-living elements in which waste products from one natural process were the fuel for another. Modern humans have intervened in this process in a way that upsets the natural balance of life. Humans have introduced non-native species from one part of the world to another, resulting in the devastation of local populations. Industrial-scale buildings can create disasters for local ecosystems, ruining habitats for animal populations. Humans remove an increasing amount of the world's resources for industrial use, too quickly for nature to recover from easily. Renewable resources must be carefully managed to maintain a balanced ecosystem; over-harvesting of forests or over-hunting of animal populations can be devastating. Pollution of the air and water with chemical pollutants has far-reaching effects on the ecosystems of the earth, including the depletion of the ozone layer that protects life on earth from ultraviolet rays. The removal of forests, which produce the earth's oxygen, further depletes the ozone layer.

Issues Concerning Management of Non-Renewable Resources

Non-renewable resources include minerals, which are created naturally over millions of years. The industrialized world extracts minerals for fuel as well as for use in electronic equipment and medicine. Increased human extraction of non-renewable resources has endangered their availability, and over-mining has created other ecological problems, including runoff and water pollution. The use of fossil fuels for energy and transportation causes air pollution and is unsustainable. Fossil fuels cannot be replaced once depleted, and they are being depleted at an increasing rate. The need to find a sustainable alternative to the use of non-renewable fossil fuels is imperative.

Review Video: Renewable and Nonrenewable Resources
Visit mometrix.com/academy and enter code: 840194

Recent Applications of Science and Technology to Health Care, the Environment, Agriculture, and Information Technology

Scientific and technological developments have led to the widespread availability of **technologies** heretofore unheard of, including cellular phones, satellite-based applications, and a worldwide network of connected computers. Some notable recent applications include:

- **Health care**: Antibiotics, genetic screening for diseases, the sequencing of the human genome. Issues include problems with health care distribution on an increasingly industrialized planet.
- **The environment**: Computerized models of climate change and pollution monitoring. Issues include increased pollution of the water, air, and soil, and the over-harvesting of natural resources with mechanized equipment.

- **Agriculture**: Genetic improvements in agricultural practices, including increased output on the same amount of arable land. Issues include unknown environmental effects of hybrid species, cross-pollination with organic species, and pollution caused by synthetic chemical fertilizers.
- **Information technology**: New Internet-based industries, increased worldwide collaboration, and access to information. Issues include the depletion of natural resources for electronics production.

Social Impacts of Recent Developments in Science and Technology

Recent **developments in science and technology** have had both positive and negative effects on human society. The issue of sustainable growth is an increasingly important one, as humans realize that the resources they use are not unlimited. Genetic research into diseases, stem cell research, and cloning technology have created great controversies as they have been introduced, and an increasing number of people reject the morality of scientific practices like animal testing in the pursuit of scientific advancement. In addition, an increasingly technology-based world has produced a new social inequality based on access to computers and Internet technology. These issues are beginning to be debated at all levels of human government, from city councils to the United Nations. Does science provide the authoritative answer to all human problems, or do ethics carry weight in scientific debates as well? Ultimately, humans must weigh the competing needs of facilitating scientific pursuits and maintaining an ethical society as they face new technological questions.

Human Impacts on Ecosystems

Human impacts on ecosystems take many forms and have many causes. They include widespread disruptions and specific niche disturbances. Humans practice many forms of environmental manipulation that affect plants and animals in many biomes and ecosystems. Many human practices involve the consumption of natural resources for food and energy production, the changing of the environment to produce food and energy, and the intrusion on ecosystems to provide shelter. These general behaviors include a multitude of specific behaviors, including the use and overuse of pesticides, the encroachment upon habitat, over hunting and over fishing, the introduction of plant and animal species into non-native ecosystems, not recycling, and the introduction of hazardous wastes and chemical byproducts into the environment. These behaviors have led to a number of consequences, such as acid rain, ozone depletion, deforestation, urbanization, accelerated species loss, genetic abnormalities, endocrine disruption in populations, and harm to individual animals.

Greenhouse Effect

The **greenhouse effect** refers to the naturally occurring and necessary process of **greenhouse gasses**, ozone, carbon dioxide, water vapor, and methane, trapping infrared radiation that is reflected toward the atmosphere. This is actually beneficial in that warm air is trapped. Without the greenhouse effect, it is estimated that the temperature on Earth would be 30 degrees less on average. The problem lies in human activity generating more greenhouse gases than are necessary. Excess greenhouse gases cause more infrared radiation to become trapped, which increases the temperature at the Earth's surface. The practices that increase the amount of greenhouse gases are the burning of natural gas and oil, farming practices that result in the release of methane and nitrous oxide, factory operations that produce gases, and deforestation practices that decrease the amount of oxygen available to offset greenhouse gases. Population growth also increases the volume of gases released.

Impact

Rising temperatures may lead to an increase in sea levels as polar ice melts, lower amounts of available fresh water as coastal areas flood, and species extinction as habitats change. They'll also cause increases in certain diseases and a decreased standard of living for humans. Less fresh water and losses of habitat for humans and other species can also lead to decreased agricultural production and food supply shortages. Increased desertification leads to habitat loss for humans and certain other species. Decreases in animal populations from losses of habitat and increased hunting by other species can lead to extinction. Increases in severe weather, such as huge sustained snowstorms, may also occur at unlikely latitudes. Even though global warming results in weather that is drier and warmer overall, it still gets cold enough to snow. There may be more moisture in the atmosphere due to evaporation. **Global warming** may cause the permanent loss of glaciers and permafrost. There might also be increases in air pollution and acid rain.

Impact of Science and Technology on Environment and Human Affairs

Since the industrial revolution, science and technology have had a profound impact on **human affairs**. There has been a rapid increase in the number of discoveries in many fields. Many major and minor discoveries have led to a great improvement in the quality of life of many people. This includes longer life spans because of better nutrition, increased access to medical care, and a decrease in workplace health hazards. Not all problems, such as health hazards and poor nutrition, have been solved, and many still exist in one form or another. For example, even though there are means to recycle, not every business does so because of economic factors. These advances, while improving the lives of many humans, have also taken their toll on the environment. A possible solution may arise when the carrying capacity for humans on Earth is reached. The population will decline, and solutions will have to be found. Otherwise, an immediate halt or decrease in the human behaviors that are causing environmental damage will need to happen.

Purpose of Studying Interactions Among Humans, Natural Hazards, and the Environment

In science class, students will learn that the **human population** on earth can be affected by various factors from both their natural environments and from the technologies they use in their daily lives. These factors can be positive or negative, so students need to learn how to prepare for, respond to, and evaluate the consequences of environmental occurrences over a long period of time. Natural disasters are a negative experience, but so are human-made disasters such as pollution and deforestation. Students need to understand that science is involved in the interactions between the human population, natural hazards, and the environment. They should know that the aim of science is to make these interactions **balanced and positive**. Science is a discipline that can help find ways to increase safety during and remediate destruction after natural disasters. Science can also advance technology and transportation in an environmentally safe manner, prevent and cure diseases, and remediate the effects of pollution and resource depletion.

Subjects Covered in Personal Health Portion of Science Class

Among the personal and social perspectives of science are the issues of **personal and public health care**. In this area, students learn such things as:

- The importance of regular **exercise** to the maintenance and improvement of health
- The need for **risk assessment** and educated decisions to prevent injuries and illnesses because of the potential for accidents and the existence of hazards
- The risk of illness and the social and psychological factors associated with the use of **tobacco products**

- The dangers of abusing **alcohol and other drug substances**, including addiction and damage to body functions
- The energy and nutrition values of various **foods**, their role in growth and development, and the requirements of the body according to variable factors
- The complexities of **human sexuality** and the dangers of sexually transmitted diseases
- The relationship between **environmental and human health**, and the need to monitor soil, water, and air standards

Risk and Benefit Analysis as Studied in Personal and Social Perspectives of Science

Risk analysis considers the type of hazard and estimates the number of people who might be exposed and the number likely to suffer consequences. The results are used to determine options for reducing or eliminating risks. For example, the Center for Disease Control must analyze the risk of a certain new virus strain causing a pandemic, how many people and what age groups need to be vaccinated first, and what precautions can be taken to guard against the spread of the disease. **Risk and benefit analysis** involves having students consider the dangers of natural (major storms), chemical (pollution), biological (pollen and bacteria), social (occupational safety and transportation), and personal (smoking, dieting, and drugs) hazards. Students then use a systematic approach to think critically about these hazards, apply probability estimates to the risks, and compare them to estimated and perceived personal and social benefits.

Interactions of Science and Technology with Society

The interactions of science and technology with society include:

- **Scientific knowledge** and the procedures used by scientists influence the way many people think about themselves, others, and the environment.
- **Technology** influences society through its products and processes. It influences quality of life and the ways people act and interact. Technological changes are often accompanied by social, political, and economic changes. Science and technology contribute enormously to economic growth and productivity. The introduction of the cell phone into society is a perfect example of technology influencing society, quality of life, human interaction, and the economy.
- **Societal challenges** often inspire questions for scientific research, and social priorities often influence research priorities through the availability of research funding.

Science and technology have been advanced through the contributions of many different people in a variety of cultures during different time periods in history. Scientists and engineers work in colleges, businesses and industries, research institutes, and government agencies, touching many lives in a variety of settings.

Science Pedagogy

The Importance of Studying Science in the Context of Personal and Social Perspectives

Learning must be **relevant**. When students study science in the context of personal and social perspectives, they are able to see the practical application of the textbook knowledge. They are given an understanding of the issues around them that can be solved by science and the means to act on those issues. Science should be taught within the **social context of history** so that students can see where society has been and how far it has come thanks to scientific advancements related to tools, medicine, transportation, and communication. Students should also understand how these advances developed in response to resources, needs, and values. Students need to review the **process of scientific inquiry** through the centuries to get a sense of the benefits of intellectual curiosity, the inter-relatedness of science, and the development of civilization. Students should question the role science has played in the development of various cultures by considering how computers, refrigeration, vaccines, microscopes, fertilizers, etc. have improved the lives of people.

Inquiry-Based Science

If learning in the science classroom is **inquiry based**, children should see themselves as being involved in the process of learning. They should feel free to express curiosity and skepticism, change ideas and procedures, take risks, and exchange information with their classmates. Inquiry-based learning in science begins with observations of details, sequences, events, changes, similarities and differences, etc. Observations are followed by investigations based on scientific standards and safety that are designed by students. Students' projects should allow for verification, extension, or dismissal of ideas. Investigations should involve choosing tools, handling materials, measuring, observing, and recording data. The results of an investigation can take the form of a journal, report, drawing, graph, or chart. The summary of the observations and investigation should include explanations, solutions, and connections to other ideas, as well as further questions, an assessment of the quality of the work, a description of any problems encountered, and a description of the strengths and weaknesses of the investigation. Finally, students should reflect together about the lessons learned from the investigation.

Research-Based Teaching Strategies for Science

Research-based teaching strategies for science emphasize student-centered learning and encourage that all new concepts be connected to prior knowledge. Research suggests that having students connect new concepts to prior knowledge allows for new information to be comprehended more easily and retained more frequently. To ensure that activities are developmentally appropriate, teachers must take into consideration the prior knowledge of students, along with students' maturity and ability levels. Students must be mature enough to handle all necessary materials and must also have the ability to complete the tasks assigned to them, with an appropriate level of scaffolding.

Considering Reading Strategies and Mathematical Practices when Choosing Science Content Material

For students to understand and make sense of science materials, certain **reading and math skills** must be attained. For example, when learning about a new science concept, students must have the ability to identify a main idea, analyze new information, interpret findings, and use decoding strategies (as well as context clues) for unknown words or phrases. During labs, students must have the ability to draw conclusions, identify cause and effect, follow written directions and answer questions. When working through specific science topics, students must use their math skills to make sense of problems, persevere through challenging scenarios, reason abstractly, model their findings, and construct arguments to explain why things happen the way they do. When choosing appropriate science content, teachers must gauge the reading and mathematical abilities of their students to ensure that developmentally appropriate materials are provided.

Differentiated Science Instruction and Assessment

Differentiated instruction is the way in which teachers modify the delivery of lessons and assessment of learning to meet the needs of all ability levels. In a science classroom, all students are exposed to the same concepts; however, the delivery of those concepts may look different for each student. Accelerated learners may be expected to read an excerpt from a science journal and answer questions based on their reading, whereas struggling learners may be given a video to watch or listen to a read-aloud to complete a guided note sheet. As an assessment, accelerated learners may be given a task with written directions and the expectation of written responses and explanations. Struggling learners might demonstrate learning of the same concept through the completion of smaller tasks, broken into more manageable chunks, where responses can be written or sketched.

Developmentally Appropriate Assessments in Science Classroom

The three types of assessments in the science classroom are diagnostic, formative, and summative. **Diagnostic assessments** are given at the start of each unit or topic in an effort to determine prior knowledge. This prior knowledge is then used as a way of making a connection to new concepts in a meaningful way. **Formative assessments** are ongoing throughout each unit of study. These assessments are used to track each student's learning and to direct future instruction. **Summative assessments** occur at the end of each unit of study to measure each student's comprehension and mastery of the skills and concepts that are being evaluated.

Physics

Laws of Thermodynamics

The **laws of thermodynamics** are generalized principles dealing with energy and heat.

- The **zeroth law** of thermodynamics states that two objects in thermodynamic equilibrium with a third object are also in equilibrium with each other. Being in thermodynamic equilibrium basically means that different objects are at the same temperature.
- The **first law** deals with conservation of energy. It states that neither mass nor energy can be destroyed; only converted from one form to another.
- The **second law** states that the entropy (the amount of energy in a system that is no longer available for work or the amount of disorder in a system) of an isolated system can only increase. The second law also states that heat is not transferred from a lower-temperature system to a higher-temperature one unless additional work is done.
- The **third law** of thermodynamics states that as temperature approaches absolute zero, entropy approaches a constant minimum. It also states that a system cannot be cooled to absolute zero.

Review Video: Laws of Thermodynamics
Visit mometrix.com/academy and enter code: 253607

Heat and Temperature

Heat is energy transfer (other than direct work) from one body or system to another due to thermal contact. Everything tends to become less organized and less orderly over time (**entropy**). In all energy transfers, therefore, the overall result is that the energy is spread out uniformly. This transfer of heat energy from hotter to cooler objects is accomplished by conduction, radiation, or convection. **Temperature** is a measurement of an object's stored heat energy. More specifically, temperature is the average kinetic energy of an object's particles. When the temperature of an object increases and its atoms move faster, kinetic energy also increases. Temperature is not energy since it changes and is not conserved. Thermometers are used to measure temperature.

Mass, Weight, Volume, Density, and Specific Gravity

Mass — Mass is a measure of the amount of substance in an object.

Weight — Weight is a measure of the gravitational pull of Earth on an object.

Volume — Volume is a measure of the amount of space occupied. There are many formulas to determine volume. For example, the volume of a cube is the length of one side cubed (a^3) and the volume of a rectangular prism is length times width times height ($l \times w \times h$). The volume of an irregular shape can be determined by how much water it displaces.

Density — Density is a measure of the amount of mass per unit volume. The formula to find density is mass divided by volume ($D = m/V$). It is expressed in terms of mass per cubic unit (e.g., grams per cubic centimeter $\frac{g}{cm^3}$).

Specific gravity — This is a measure of the ratio of a substance's density compared to the density of water.

> **Review Video: Mass, Weight, Volume, Density, and Specific Gravity**
> Visit mometrix.com/academy and enter code: 920570

Thermal Contact

Thermal contact refers to energy transferred to a body by a means other than work. A system in thermal contact with another can exchange energy with it through the process of heat transfer. Thermal contact does not necessarily involve direct physical contact. **Heat** is energy that can be transferred from one body or system to another without work being done. Everything tends to become less organized and less useful over time (entropy). In all energy transfers, therefore, the overall result is that the heat is spread out so that objects are in thermodynamic equilibrium and the heat can no longer be transferred without additional work.

Models for Flow of Electric Charge

Models that can be used to explain the **flow of electric current, potential, and circuits** include water, gravity, and roller coasters. For example, just as a mass can have a potential for energy based on its location, so can a charge within an electrical field. Just as a force is required to move an object uphill, a force is also required to move a charge from a low to high potential. Another example is water. Water does not flow when it is level. If it is lifted to a point and then placed on a downward path, it will flow. A roller coaster car requires work to be performed to transport it to a point where it has potential energy (the top of a hill). Once there, gravity provides the force for it to flow (move) downward. If either path is broken, the flow or movement stops or is not completed.

Atomic Structures

Magnetic Fields

The motions of subatomic structures (nuclei and electrons) produce a **magnetic field**. It is the direction of the spin and orbit that indicates the direction of the field. The strength of a magnetic field is known as the **magnetic moment**. As electrons spin and orbit a nucleus, they produce a magnetic field. Pairs of electrons that spin and orbit in opposite directions cancel each other out, creating a net magnetic field of zero. Materials that have an unpaired electron are magnetic. Those with a weak attractive force are referred to as paramagnetic materials, while ferromagnetic materials have a strong attractive force. A diamagnetic material has electrons that are paired and, therefore, does not typically have a magnetic moment. There are, however, some diamagnetic materials that have a weak magnetic field.

Electric Charges

The attractive force between the electrons and the nucleus is called the **electric force**. A positive (+) charge or a negative (−) charge creates a field of sorts in the empty space around it, which is known as an **electric field**. The direction of a positive charge is away from the electric field and the direction of a negative charge is towards it. An electron within the force of the field is pulled towards a positive charge because an electron has a negative charge. A particle with a positive charge is pushed away, or repelled, by another positive charge. Like charges repel each other and opposite charges attract. Lines of force show the paths of charges. The **electric force** between two objects is directly proportional to the product of the charge magnitudes and inversely proportional to the square of the distance between the two objects. **Electric charge** is measured with the unit

Coulomb (C). It is the amount of charge moved in one second by a steady current of one ampere (1C = 1A × 1s).

Review Video: Electric Charge
Visit mometrix.com/academy and enter code: 323587

Electric Current Movement Through Circuits

Electric current is the sustained flow of electrons that are part of an electric charge moving along a path in a circuit. This differs from a static electric charge, which is a constant non-moving charge rather than a continuous flow. The **rate of flow of electric charge** is expressed using the ampere (amp or A) and can be measured using an ammeter. A current of 1 ampere means that 1 coulomb of charge passes through a given area every second. Electric charges typically only move from areas of high electric potential to areas of low electric potential. To get charges to flow into a high potential area, you must connect it to an area of higher potential by introducing a battery or other voltage source.

Simple Circuits

Movement of electric charge along a path between areas of high electric potential and low electric potential, with a resistor or load device between them, is the definition of a **simple circuit**. It is a closed conducting path between the high and low potential points, such as the positive and negative terminals on a battery. One example of a circuit is the flow from one terminal of a car battery to the other. The electrolyte solution of water and sulfuric acid provides work in chemical form to start the flow. A frequently used classroom example of circuits involves using a D cell (1.5 V) battery, a small light bulb, and a piece of copper wire to create a circuit to light the bulb.

Review Video: Resistance of Electric Currents
Visit mometrix.com/academy and enter code: 668423

Magnets

A **magnet** is a piece of metal, such as iron, steel, or magnetite (lodestone) that can affect another substance within its **field of force** that has like characteristics. Magnets can either attract or repel other substances. Magnets have two **poles**: north and south. Like poles repel and opposite poles (pairs of north and south) attract. The magnetic field is a set of invisible lines representing the paths of attraction and repulsion. Magnetism can occur naturally, or ferromagnetic materials can be magnetized. Certain matter that is magnetized can retain its magnetic properties indefinitely and become a permanent magnet. Other matter can lose its magnetic properties. For example, an iron nail can be temporarily magnetized by stroking it repeatedly in the same direction using one pole of another magnet. Once magnetized, it can attract or repel other magnetically inclined materials, such as paper clips. Dropping the nail repeatedly will cause it to lose its charge.

Review Video: Magnets
Visit mometrix.com/academy and enter code: 570803

Magnetic Fields, Current, and Magnetic Domains

A **magnetic field** can be formed not only by a magnetic material, but also by electric current flowing through a wire. When a coiled wire is attached to the two ends of a battery, for example, an electromagnet can be formed by inserting a ferromagnetic material such as an iron bar within the coil. When electric current flows through the wire, the bar becomes a magnet. If there is no current, the magnetism is lost. A **magnetic domain** occurs when the magnetic fields of atoms are grouped and aligned. These groups form what can be thought of as miniature magnets within a material.

This is what happens when an object like an iron nail is temporarily magnetized. Prior to magnetization, the organization of atoms and their various polarities are somewhat random with respect to where the north and south poles are pointing. After magnetization, a significant percentage of the poles are lined up in one direction, which is what causes the magnetic force exerted by the material.

Motion and Displacement

Motion is a change in the location of an object and is the result of an unbalanced net force acting on the object. Understanding motion requires an understanding of three basic quantities: displacement, velocity, and acceleration.

When something moves from one place to another, it has undergone **displacement**. Displacement along a straight line is a very simple example of a vector quantity. If an object travels from position $x = -5$ cm to $x = 5$ cm, it has undergone a displacement of 10 cm. If it traverses the same path in the opposite direction, its displacement is -10 cm. A vector that spans the object's displacement in the direction of travel is known as a displacement vector.

Review Video: Displacement
Visit mometrix.com/academy and enter code: 236197

Gravitational Force

Gravitational force is a universal force that causes every object to exert a force on every other object. The gravitational force between two objects can be described by the formula, $F = Gm_1m_2/r^2$, where m_1 and m_2 are the masses of two objects, r is the distance between them, and G is the gravitational constant, $G = 6.672 \times 10^{-11}\ \text{N m}^2/\text{kg}^2$. In order for this force to have a noticeable effect, one or both of the objects must be extremely large, so the equation is generally only used in problems involving planetary bodies. For problems involving objects on the earth being affected by earth's gravitational pull, the force of gravity is simply calculated as $F = mg$, where g is 9.81 m/s^2 toward the ground.

Review Video: What is Acceleration Due to Gravity?
Visit mometrix.com/academy and enter code: 938774

Newton's First Two Laws of Motion

Newton's First Law

An object at rest or in motion will remain at rest or in motion unless acted upon by an external force.

This phenomenon is commonly referred to as **inertia**, the tendency of a body to remain in its present state of motion. In order for the body's state of motion to change, it must be acted on by an unbalanced force.

Review Video: Newton's First Law of Motion
Visit mometrix.com/academy and enter code: 590367

Newton's Second Law

An object's acceleration is **directly proportional** to the net force acting on the object and **inversely proportional** to the object's mass.

This law is generally written in equation form $F = ma$, where F is the net force acting on a body, m is the mass of the body, and a is its acceleration. Note that since the mass is always a positive quantity, the acceleration is always in the same direction as the force.

Review Video: Newton's Second Law of Motion
Visit mometrix.com/academy and enter code: 737975

Simple Machines

Simple machines include the inclined plane, lever, wheel and axle, and pulley. These simple machines have no internal source of energy. More **complex or compound machines** can be formed from them. Simple machines provide a force known as a mechanical advantage and make it easier to accomplish a task. The **inclined plane** enables a force less than the object's weight to be used to push an object to a greater height. A **lever** enables a multiplication of force. The wheel and axle allows for movement with less resistance. Single or double **pulleys** allow for easier direction of force. The wedge and screw are forms of the inclined plane. A **wedge** turns a smaller force working over a greater distance into a larger force. The **screw** is similar to an incline that is wrapped around a shaft.

Review Video: Simple Machines
Visit mometrix.com/academy and enter code: 950789

Friction

Friction is a force that arises as a **resistance to motion** where two surfaces are in contact. The maximum magnitude of the frictional force (f) can be calculated as $f = F_c\mu$, where F_c is the contact force between the two objects and μ is a coefficient of friction based on the surfaces' material composition. Two types of friction are static and kinetic. To illustrate these concepts, imagine a book resting on a table. The force of its weight (W) is equal and opposite to the force of the table on the book, or the normal force (N). If we exert a small force (F) on the book, attempting to push it to one side, a frictional force (f) would arise, equal and opposite to our force. At this point, it is a **static frictional force** because the book is not moving. If we increase our force on the book, we will eventually cause it to move. At this point, the frictional force opposing us will be a **kinetic frictional force**. Generally, the kinetic frictional force is lower than static frictional force (because the frictional coefficient for static friction is larger), which means that the amount of force needed to maintain the movement of the book will be less than what was needed to start it moving.

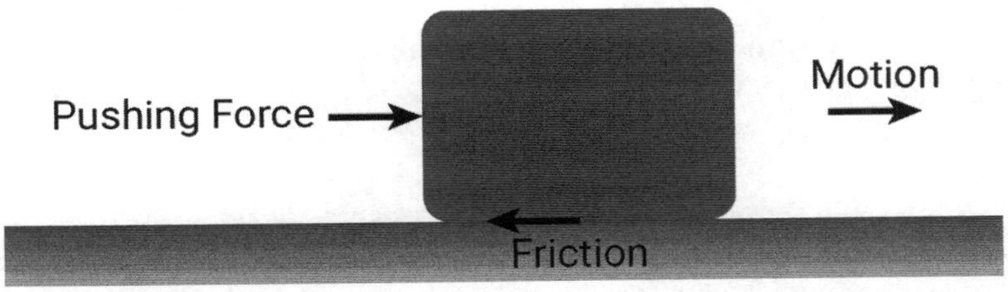

Review Video: Friction
Visit mometrix.com/academy and enter code: 716782

Sound

Sound is a pressure disturbance that moves through a medium in the form of mechanical waves, which transfer energy from one particle to the next. Sound requires a medium to travel through, such as air, water, or other matter since it is the vibrations that transfer energy to adjacent particles, not the actual movement of particles over a great distance. Sound is transferred through the movement of atomic particles, which can be atoms or molecules. Waves of sound energy move outward in all directions from the source. Sound waves consist of compressions (particles are forced together) and rarefactions (particles move farther apart and their density decreases). A wavelength consists of one compression and one rarefaction. Different sounds have different wavelengths. Sound is a form of kinetic energy.

Review Video: Sound
Visit mometrix.com/academy and enter code: 562378

Pitch, Loudness, Sound Intensity, Timbre, and Oscillation

Pitch — Pitch is the quality of sound determined by frequency. For example, a musical note can be tuned to a specific frequency. A, for instance, has a frequency of 440 Hz, which is a higher frequency than middle C. Humans can detect frequencies between about 20 Hz to 20,000 Hz.

Loudness — Loudness is a human's perception of sound intensity.

Sound intensity — Sound intensity is measured as the sound power per unit area and can be expressed in decibels.

Timbre — This is a human's perception of the type or quality of sound.

Oscillation — This is a measurement, usually of time, against a basic value, equilibrium, or rest point.

Doppler Effect

The **Doppler effect** refers to the effect the relative motion of the source of the wave and the location of the observer has on waves. The Doppler effect is easily observable in sound waves. What a person hears when a train approaches or a car honking its horn passes by are examples of the Doppler effect. The pitch of the sound is different not because the *emitted frequency* has changed, but because the *received frequency* has changed. The frequency is higher (as is the pitch) as the train approaches, the same as emitted just as it passes, and lower as the train moves away. This is because the wavelength changes. The Doppler effect can occur when an observer is stationary, and can also occur when two trains approach and pass each other. **Electromagnetic waves** are also affected in this manner. The motion of the medium can also affect the wave. For waves that do not travel in a medium, such as light waves, it is the difference in velocity that determines the outcome.

Waves

Waves have energy and can transfer energy when they interact with matter. Although waves transfer energy, they do not transport matter. They are a disturbance of matter that transfers energy from one particle to an adjacent particle. There are many types of waves, including sound, seismic, water, light, micro, and radio waves. The two basic categories of waves are mechanical and electromagnetic. **Mechanical waves** are those that transmit energy through matter. **Electromagnetic waves** can transmit energy through a vacuum. A **transverse wave** provides a good illustration of the features of a wave, which include crests, troughs, amplitude, and wavelength.

ELECTROMAGNETIC SPECTRUM

The electromagnetic spectrum is defined by frequency (f) and wavelength (λ). Frequency is typically measured in hertz and wavelength is usually measured in meters. Because light travels at a fairly constant speed, frequency is inversely proportional to wavelength, a relationship expressed by the formula $f = c/\lambda$, where c is the speed of light (about 3.0×10^8 m/s). Frequency multiplied by wavelength equals the speed of the wave; for electromagnetic waves, this is the speed of light, with some variance for the medium in which it is traveling. Electromagnetic waves include (from largest to smallest wavelength) radio waves, microwaves, infrared radiation (radiant heat), visible light, ultraviolet radiation, x-rays, and gamma rays. The energy of electromagnetic waves is carried in packets that have a magnitude inversely proportional to the wavelength. Radio waves have a range of wavelengths, from about 10^{-3} to 10^5 meters, while their frequencies range from 10^3 to about 10^{11} Hz.

Review Video: Electromagnetic Spectrum
Visit mometrix.com/academy and enter code: 771761

VISIBLE LIGHT

Light is the portion of the electromagnetic spectrum that is visible because of its ability to stimulate the retina. It is absorbed and emitted by electrons, atoms, and molecules that move from one energy level to another. **Visible light** interacts with matter through molecular electron excitation (which occurs in the human retina) and through plasma oscillations (which occur in metals). Visible light is between ultraviolet and infrared light on the spectrum. The wavelengths of visible light cover a range from 380 nm (violet) to 760 nm (red). Different wavelengths correspond to different colors.

REFLECTION AND REFRACTION

Reflection is the rebound of a light wave from a surface back toward the medium from where it came. A light wave that hits a reflecting surface at a 90-degree angle retraces its original path back to its source. Striking the surface at any other angle results in reflection of the wave at an angle in the opposite direction. Reflectance is the amount of light a material reflects; metals have high reflectance. The smoother a surface, the higher its reflectance. **Refraction** is the change in the direction of a light wave when it passes through a transparent medium with a different optical density from the one in which the wave had been traveling. This results in a change in the wave's velocity. The ratio of the sine of the angle of the incoming ray to the sine of the angle of refraction is equal to the ratio of the speed of light in the original medium to the speed of light in the refracting medium.

$$\frac{\sin\theta_{in}}{\sin\theta_{ref}} = \frac{v_{in}}{v_{ref}}$$

Review Video: Reflection, Transmission, and Absorption of Light
Visit mometrix.com/academy and enter code: 109410

Chemistry

Past Atomic Models and Theories

There have been many revisions to theories regarding the structure of **atoms** and their **particles**. Part of the challenge in developing an understanding of matter is that atoms and their particles are too small to be seen. It is believed that the first conceptualization of the atom was developed by **Democritus** in 400 B.C. Some of the more notable models are the solid sphere or billiard ball model postulated by John Dalton, the plum pudding or raisin bun model by J.J. Thomson, the planetary or nuclear model by Ernest Rutherford, the Bohr or orbit model by Niels Bohr, and the electron cloud or quantum mechanical model by Louis de Broglie and Erwin Schrodinger. Rutherford directed the alpha scattering experiment that discounted the plum pudding model. The shortcoming of the Bohr model was the belief that electrons orbited in fixed rather than changing ecliptic orbits.

Review Video: Atomic Models
Visit mometrix.com/academy and enter code: 434851

Models of Atoms

Atoms are extremely small. A hydrogen atom is about 5×10^{-8} mm in diameter. According to some estimates, five trillion hydrogen atoms could fit on the head of a pin. **Atomic radius** refers to the average distance between the nucleus and the outermost electron. Models of atoms that include the proton, nucleus, and electrons typically show the electrons very close to the nucleus and revolving around it, similar to how the Earth orbits the sun. However, another model relates the Earth as the nucleus and its atmosphere as electrons, which is the basis of the term "**electron cloud**." Another description is that electrons swarm around the nucleus. It should be noted that these atomic models are not to scale. A more accurate representation would be a nucleus with a diameter of about 2 cm in a stadium. The electrons would be in the bleachers. This model is similar to the not-to-scale solar system model. In reference to the periodic table, atomic radius increases as energy levels are added and decreases as more protons are added (because they pull the electrons closer to the nucleus). Essentially, atomic radius increases toward the left and toward the bottom of the periodic table (i.e., Francium (Fr) has the largest atomic radius while Helium (He) has the smallest).

Structure of Atoms

All matter consists of **atoms**. Atoms consist of a nucleus and electrons. The **nucleus** consists of protons and neutrons. The properties of these are measurable; they have mass and an electrical charge. The nucleus is positively charged due to the presence of protons. **Electrons** are negatively charged and orbit the nucleus. The nucleus has considerably more mass than the surrounding electrons. Atoms can bond together to make **molecules**. Atoms that have an equal number of protons and electrons are electrically neutral. If the number of protons and electrons in an atom is not equal, the atom has a positive or negative charge and is an ion.

Atomic Number, Neutrons, Nucleon, and Element

- **Atomic number** (proton number) — The atomic number of an element refers to the number of protons in the nucleus of an atom. It is a unique identifier. It can be represented as Z. Atoms with a neutral charge have an atomic number that is equal to the number of electrons.
- **Neutrons** — Neutrons are the uncharged atomic particles contained within the nucleus. The number of neutrons in a nucleus can be represented as "N."
- **Nucleon** — This refers collectively to both neutrons and protons.

- **Element** — An element is matter with one particular type of atom. It can be identified by its atomic number or the number of protons in its nucleus. There are approximately 117 elements currently known, 94 of which occur naturally on Earth. Elements from the periodic table include hydrogen, carbon, iron, helium, mercury, and oxygen.

Molecules

Electrons in an atom can orbit different levels around the nucleus. They can absorb or release energy, which can change the location of their orbit or even allow them to break free from the atom. The outermost layer is the **valence layer**, which contains the valence electrons. The valence layer tends to have or share eight electrons. **Molecules** are formed by a chemical bond between atoms, a bond that occurs at the valence level. Two basic types of bonds are covalent and ionic. A **covalent bond** is formed when atoms share electrons. An **ionic bond** is formed when an atom transfers an electron to another atom. A cation or positive ion is formed when an atom loses one or more electrons. An anion or negative ion is formed when an atom gains one or more electrons. A **hydrogen bond** is a weak bond between a hydrogen atom of one molecule and an electronegative atom (such as nitrogen, oxygen, or fluorine) of another molecule. The **Van der Waals force** is a weak force between molecules. This type of force is much weaker than actual chemical bonds between atoms.

Review Video: Molecules
Visit mometrix.com/academy and enter code: 349910

Interaction of Atoms to Form Compounds

Atoms interact by **transferring** or sharing the electrons furthest from the nucleus. Known as the outer or **valence electrons**, they are responsible for the chemical properties of an element. **Bonds** between atoms are created when electrons are paired up by being transferred or shared. If electrons are transferred from one atom to another, the bond is ionic. If electrons are shared, the bond is covalent. Atoms of the same element may bond together to form molecules or crystalline solids. When two or more different types of atoms bind together chemically, a compound is made. The physical properties of compounds reflect the nature of the interactions among their molecules. These interactions are determined by the structure of the molecule, including the atoms they consist of and the distances and angles between them.

Matter

Matter refers to substances that have mass and occupy space (or volume). The traditional definition of matter describes it as having three states: solid, liquid, and gas. These different states are caused by differences in the distances and angles between molecules or atoms, which result in differences in the energy that binds them. **Solid** structures are rigid or nearly rigid and have strong bonds. Molecules or atoms of **liquids** move around and have weak bonds, although they are not weak enough to readily break. Molecules or atoms of **gases** move almost independently of each other, are typically far apart, and do not form bonds. The current definition of matter describes it as having four states. The fourth is **plasma**, which is an ionized gas that has some electrons that are described as free because they are not bound to an atom or molecule.

Review Video: States of Matter
Visit mometrix.com/academy and enter code: 742449

Most Abundant Elements in the Universe and on Earth

Aside from dark energy and dark matter, which are thought to account for all but four percent of the universe, the two most abundant elements in the universe are **hydrogen** (H) and **helium** (He).

After hydrogen and helium, the most abundant elements are oxygen, neon, nitrogen, carbon, silicon, and magnesium. The most abundant isotopes in the solar system are hydrogen-1 and helium-4. Measurements of the masses of elements in the Earth's crust indicate that oxygen (O), silicon (Si), and aluminum (Al) are the most abundant on Earth. Hydrogen in its plasma state is the most abundant chemical element in stars in their main sequences but is relatively rare on planet Earth.

Energy Transformations

The following are some examples of energy transformations:

- **Electric to mechanical**: Ceiling fan
- **Chemical to heat**: A familiar example of a chemical to heat energy transformation is the internal combustion engine, which transforms the chemical energy (a type of potential energy) of gas and oxygen into heat. This heat is transformed into propulsive energy, which is kinetic. Lighting a match and burning coal are also examples of chemical to heat energy transformations.
- **Chemical to light**: Phosphorescence and luminescence (which allow objects to glow in the dark) occur because energy is absorbed by a substance (charged) and light is re-emitted comparatively slowly. This process is different from the one involved with glow sticks. They glow due to chemiluminescence, in which an excited state is created by a chemical reaction and transferred to another molecule.
- **Heat to electricity**: Examples include thermoelectric, geothermal, and ocean thermal.
- **Nuclear to heat**: Examples include nuclear reactors and power plants.
- **Mechanical to sound**: Playing a violin or almost any instrument
- **Sound to electric**: Microphone
- **Light to electric**: Solar panels
- **Electric to light**: Light bulbs

Relationship Between Conservation of Matter and Atomic Theory

Atomic theory is concerned with the characteristics and properties of atoms that make up matter. It deals with matter on a *microscopic level* as opposed to a *macroscopic level*. Atomic theory, for instance, discusses the kinetic motion of atoms in order to explain the properties of macroscopic quantities of matter. John Dalton (1766-1844) is credited with making many contributions to the field of atomic theory that are still considered valid. This includes the notion that all matter consists of atoms and that atoms are indestructible. In other words, atoms can be neither created nor destroyed. This is also the theory behind the conservation of matter, which explains why chemical reactions do not result in any detectable gains or losses in matter. This holds true for chemical reactions and smaller-scale processes. When dealing with large amounts of energy, however, atoms can be destroyed by nuclear reactions. This can happen in particle colliders or atom smashers.

Review Video: Chemical Reactions
Visit mometrix.com/academy and enter code: 579876

Review Video: John Dalton
Visit mometrix.com/academy and enter code: 565627

Difference Between Atoms and Molecules

Elements from the periodic table such as hydrogen, carbon, iron, helium, mercury, and oxygen are **atoms**. Atoms combine to form molecules. For example, two atoms of hydrogen (H) and one atom of oxygen (O) combine to form one molecule of water (H_2O).

Chemical and Physical Properties

Matter has both physical and chemical properties. **Physical properties** can be seen or observed without changing the identity or composition of matter. For example, the mass, volume, and density of a substance can be determined without permanently changing the sample. Other physical properties include color, boiling point, freezing point, solubility, odor, hardness, electrical conductivity, thermal conductivity, ductility, and malleability. **Chemical properties** cannot be measured without changing the identity or composition of matter. Chemical properties describe how a substance reacts or changes to form a new substance. Examples of chemical properties include flammability, corrosivity, oxidation states, enthalpy of formation, and reactivity with other chemicals.

Chemical and Physical Changes

Physical changes do not produce new substances. The atoms or molecules may be rearranged, but no new substances are formed. Phase changes or changes of state such as melting, freezing, and sublimation are physical changes. For example, physical changes include the melting of ice, the boiling of water, sugar dissolving into water, and the crushing of a piece of chalk into a fine powder. **Chemical changes** involve a chemical reaction and do produce new substances. When iron rusts, iron oxide is formed, indicating a chemical change. Other examples of chemical changes include baking a cake, burning wood, digesting a cracker, and mixing an acid and a base.

Physical and Chemical Properties and Changes

Both physical changes and chemical reactions are everyday occurrences. **Physical changes** do not result in different substances. For example, when water becomes ice it has undergone a physical change, but not a chemical change. It has changed its form, but not its composition. It is still H_2O. **Chemical properties** are concerned with the constituent particles that make up the physicality of a substance. Chemical properties are apparent when **chemical changes** occur. The chemical properties of a substance are influenced by its electron configuration, which is determined in part by the number of protons in the nucleus (the atomic number). Carbon, for example, has 6 protons and 6 electrons. It is an element's outermost valence electrons that mainly determine its chemical properties. Chemical reactions may release or consume energy.

Review Video: Chemical and Physical Properties of Matter
Visit mometrix.com/academy and enter code: 717349

Elements, Compounds, Solutions, and Mixtures

- **Elements** — These are substances that consist of only one type of atom.
- **Compounds** — These are substances containing two or more elements. Compounds are formed by chemical reactions and frequently have different properties than the original elements. Compounds are decomposed by a chemical reaction rather than separated by a physical one.
- **Solutions** — These are homogeneous mixtures composed of two or more substances that have become one.
- **Mixtures** — Mixtures contain two or more substances that are combined but have not reacted chemically with each other. Mixtures can be separated using physical methods, while compounds cannot.

Heat, Energy, Work, and Thermal Energy

- **Heat** — Heat is the transfer of energy from a body or system as a result of thermal contact. Heat consists of random motion and the vibration of atoms, molecules, and ions. The higher the temperature is, the greater the atomic or molecular motion will be.
- **Energy** — Energy is the capacity to do work.
- **Work** — Work is the quantity of energy transferred by one system to another due to changes in a system that is the result of external forces, or macroscopic variables. Another way to put this is that work is the amount of energy that must be transferred to overcome a force. Lifting an object in the air is an example of work. The opposing force that must be overcome is gravity. Work is measured in joules (J). The rate at which work is performed is known as power.
- **Thermal energy** — Thermal energy is the energy present in a system due to temperature.

Types of Energy

Some discussions of energy consider only two types of energy: **kinetic energy** (the energy of motion) and **potential energy** (which depends on relative position or orientation). There are, however, other types of energy. **Electromagnetic waves**, for example, are a type of energy contained by a field. Another type of potential energy is electrical energy, which is the energy it takes to pull apart positive and negative electrical charges. **Chemical energy** refers to the manner in which atoms form into molecules, and this energy can be released or absorbed when molecules regroup. **Solar energy** comes in the form of visible light and non-visible light, such as infrared and ultraviolet rays. **Sound energy** refers to the energy in sound waves.

Chemical Reactions

Chemical reactions measured in human time can take place quickly or slowly. They can take fractions of a second or billions of years. The rates of chemical reactions are determined by how frequently reacting atoms and molecules interact. Rates are also influenced by the temperature and various properties (such as shape) of the reacting materials. **Catalysts** accelerate chemical reactions, while inhibitors decrease reaction rates. Some types of reactions release energy in the form of heat and light. Some types of reactions involve the transfer of either electrons or hydrogen ions between reacting ions, molecules, or atoms. In other reactions, chemical bonds are broken down by heat or light to form reactive radicals with electrons that will readily form new bonds. Processes such as the formation of ozone and greenhouse gases in the atmosphere and the burning and processing of fossil fuels are controlled by radical reactions.

Review Video: Catalysts
Visit mometrix.com/academy and enter code: 288189

Reading Chemical Equations

Chemical equations describe chemical reactions. The reactants are on the left side before the arrow. The products are on the right side after the arrow. The arrow is the mark that points to the reaction or change. The coefficient is the number before the element. This gives the ratio of reactants to products in terms of moles.

The equation for making water from hydrogen and oxygen is $2H_{2(g)} + O_{2(g)} \rightarrow 2H_2O_{(l)}$. The number 2 before hydrogen and water is the coefficient. This means that there are 2 moles of hydrogen and 2 of water. There is 1 mole of oxygen. This does not need to have the number 1 before the symbol for the element. For additional information, the following subscripts are often included to indicate the state of the substance: (g) stands for gas, (l) stands for liquid, (s) stands for solid, and (aq) stands for aqueous. Aqueous means the substance is dissolved in water. Charges are shown by superscript for individual ions, not for ionic compounds. Polyatomic ions are separated by parentheses. This is done so the kind of ion will not be confused with the number of ions.

BALANCING EQUATIONS

An **unbalanced equation** is one that does not follow the **law of conservation of mass**, which states that matter can only be changed, not created or destroyed. If an equation is unbalanced, the numbers of atoms indicated by the stoichiometric coefficients on each side of the arrow will not be equal. Start by writing the formulas for each species in the reaction. Count the atoms on each side and determine if the number is equal. Coefficients must be whole numbers. Fractional amounts, such as half a molecule, are not possible. Equations can be balanced by adjusting the coefficients of each part of the equation to the smallest possible whole number coefficient. $H_2 + O_2 \rightarrow H_2O$ is an example of an unbalanced equation. The balanced equation is $2H_2 + O_2 \rightarrow 2H_2O$, which indicates that it takes two moles of hydrogen and one of oxygen to produce two moles of water.

Review Video: How Do You Balance Chemical Equations?
Visit mometrix.com/academy and enter code: 341228

PERIODIC TABLE

The **periodic table** groups elements with similar chemical properties together. The grouping of elements is based on **atomic structure**. It shows periodic trends of physical and chemical properties and identifies families of elements with similar properties. It is a common model for organizing and understanding elements. In the periodic table, each element has its own cell that includes varying amounts of information presented in symbol form about the properties of the element. Cells in the table are arranged in **rows** (periods) and **columns** (groups or families). At minimum, a cell includes the symbol for the element and its atomic number. The cell for hydrogen, for example, which appears first in the upper left corner, includes an "H" and a "1" above the letter. Elements are ordered by atomic number, left to right, top to bottom.

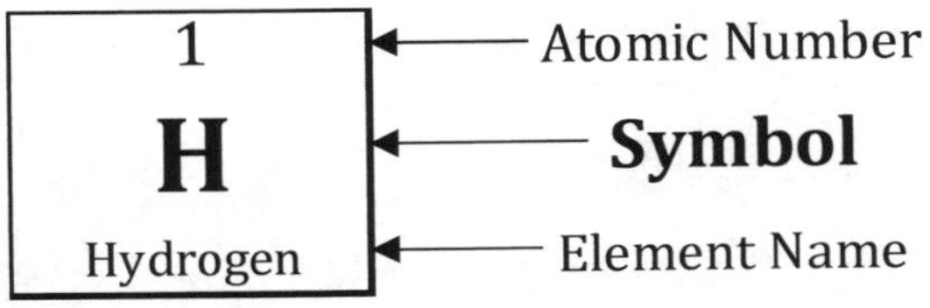

Review Video: Periodic Table
Visit mometrix.com/academy and enter code: 154828

SOLUTIONS

A **solution** is a homogeneous mixture. A **mixture** is two or more different substances that are mixed together, but not combined chemically. Homogeneous mixtures are those that are uniform in their composition. Solutions consist of a solute (the substance that is dissolved) and a solvent (the substance that does the dissolving). An example is sugar water. The solvent is the water and the solute is the sugar. The intermolecular attraction between the solvent and the solute is called solvation. **Hydration** refers to solutions in which water is the solvent. Solutions are formed when the forces between the molecules of the solute and the solvent are as strong as the forces holding the solute together. An example is that salt (NaCl) dissolves in water to create a solution. The Na^+

and the Cl^- ions in salt interact with the molecules of water and vice versa to overcome the intramolecular forces of the solute.

Review Video: Solutions
Visit mometrix.com/academy and enter code: 995937

Review Video: Concentration of Solution Percent by Volume
Visit mometrix.com/academy and enter code: 400152

Mixtures, Suspensions, Colloids, Emulsions, and Foams

A **mixture** is a combination of two or more substances that are not bonded. **Suspensions** are mixtures of heterogeneous materials. Particles in suspensions are usually larger than those found in true solutions. Dirt mixed vigorously with water is an example of a suspension. The dirt is temporarily suspended in water, but the two separate once the mixing is ceased. A mixture of large (1 nm to 500 nm) particles is called a **colloidal suspension**. The particles are termed dispersants and the dispersing medium is similar to the solvent in a solution. Sol refers to a liquid or a solid that also has solids dispersed through it, such as milk or gelatin. An aerosol spray is a colloid suspension of gas and the solid or liquid being dispersed. An **emulsion** refers to a liquid or a solid that has small droplets of another liquid dispersed through it. A **foam** is a liquid that has gas dispersed through it.

pH

The **potential of hydrogen** (pH) is a measurement of the concentration of hydrogen ions in a substance in terms of the number of moles of H^+ per liter of solution. All substances fall between 0 and 14 on the pH scale. A lower pH indicates a higher H^+ concentration, while a higher pH indicates a lower H^+ concentration. Pure water has a neutral pH, which is 7. Anything with a pH lower than water (0-7) is considered acidic. Anything with a pH higher than water (7-14) is a base. Drain cleaner, soap, baking soda, ammonia, egg whites, and sea water are common bases. Urine, stomach acid, citric acid, vinegar, hydrochloric acid, and battery acid are acids. A pH indicator is a substance that acts as a detector of hydrogen or hydronium ions. It is halochromic, meaning it changes color to indicate that hydrogen or hydronium ions have been detected.

Review Video: pH
Visit mometrix.com/academy and enter code: 187395

Properties of Acids

When they are dissolved in aqueous solutions, some properties of **acids** are that they conduct electricity, change blue litmus paper to red, have a sour taste, react with bases to neutralize them, and react with active metals to free hydrogen. A **weak acid** is one that does not donate all of its protons or disassociate completely. **Strong acids** include hydrochloric, hydriodic, hydrobromic, perchloric, nitric, and sulfuric. They ionize completely. **Superacids** are those that are stronger than 100 percent sulfuric acid. They include fluoroantimonic, magic, and perchloric acids. Acids can be used in pickling, a process used to remove rust and corrosion from metals. They are also used as catalysts in the processing of minerals and the production of salts and fertilizers. Phosphoric acid (H_3PO_4) is added to sodas and other acids are added to foods as preservatives or to add taste.

Review Video: Properties of Acids
Visit mometrix.com/academy and enter code: 645283

Properties of Bases

When they are dissolved in aqueous solutions, some properties of **bases** are that they conduct electricity, change red litmus paper to blue, feel slippery, and react with acids to neutralize their properties. A **weak base** is one that does not completely ionize in an aqueous solution, and usually has a low pH. **Strong bases** can free protons in very weak acids. Examples of strong bases are hydroxide compounds such as potassium, barium, and lithium hydroxides. Most are in the first and second groups of the periodic table. A **superbase** is extremely strong compared to sodium hydroxide and cannot be kept in an aqueous solution. Superbases are organized into organic, organometallic, and inorganic classes. Bases are used as insoluble catalysts in heterogeneous reactions and as catalysts in hydrogenation.

Properties of Salts

Some properties of **salts** are that they are formed from acid base reactions, are ionic compounds consisting of metallic and nonmetallic ions, dissociate in water, and are comprised of tightly bonded ions. Some common salts are sodium chloride (NaCl), sodium bisulfate ($NaHSO_4$), potassium dichromate ($K_2Cr_2O_7$), and calcium chloride ($CaCl_2$). Calcium chloride is used as a drying agent, and may be used to absorb moisture when freezing mixtures. Potassium nitrate (KNO_3) is used to make fertilizer and in the manufacturing of explosives. Sodium nitrate ($NaNO_3$) is also used in the making of fertilizer. Baking soda [sodium bicarbonate ($NaHCO_3$)] is a salt, as are Epsom salts [magnesium sulfate ($MgSO_4$)]. Salt and water can react to form a base and an acid. This is called a **hydrolysis reaction**.

Unique Properties of Water

The important properties of water (H_2O) are high polarity, hydrogen bonding, cohesiveness, adhesiveness, high specific heat, high latent heat, and high heat of vaporization. Water is vital to life as we know it. The reason is that water is one of the main parts of many living things.

Water is a liquid at room temperature. The high specific heat of water means that it does not easily break its hydrogen bonds. Also, it resists heat and motion. This is why it has a high boiling point and high vaporization point.

Most substances are denser in their solid forms. However, water is different because its solid-state floats in its liquid state. Water is cohesive. This means that it is drawn to itself. It is also adhesive. This means that it draws in other molecules. If water will attach to another substance, the substance is said to be hydrophilic. Because of its cohesive and adhesive properties, water makes a good solvent. Substances with polar ions and molecules easily dissolve in water.

Review Video: Properties of Water
Visit mometrix.com/academy and enter code: 279526

Kinetic Theory of Gases

The **kinetic theory of gases** assumes that gas molecules are small compared to the distances between them and that they are in constant random motion. The attractive and repulsive forces between gas molecules are negligible. Their kinetic energy does not change with time as long as the temperature remains the same. The higher the temperature is, the greater the motion will be. As the temperature of a gas increases, so does the kinetic energy of the molecules. In other words, gas will occupy a greater volume as the temperature is increased and a lesser volume as the temperature is decreased. In addition, the same amount of gas will occupy a greater volume as the temperature increases, but pressure remains constant. At any given temperature, gas molecules have the same average kinetic energy. The **ideal gas law** is derived from the kinetic theory of gases.

Review Video: Ideal Gas Law
Visit mometrix.com/academy and enter code: 381353

Organic Compounds

Two of the main characteristics of **organic compounds** are that they **include carbon** and are formed by **covalent bonds**. Carbon can form long chains, double and triple bonds, and rings. While inorganic compounds tend to have high melting points, organic compounds tend to melt at temperatures below 300° C. They also tend to boil, sublimate, and decompose below this temperature. Unlike inorganic compounds, they are not very water-soluble. Organic molecules are organized into functional groups based on their specific atoms, which helps determine how they will react chemically. A few groups are alkanes, nitro, alkenes, sulfides, amines, and carbolic acids. The hydroxyl group ($-OH$) consists of alcohols. These molecules are polar, which increases their solubility. By some estimates, there are more than 16 million organic compounds.

Review Video: Organic Compounds
Visit mometrix.com/academy and enter code: 264922

Hydrogen Bonds

Hydrogen bonds are weaker than covalent and ionic bonds and refer to the type of attraction in an electronegative atom such as oxygen, fluorine, or nitrogen. Hydrogen bonds can form within a single molecule or between molecules. A water molecule is **polar**, meaning it is partially positively charged on one end (the hydrogen end) and partially negatively charged on the other (the oxygen end). This is because the hydrogen atoms are arranged around the oxygen atom in a close tetrahedron. Hydrogen is **oxidized** (its number of electrons is reduced) when it bonds with oxygen to form water. Hydrogen bonds tend not only to be weak but also short-lived. They also tend to be numerous. Hydrogen bonds give water many of its important properties, including its high specific heat and high heat of vaporization, its solvent qualities, its adhesiveness and cohesiveness, its hydrophobic qualities, and its ability to float in its solid form. Hydrogen bonds are also an important component of proteins, nucleic acids, and DNA.

Inorganic Compounds

The main trait of **inorganic compounds** is that they lack carbon. Inorganic compounds include mineral salts, metals and alloys, non-metallic compounds such as phosphorus, and metal complexes. A metal complex has a central atom (or ion) bonded to surrounding ligands (molecules or anions). The ligands sacrifice the donor atoms (in the form of at least one pair of electrons) to the central atom. Many inorganic compounds are ionic, meaning they form ionic bonds rather than share electrons. They may have high melting points because of this. They may also be colorful, but this is not an absolute identifier of an inorganic compound. Salts, which are inorganic compounds, are an example of inorganic bonding of cations and anions. Some examples of salts are magnesium chloride ($MgCl_2$) and sodium oxide (Na_2O). Oxides, carbonates, sulfates, and halides are classes of inorganic compounds. They are typically poor conductors, are very water soluble, and crystallize easily. Minerals and silicates are also inorganic compounds.

Biology

Subfields of Biology

There are a number of subfields of biology:

- **Zoology** – The study of animals
- **Botany** – The study of plants
- **Biophysics** – The application of the laws of physics to the processes of organisms and the application of the facts about living things to human processes and inventions
- **Biochemistry** – The study of the chemistry of living organisms, including diseases and the pharmaceutical drugs used to cure them
- **Cytology** – The study of cells
- **Histology** – The study of the tissues of plants and animals
- **Organology** – The study of tissues organized into organs
- **Physiology** – The study of the way organisms function, including metabolism, the exchange of matter and energy in nutrition, the senses, reproduction and development, and the work of the nervous system and brain
- **Genetics** – The study of heredity as it relates to the transmission of genes
- **Ethology** – The study of animal behavior
- **Ecology** – The study of the relationship of living organisms to their environments

Classification of Life Forms

All living creatures can be classified into one of three domains and then into one of six kingdoms:

- Domain Bacteria
    - **Kingdom Eubacteria**—single celled prokaryotes with little internal complexity, contains peptidoglycan. Members have just one chromosome, reproduce asexually, may have flagella, and are very simple in form.
- Domain Archaea
    - **Kingdom Archaebacteria**—single celled prokaryotes with little internal complexity, does not contain peptidoglycan. Members have just one chromosome, reproduce asexually, may have flagella, and are very simple in form.
- Domain Eukarya
    - **Kingdom Protista**—single celled eukaryotes with greater internal complexity than Bacteria or Archaea. They have a true nucleus surrounded by a membrane that separates it from the cytoplasm. Most are one-celled and have no complex tissues like plants.
    - **Kingdom Fungi**—single celled or multicellular with considerable variation and complexity. Members have no chlorophyll, so they don't make their own food like plants. They reproduce using spores. Fungi are made up of filaments called hyphae that, in larger fungi, can interlace to form a tissue called mycelium.

- **Kingdom Plantae**—multicellular with great variation and complexity, rigid cell walls. This group consists of organisms that have chlorophyll and make their own food. Plants have differentiated tissues and reproduce either sexually or asexually.
- **Kingdom Animalia**—multicellular with much variation and complexity, cell membrane. This group consists of organisms that move around and have to feed on existing organic material.

Review Video: Kingdom Animalia
Visit mometrix.com/academy and enter code: 558413

Review Video: Kingdom Fungi
Visit mometrix.com/academy and enter code: 315081

Review Video: Kingdom Plantae
Visit mometrix.com/academy and enter code: 710084

Characteristics of Invertebrates

Invertebrates are animals with no internal skeletons. They can be divided into three groups:

1. **Marine Invertebrates** – Members of this group live in oceans and seas. Marine invertebrates include sponges, corals, jellyfish, snails, clams, octopuses, squids, and crustaceans, none of which live on the surface.
2. **Freshwater Invertebrates** – Members of this group live in lakes and rivers. Freshwater invertebrates include worms on the bottom, microscopic crustaceans, and terrestrial insect larvae that live in the water column, but only where there is no strong current. Some live on the surface of the water.
3. **Terrestrial Invertebrates** – Members of this group live on dry ground. Terrestrial invertebrates include insects, mollusks (snails, slugs), arachnids, and myriapods (centipedes and millipedes). Terrestrial invertebrates breathe through a series of tubes that penetrate into the body (trachea) and deliver oxygen into tissues. Underground terrestrial invertebrates are generally light-colored with atrophied eyes and no cuticle to protect them from desiccation. They include worms that live underground and in caves and rock crevices. This group also includes insects such as ants that create colonies underground.

Characteristics of Vertebrate Groups

The **vertebrates**, animals with an internal skeleton, are divided into four groups:

1. **Fish** – This group is the most primitive, but is also the group from which all other groups evolved. Fish live in water, breathe with gills, are cold-blooded, have fins and scales, and are typically oviparous, which means they lay eggs. Fish typically have either cartilaginous skeletons (such as rays and sharks) or bony skeletons.
2. **Amphibians** – The skin of animals in this group is delicate and permeable, so they need water to keep it moist. Amphibians are oviparous. The young start out in water with gills, but the adults use lungs.
3. **Reptiles and birds** – The skin of animals in this group has very hard, horn-like scales. Birds have exchanged scales for feathers. Reptiles and birds are oviparous, although birds care for their eggs and reptiles do not. Members have a cloaca, an excretory and reproductive cavity that opens to the outside. Reptiles are cold-blooded, but birds are warm-blooded.

4. **Mammals** – These are the most highly evolved vertebrates. Mammals have bodies covered with fur; are warm-blooded; are viviparous, meaning they give birth to live young which are fed with milk from female mammary glands; and are tetrapods (four-legged). Most live on the ground (except whales and dolphins) and a few fly (bats).

Hunters and Prey Animals

The interaction between **predators** and their **prey** is important to controlling the balance of an ecosystem. **Hunters** are **carnivorous** animals at the top of the ecological pyramid that eat other animals. Hunters tend to be territorial, leaving signs to warn others to stay out or risk a fight. Hunters are equipped to capture with claws, curved beaks, spurs, fangs, etc. They try to use a minimum amount of energy for each capture, so they prey upon the more vulnerable (the old, ill, or very young) when given a choice. Predators never kill more than they can eat. Some hunters have great speed, some stalk, and some hunt in groups. **Prey** animals are those that are captured by predators for food. They are usually **herbivores** further down the ecological pyramid. Prey animals have special characteristics to help them flee from predators. They may hide in nests or caves, become totally immobile to escape detection, have protective coloration or camouflage, have warning coloration to indicate being poisonous, or have shells or quills for protection.

Life Processes That All Living Things Have in Common

Living things share many **processes** that are necessary to survival, but the ways these processes and interactions occur are highly diverse. Processes include those related to:

- **Nutrition** – the process of obtaining, ingesting, and digesting foods; excreting unused or excess substances; and extracting energy from the foods to maintain structure.
- **Transport** (circulation) – the process of circulating essential materials such as nutrients, cells, hormones, and gases (oxygen and hydrogen) to the places they are needed by moving them through veins, arteries, and capillaries. Needed materials do not travel alone, but are "piggybacked" on transporting molecules.
- **Respiration** – the process of breathing, which is exchanging gases between the interior and exterior using gills, trachea (insects), or lungs.
- **Regulation** – the process of coordinating life activities through the nervous and endocrine systems.
- **Reproduction and growth** – the process of producing more of one's own kind and growing from birth to adulthood. The more highly evolved an animal is, the longer its growth time is.
- **Locomotion** (in animals) – the process of moving from place to place in the environment by using legs, flight, or body motions.

Organisms That Interfere with Cell Activity

Viruses, bacteria, fungi, and other parasites may infect plants and animals and interfere with normal life functions, create imbalances, or disrupt the operations of cells.

- **Viruses** – These enter the body by inhalation (airborne) or through contact with contaminated food, water, or infected tissues. They affect the body by taking over the cell's protein synthesis mechanism to make more viruses. They kill the host cell and impact tissue and organ operations. Examples of viruses include measles, rabies, pneumonia, and AIDS.
- **Bacteria** – These enter the body through breaks in the skin or contaminated food or water, or by inhalation. They reproduce rapidly and produce toxins that kill healthy host tissues. Examples include diphtheria, bubonic plague, tuberculosis, and syphilis.

- **Fungi** – These feed on healthy tissues of the body by sending rootlike tendrils into the tissues to digest them extracellularly. Examples include athlete's foot and ringworm.
- **Parasites** – These enter the body through the skin, via insect bites, or through contaminated food or water. Examples include tapeworms, malaria, or typhus.

HYDROCARBONS AND CARBOHYDRATES

Carbon is an element found in all living things. Two types of carbon molecules that are essential to life are hydrocarbons and carbohydrates. **Hydrocarbons**, composed only of hydrogen and carbon, are the simplest organic molecules. The simplest of these is methane, which has one carbon atom and four hydrogen atoms. Methane is produced by the decomposition of animal or vegetable matter, and is part of petroleum and natural gas. **Carbohydrates** are compounds made of hydrogen, carbon, and oxygen. There are three types of these macromolecules (large molecules):

1. **Sugars** are soluble in water and, although they have less energy than fats, provide energy more quickly.
2. **Starches**, insoluble in water, are long chains of glucose that act as reserve substances. Potatoes and cereals are valuable foods because they are rich in starch. Animals retain glucose in their cells as glycogen, a special type of starch.
3. **Cellulose**, composed of glucose chains, makes up the cells and tissues of plants. It is one of the most common organic materials.

Review Video: Basics of Hydrocarbons
Visit mometrix.com/academy and enter code: 824749

LIPIDS, PROTEINS, AND NUCLEIC ACIDS

Besides hydrocarbons and carbohydrates, there are three other types of carbon molecules that are essential to life: lipids, proteins, and nucleic acids. **Lipids** are compounds that are insoluble or only partially soluble in water. There are three main types: fats, which act as an energy reserve for organisms; phospholipids, which are one of the essential components of cell membranes; and steroids such as cholesterol and estrogen, which are very important to metabolism. **Proteins** are complex substances that make up almost half the dry weight of animal bodies. These molecules contain hydrogen, carbon, oxygen, and other elements, chiefly nitrogen and sulfur. Proteins make up muscle fibers and, as enzymes, act as catalysts. **Nucleic acids** are large molecules (polymers) composed of a large number of simpler molecules (nucleotides). Each one has a sugar containing five carbons (pentose), a phosphorous compound (phosphate group), and a nitrogen compound (nitrogenated base). Nucleic acids facilitate perpetuation of the species because they carry genetic information as DNA and RNA.

CELL

The **cell** is the basic organizational unit of all living things. Each piece within a cell has a function that helps organisms grow and survive. There are many different types of cells, but cells are unique to each type of organism. The one thing that all cells have in common is a **membrane**, which is comparable to a semi-permeable plastic bag. The membrane is composed of phospholipids. There are also some **transport holes**, which are proteins that help certain molecules and ions move in and out of the cell. The cell is filled with a fluid called **cytoplasm** or cytosol. Within the cell are a variety of **organelles**, groups of complex molecules that help a cell survive, each with its own unique membrane that has a different chemical makeup from the cell membrane. The larger the cell, the more organelles it will need to live.

Review Video: Plant and Animal Cells
Visit mometrix.com/academy and enter code: 115568

Review Video: An Introduction to Cellular Biology
Visit mometrix.com/academy and enter code: 629967

Review Video: Cell Structure
Visit mometrix.com/academy and enter code: 591293

Nucleus and Mitochondria in Eukaryotic Cells

Eukaryotic cells have a nucleus, a big dark spot floating somewhere in the center that acts like the brain of the cell by controlling eating, movement, and reproduction. A **nuclear envelope** surrounds the nucleus and its contents, but allows RNA and proteins to pass through. **Chromatin**, made up of DNA, RNA, and nuclear proteins, is present in the nucleus. The nucleus also contains a nucleolus made of RNA and protein. **Mitochondria** are very small organelles that take in nutrients, break them down, and create energy for the cell through a process called cellular respiration. There might be thousands of mitochondria depending on the cell's purpose. A muscle cell needs more energy for movement than a cell that transmits nerve impulses, for example. Mitochondria have two membranes: a **cover** and the **inner cristae** that folds over many times to increase the surface work area. The fluid inside the mitochondria, the matrix, is filled with water and enzymes that take food molecules and combine them with oxygen so they can be digested.

Review Video: Mitochondria
Visit mometrix.com/academy and enter code: 444287

Review Video: Cellular Energy Production
Visit mometrix.com/academy and enter code: 743401

Review Video: Cell Functions
Visit mometrix.com/academy and enter code: 883787

Chloroplasts of Plant Cells

Chloroplasts, which make plants green, are the food producers of a plant cell. They differ from an animal cell's mitochondria, which break down sugars and nutrients. **Photosynthesis** occurs when the energy from the sun hits a chloroplast and the chlorophyll uses that energy to combine carbon dioxide and water to make sugars and oxygen. The nutrition and oxygen obtained from plants makes them the basis of all life on earth. A chloroplast has two membranes to contain and protect the inner parts. The **stroma** is an area inside the chloroplast where reactions occur and starches are created. A **thylakoid** has chlorophyll molecules on its surface, and a stack of thylakoids is called a granum. The stacks of sacs are connected by **stromal lamellae**, which act like the skeleton of the chloroplast, keeping all the sacs a safe distance from each other and maximizing the efficiency of the organelle.

Passive and Active Transport

Passive transport within a cell does not require energy and work. For example, when there is a large concentration difference between the outside and the inside of a cell, the pressure of the greater concentration, not energy, will move molecules across the lipid bilayer into the cell. Another example of passive transport is osmosis, which is the movement of water across a membrane. Too much water in a cell can cause it to burst, so the cell moves ions in and out to help equalize the amount of water. **Active transport** is when a cell uses energy to move individual molecules across the cell membrane to maintain a proper balance. **Proteins** embedded in the lipid bilayer do most of the transport work. There are hundreds of different types of proteins because they are specific. For instance, a protein that moves glucose will not move calcium. The activity of these proteins can be stopped by inhibitors or poisons, which can destroy or plug up a protein.

Review Video: Passive Transport: Diffusion and Osmosis
Visit mometrix.com/academy and enter code: 642038

Mitotic Cell Replication

Mitosis is the duplication of a cell and all its parts, including the DNA, into two identical daughter cells. There are five phases in the life cycle of a cell:

1. **Prophase** – This is the process of duplicating everything in preparation for division.
2. **Metaphase** – The cell's different pieces align themselves for the split. The DNA lines up along a central axis and the centrioles send out specialized tubules that connect to the centromere. The centromere has two strands of a chromosome (condensed DNA) attached to it.
3. **Anaphase** – Half of the chromosomes go one way and half go another.
4. **Telophase** – When the chromosomes get to the side of the cell, the cell membrane closes in and splits the cell into two pieces. This results in two separate cells, each with half of the original DNA.
5. **Interphase** – This is the normal state of the cell, or the resting stage between divisions. During this stage, the cell duplicates nucleic acids in preparation for the next division.

Review Video: Mitosis
Visit mometrix.com/academy and enter code: 849894

Microbes

Microbes are the smallest, simplest, and most abundant organisms on earth. Their numbers are incalculable, and a microscope is required to see them. There is a huge variety of microbes, including bacteria, fungi, some algae, and protozoa. Microbes can be harmful or helpful.

Microbes can be **heterotrophic** (eat other things) or **autotrophic** (make food for themselves). They can be solitary or colonial, sexual or asexual. Examples include mold, a multi-cellular type of fungus, and yeasts, which are single-celled (but may live in colonies). A **mushroom** is a fungus that lives as a group of strands underground called hyphae that decompose leaves or bark on the ground. When it reproduces, it develops a mushroom whose cap contains spores. **Mold** is a type of zygote fungi that reproduces with a stalk, but releases zygospores. **Good bacteria** can be those that help plants absorb the nitrogen needed for growth or help grazing animals break down the cellulose in plants. Some **bad bacteria** are killed by the penicillin developed from a fungus.

Roots, Stems, and Leaves

Roots are structures designed to pull water and minerals from soil or water. In large plants such as trees, the roots usually go deep into the ground to not only reach the water, but also to support and stabilize the tree. There are some plant species that have roots above ground, and there are also plants called epiphytes that live in trees with their roots clinging to the branches. Some roots, like carrots and turnips, serve as food. Roots are classified as **primary** and **lateral** (like a trunk and branches). The **apical meristem** is the tip of a root or shoot that helps the plant increase in length.

Root hairs are fuzzy root extensions that help with the absorption of water and nutrients. The majority of the plant above ground is made up of the stems (trunk and branches) and leaves. **Stems** transport food and water and act as support structures. **Leaves** are the site for photosynthesis, and are connected to the rest of the plant by a vascular system.

Gymnosperms, Cycads, and Conifers

Gymnosperms are plants with vascular systems and seeds but no flowers (flowers are an evolutionary advancement). The function of the seed is to ensure offspring can be produced by the plant by providing a protective coating that lets the plant survive for long periods until it germinates. It also stores food for the new plant to use until it can make its own. Seeds can be spread over a wide area. **Cycads** are sturdy plants with big, waxy fronds that make them look like ferns or palms. They can survive in harsh conditions if there is warm weather. For reproduction, they have big cones located in the center of the plant. The female plant grows a fruit in the middle of the stem. **Conifers** are trees that thrive in northern latitudes and have cones. Examples of conifers are pine, cedar, redwood, and spruce. Conifers are evergreens because they have needles that take full advantage of the sun year-round. They are also very tall and strong because of the chemical substance xylem in their systems.

Angiosperms

Angiosperms are plants that have flowers. This is advantageous because the plant's seeds and pollen can be spread not only by gravity and wind, but also by insects and animals. Flowers are able to attract organisms that can help pollinate the plant and distribute seeds. Some flowering plants also produce fruit. When an animal eats the fruit, the plant seeds within will be spread far and wide in the animal's excrement. There are two kinds of angiosperm seeds: monocotyledons (monocots) and dicotyledons (dicots). A **cotyledon** is the seed leaf or food package for the developing plant. **Monocots** are simple flowering plants such as grasses, corn, palm trees, and lilies. They always have three petals on their flowers, and their leaves are long strands (like a palm frond). A **dicot** has seeds with two cotyledons, or two seed leaves of food. Most everyday flowers are dicots with four or five petals and extremely complex leaves with veins. Examples include roses, sunflowers, cacti, and cherry trees.

Arthropods

Arthropods have a number of unique characteristics:

- They have an **exoskeleton** (outside instead of inside).
- They **molt**. As the arthropod grows, it must shed its old shell and grow a new one.
- They have several **legs**, which are jointed.
- Their advanced **nervous systems** allow for hunting, moving around, finding a mate, and learning new behaviors for adaptation.
- They develop through **metamorphosis**. As arthropods develop, they change body shape. There are two types of metamorphosis:
    - *Complete* – The entire body shape changes. An example is butterflies, which change from worm-like larvae to insects with wings.
    - *Gradual* – The arthropod starts off small with no wings, and then molts and grows wings. Example: Grasshoppers.

Arthropods include spiders, crustaceans, and the enormous insect species (26 orders) called uniramians. Ranging from fleas to mosquitoes, beetles, dragonflies, aphids, bees, flies, and many more, uniramians have exoskeletons made of chitin, compound eyes, complex digestive systems, and usually six legs. This group is extremely diverse. Some can fly, some have toxins or antennae, and some can make wax, silk, or honey.

Reptiles

One group of vertebrates is the **reptile**. This group includes:

- **Crocodilia** – This is a group of reptiles that can grow quite large, and includes alligators and crocodiles. Normally found near the water in warmer climates, Crocodilia might be more closely related to birds than other reptiles.
- **Squamata** – This is the order of reptiles that includes snakes and lizards. Snakes are special because they have no legs and no ears. They feel vibrations, smell with their tongues, have specialized scales, and can unhinge their jaws to swallow prey that is larger than they are. Like snakes, lizards have scales, but they differ in that they have legs, can dig, can climb trees, and can grab things.
- **Chelonia** – This is the order of reptiles that includes turtles and tortoises. It is a special group because its members have shells. Different varieties live in forests, water, and deserts, or anywhere the climate is warm enough. They also live a long time, up to hundreds of years. Turtles are typically found near water and tortoises on land, even dry areas.

Reproduction in Mammals

When classified according to how they reproduce, there are three types of mammals:

1. **Monotremes** are rare mammals that lay eggs. These were the first mammals, and are more closely related to reptiles than other mammals. Examples include the duck-billed platypus and the spiny anteater.
2. **Marsupials** are special mammals. They give birth to live young, but the babies mature in pouches, where they are carried and can feed on milk. Many are found in Australia. The isolation of this island continent prevented placental mammals from taking hold. Examples of marsupials include kangaroos, possums, and koalas.
3. **Placental mammals** give birth from the females' placenta to live young. The young may be able to walk immediately, or they may need to be carried. They are still dependent on parental care for at least a short time. Placental mammals are the dominant form of mammals. Members of this group include cetaceans such as whales and dolphins, which are mammals that evolved but returned to the ocean.

Respiratory System

The **respiratory system** exchanges gases with the environment. Amphibians exchange gases through their moist skin, and fish use gills, but mammals, birds, and reptiles have lungs. The human respiratory system is made up of the nose, mouth, pharynx, trachea, and two lungs. The purpose of the respiratory system is to bring oxygen into the body and expel carbon dioxide. The respiratory system can inhale viruses, bacteria, and dangerous chemicals, so it is vulnerable to toxins and diseases such as pneumonia, which causes the lungs to fill with fluid until they cannot take in enough oxygen to support the body. **Emphysema**, often caused by smoking tobacco, destroys the tissues in the lungs, which cannot be regenerated. The respiratory system interacts with the **digestive system** in that the mouth and pharynx are used to swallow food and drink, as well as to breathe. It interacts with the circulatory system in that it provides fresh oxygen through blood vessels that pass through the lungs. This oxygen is then carried by the circulatory system throughout the body.

Review Video: Respiratory System
Visit mometrix.com/academy and enter code: 783075

Skeletal System

The human body has an **endoskeleton**, meaning it is inside the body. It is made up of bones instead of the hard plate of exoskeletons or fluids in tubes, which comprise the hydrostatic system of the starfish. The purpose of the skeleton is to support the body, provide a framework to which the muscles and organs can connect, and protect the inner organs. The skull protects the all-important brain and the ribs protect the internal organs from impact. The skeletal system interacts with the muscular system to help the body move, and softer cartilage works with the calcified bone to allow smooth movement of the body. The skeletal system also interacts with the circulatory system in that the marrow inside the bones helps produce both white and red blood cells.

Review Video: Skeletal System
Visit mometrix.com/academy and enter code: 256447

Nervous System

The **nervous system** is divided into two parts: the **central nervous system** (brain and spinal cord) and the **peripheral nervous system** (a network of billions of neurons of different types throughout the entire body). The neurons are connected end to end, and transmit electrical impulses to each other. **Efferent neurons** send impulses from the central system to the limbs and organs. **Afferent neurons** receive sensory information and transmit it back to the central system. The nervous system is concerned with **senses and action**. In other words, it senses something and then acts upon it. An example is a predator sensing prey and attacking it. The nervous system also automatically senses activity inside the body and reacts to stimuli. For example, the first bite of a meal sets the whole digestive system into motion. The nervous system **interacts** with every other system in the body because all the tissues and organs need instruction, even when individuals are not aware of any activity occurring. For instance, the endocrine system is constantly working to produce hormones or adrenaline as needed.

Review Video: The Nervous System
Visit mometrix.com/academy and enter code: 708428

Genetics, Genes, and Chromosomes

Genetics is the science devoted to the study of how characteristics are transmitted from one generation to another. In the 1800s, Gregor Mendel discovered the three laws of heredity that explain how genetics works. Genes are the hereditary units of material that are transmitted from one generation to the next. They are capable of undergoing mutations, can be recombined with other genes, and can determine the nature of an organism, including its color, shape, and size. **Genotype** is the genetic makeup of an individual based on one or more characteristics, while phenotype is the external manifestation of the genotype. For example, genotype determines hair color genes, whereas phenotype is the actual color of the hair observed. **Chromosomes** are the structures inside the nucleus of a cell made up primarily of deoxyribonucleic acid (DNA) and proteins. The chromosomes carry the genes. The numbers vary according to the species, but they are always the same for each species. For example, the human has 46 chromosomes, and the water lily has 112.

Review Video: Gene & Alleles
Visit mometrix.com/academy and enter code: 363997

Review Video: Genetic vs. Environmental Traits
Visit mometrix.com/academy and enter code: 750684

Review Video: Chromosomes
Visit mometrix.com/academy and enter code: 132083

Mendel's Contributions to Genetics

Johann Gregor Mendel is known as the father of **genetics**. Mendel was an Austrian monk who performed thousands of experiments involving the breeding of the common pea plant in the garden of his monastery. Mendel kept detailed records including seed color, pod color, seed type, flower color, and plant height for eight years and published his work in 1865. Unfortunately, his work was largely ignored until the early 1900s. Mendel's work showed that genes come in pairs and that dominant and recessive traits are inherited independently of each other. His work established the law of segregation, the law of independent assortment, and the law of dominance.

Darwin's Contributions to the Theory of Evolution

Charles Darwin's theory of evolution is the unifying concept in biology today. From 1831 to 1836, Darwin traveled as a naturalist on a five-year voyage on the *H.M.S. Beagle* around the tip of South America and to the Galápagos Islands. He studied finches, took copious amounts of meticulous notes, and collected thousands of plant and animal specimens. He collected 13 species of finches each with a unique bill for a distinct food source, which led him to believe, due to similarities between the finches, that the finches shared a common ancestor. The similarities and differences of fossils of extinct rodents and modern mammal fossils led him to believe that the mammals had changed over time. Darwin believed that these changes were the result of random genetic changes called mutations. He believed that mutations could be beneficial and eventually result in a different organism over time. In 1859, in his first book, *On the Origin of Species*, Darwin proposed that natural selection was the means by which adaptations would arise over time. He coined the term "natural selection" and said that it is the mechanism of evolution. Because variety exists among individuals of a species, he stated that those individuals must compete for the same limited resources. Some would die, and others would survive. According to Darwin, evolution is a slow, gradual process. In 1871, Darwin published his second book, *Descent of Man, and Selection in Relation to Sex*, in which he discussed the evolution of man.

Review Video: Darwin's Contributions to Theory of Evolution
Visit mometrix.com/academy and enter code: 898980

Contribution to Genetics Made by Alfred Hershey and Martha Chase

Alfred Hershey and Martha Chase did a series of experiments in 1952 known as the **Hershey-Chase experiments**. These experiments showed that deoxyribonucleic acid (DNA), not protein, is the genetic material that transfers information for inheritance. The Hershey-Chase experiments used a bacteriophage, a virus that infects bacteria, to infect the bacteria *Escherichia coli.* The bacteriophage T2 is basically a small piece of DNA enclosed in a protein coating. The DNA contains phosphorus, and the protein coating contains sulfur. In the first set of experiments, the T2 was marked with radioactive phosphorus-32. In the second set of experiments, the T2 was marked with radioactive sulfur-35. For both sets of experiments, after the *E. coli* was infected by the T2, the *E. coli* was isolated using a centrifuge. In the first set of experiments, the radioactive isotope (P-32) was found in the *E. coli*, showing that the genetic information was transferred by the DNA. In the second set of experiments, the radioactive isotope (S-35) was not found in the *E. coli*, showing that the genetic information was not transferred by the protein as was previously thought. Hershey and Chase conducted further experiments allowing the bacteria from the first set of experiments to reproduce, and the offspring was also found to contain the radioactive isotope (P-32) further confirming that the DNA transferred the genetic material.

Ecology

Autotrophs, Producers, Herbivores, Carnivores, Omnivores, and Decomposers

Energy flows in one direction: from the sun, through photosynthetic organisms such as green plants (producers) and algae (autotrophs), and then to herbivores, carnivores, and decomposers. **Autotrophs** are organisms capable of producing their own food. The organic molecules they produce are food for all other organisms (heterotrophs). **Producers** are green plants that manufacture food by photosynthesis. **Herbivores** are animals that eat only plants (deer, rabbits, etc.). Since they are the first animals to receive the energy captured by producers, herbivores are called primary consumers. **Carnivores**, or secondary consumers, are animals that eat the bodies of other animals for food. Predators (wolves, lions, etc.) kill other animals, while scavengers consume animals that are already dead from predation or natural causes (buzzards). **Omnivores** are animals that eat both plants and other animals (humans). **Decomposers** include saprophytic fungi and bacteria that break down the complex structures of the bodies of living things into simpler forms that can be used by other living things. This recycling process releases energy from organic molecules.

Abiotic Factors and Biotic Factors

Abiotic factors are the physical and chemical factors in the environment that are nonliving but upon which the growth and survival of living organisms depends. These factors can determine the types of plants and animals that will establish themselves and thrive in a particular area. Abiotic factors include:

- Light intensity available for photosynthesis
- Temperature range
- Available moisture
- Type of rock substratum
- Type of minerals
- Type of atmospheric gases
- Relative acidity (pH) of the system

Biotic factors are the living components of the environment that affect, directly or indirectly, the ecology of an area, possibly limiting the type and number of resident species. The relationships of predator/prey, producer/consumer, and parasite/host can define a community. Biotic factors include:

- Population levels of each species
- The food requirements of each species
- The interactions between species
- The wastes produced

How Plants Manufacture Food

Plants are the only organisms capable of transforming **inorganic material** from the environment into **organic matter** by using water and solar energy. This transformation is made possible by chloroplasts, flat structures inside plant cells. **Chloroplasts**, located primarily in leaves, contain chlorophyll (the pigment capable of absorbing light and storing it in chemical compounds), DNA, ribosomes, and numerous enzymes. Chloroplasts are surrounded by a membrane. The leaves of plants are the main producers of oxygen, which helps purify the air. The **chlorophyll** in chloroplasts is responsible for the light, or luminous, phase of photosynthesis. The energy it absorbs breaks down water absorbed through the roots into hydrogen and oxygen to form ATP molecules that store energy. In the dark phase, when the plant has no light, the energy molecules are used to attach carbon dioxide to water and form glucose, a sugar.

Producers, Consumers, and Decomposers

The **food chain**, or food web, is a series of events that happens when one organism consumes another to survive. Every organism is involved in dozens of connections with others, so what happens to one affects the environment of the others. In the food chain, there are three main categories:

- **Producers** – Plants and vegetables are at the beginning of the food chain because they take energy from the sun and make food for themselves through photosynthesis. They are food sources for other organisms.
- **Consumers** – There are three levels of consumers: the organisms that eat plants (primary consumers, or herbivores); the organisms that eat the primary consumers (secondary consumers, or carnivores); and, in some ecosystems, the organisms that eat both plants and animals (tertiary consumers, or omnivores).
- **Decomposers** – These are the organisms that eat dead things or waste matter and return the nutrients to the soil, thus returning essential molecules to the producers and completing the cycle.

Review Video: Food Webs
Visit mometrix.com/academy and enter code: 853254

System of Classification for Living Organisms

The main characteristic by which living organisms are classified is the degree to which they are **related**, not the degree to which they resemble each other. The science of classification is called **taxonomy**. This classification is challenging since the division lines between groups is not always clear. Some animals have characteristics of two separate groups. The current system of taxonomy involves placing an organism into a **domain** (Bacteria, Archaea, and Eukarya), and then into a **kingdom** (Eubacteria, Archaeabacteria, Protista, Fungi, Plantae, and Animalia). The kingdoms are divided into phyla, then classes, then orders, then families, and finally genuses and species. For example, the family cat is in the domain of eukaryotes, the kingdom of animals, the phylum of chordates, the class of mammals, the order of carnivores, the family of felidae, and the genus of felis. All species of living beings can be identified with Latin scientific names that are assigned by the worldwide binomial system. The genus name comes first, and is followed by the name of the species. The family cat is *felis domesticus*.

Review Video: Biological Classification Systems
Visit mometrix.com/academy and enter code: 736052

Properties That Contribute to Earth's Life-Sustaining System

Life on earth is dependent on:

- All three states of **water** – gas (water vapor), liquid, and solid (ice)
- A variety of forms of **carbon**, the basis of life (carbon-based units)
- In the atmosphere, carbon dioxide, in the forms of methane and black carbon soot, produces the **greenhouse effect** that provides a habitable atmosphere.
- The earth's **atmosphere and electromagnetic field**, which shield the surface from harmful radiation and allow useful radiation to go through.

- The **earth's relationship to the sun and the moon**, which creates the four seasons and the cycles of plant and animal life.
- The combination of **water, carbon, and nutrients** that provides sustenance for life and regulates the climate system in a habitable temperature range with non-toxic air.

Geology

Earth System Science

The complex and interconnected dynamics of the continents, atmosphere, oceans, ice, and life forms are the subject of **earth system science**. These interconnected dynamics require an interdisciplinary approach that includes chemistry, physics, biology, mathematics, and applied sciences in order to study the Earth as an integrated system and determine (while considering human impact and interaction) the past, present, and future states of the earth. Scientific inquiry in this field includes exploration of:

- Extreme weather events as they pertain to a changing climate
- Earthquakes and volcanic eruptions as they pertain to tectonic shifts
- Losses in biodiversity in relation to the changes in the earth's ecosystems
- Causes and effects in the environment
- The sun's solar variability in relation to the earth's climate
- The atmosphere's increasing concentrations of carbon dioxide and aerosols
- Trends in the earth's systems in terms of changes and their consequences

Traditional Earth Science Disciplines

Modern science is approaching the study of the earth in an integrated fashion that sees the earth as an interconnected system that is impacted by humankind and, therefore, must include social dimensions. Traditionally, though, the following were the earth science disciplines:

- **Geology** – This is the study of the origin and structure of the earth and of the changes it has undergone and is in the process of undergoing. Geologists work from the crust inward.
- **Meteorology** – This is the study of the atmosphere, including atmospheric pressure, temperature, clouds, winds, precipitation, etc. It is also concerned with describing and explaining weather.
- **Oceanography** – This is the study of the oceans, which includes studying their extent and depth, the physics and chemistry of ocean waters, and the exploitation of their resources.
- **Ecology** – This is the study of living organisms in relation to their environment and to other living things. It is the study of the interrelations between the different components of the ecosystem.

Geological Eras

Geologists divide the history of the earth into units of time called **eons**, which are divided into **eras**, then into **periods**, then into **epochs** and finally into **ages**. Dates are approximate of course, and there may be variations of a few million years. (Million years ago is abbreviated as Ma.) Some of the most commonly known time periods are:

- **Hadean Eon** – About 4.5 to 3.8 billion years ago
- **Archaean Eon** – 3.8 to 2.5 billion years ago
- **Proterozoic Eon** – 2.5 billion to 542 Ma
- **Phanerozoic Eon** – 542 Ma to the present
    - **Paleozoic Era** – 542 Ma to 251 Ma
        - **Cambrian Period** – 542 to 488 Ma
        - **Ordovician Period** – 488 to 443 Ma
        - **Silurian Period** – 443 to 416 Ma
        - **Devonian Period** – 416 to 359 Ma

- ❖ **Carboniferous Period** – 359 to 290 Ma
- ❖ **Permian Period** – 290 to 252 Ma

- o **Mesozoic Era** – 252 to 65 Ma
  - ❖ **Triassic Period** – 252 to 200 Ma
  - ❖ **Jurassic Period** – 200 to 150 Ma
  - ❖ **Cretaceous Period** – 150 to 65 Ma
- o **Cenozoic Era** – 65 Ma to the present
  - ❖ **Paleogene Period** – 65 to 28 Ma
  - ❖ **Neogene Period** – 28 to 2 Ma
  - ❖ **Quaternary Period** – about 2 Ma to the present

Development of Life on Earth According to Time Periods

The **evolution** of life on earth is believed to have occurred as follows:

- Igneous rocks formed. (Hadean Eon)
- The continents formed. (Archaean Eon)
- The first multi-cellular creatures such as hydras, jellyfish, and sponges appeared about 600 Ma.
- Flatworms, roundworms, and segmented worms appeared about 550 Ma.
- Moss, arthropods, octopus, and eels appeared. (Cambrian Period)
- Mushrooms, fungi, and other primitive plants appeared; sea animals began to use calcium to build bones and shells. (Ordovician Period)
- Fish with jaws appeared. (Silurian Period)
- Fish developed lungs and legs (frogs) and went on land; ferns appeared. (Devonian period)
- Reptiles developed the ability to lay eggs on land and pine trees appeared. (Carboniferous Period)
- Dinosaurs dominated the land during the Triassic and Jurassic Periods.
- Flying insects, birds, and the first flowering plants appeared; dinosaurs died out. (Cretaceous Period)
- Mammals evolved and dominated; grasses became widespread. (50 Ma)
- Hominids appeared more than 2 Ma.

Hydrosphere and Hydrologic Cycle

The **hydrosphere** is anything on earth that is related to water, whether it is in the air, on land, or in a plant or animal system. A water molecule consists of only two atoms of hydrogen and one of oxygen, yet it is what makes life possible. Unlike the other planets, earth is able to sustain life because its temperature allows water to be in its liquid state most of the time. Water vapor and ice are of no use to living organisms. The **hydrologic cycle** is the journey water takes as it assumes different forms. Liquid surface water evaporates to form the gaseous state of a cloud, and then becomes liquid again in the form of rain. This process takes about 10 days if water becomes a cloud. Water at the bottom of the ocean or in a glacier is not likely to change form, even over periods of thousands of years.

Review Video: Hydrologic Cycle
Visit mometrix.com/academy and enter code: 426578

Aquifers

An **aquifer** is an underground water reservoir formed from groundwater that has infiltrated from the surface by passing through the soil and permeable rock layers (the zone of aeration) to a zone of saturation where the rocks are impermeable. There are two types of aquifers. In one, the water is under pressure (**confined**) as the supply builds up between layers of impermeable rocks and has to move back towards the surface, resulting in a spring or artesian well. The second type of aquifer is called "**unconfined**" because it has room to expand and contract, and the water has to be pumped out. The highest level of the aquifer is called the water table. If water is pumped out of the aquifer such that the water table dips in a specific area, that area is called a cone of depression.

Biosphere

Biosphere is the term used by physical geographers to describe the living world of trees, bugs, and animals. It refers to any place where life exists on earth, and is the intersection of the hydrosphere, the atmosphere, the land, and the energy that comes from space. The biosphere includes the upper areas of the atmosphere where birds and insects can travel, areas deep inside caves, and hydrothermal vents at the bottom of the ocean.

Factors that affect the biosphere include:

- The **distance and tilt** between the earth and the sun – This produces temperatures that are conducive to life and causes the seasons.
- **Climate, daily weather, and erosion** – These change the land and the organisms on and in it.
- Earthquakes, tornadoes, volcanoes, tsunamis, and other **natural phenomena** – These all change the land.
- **Chemical erosion** – This changes the composition of rocks and organic materials.
- **Biological erosion** – This is bacteria and single-celled organisms breaking down organic and inorganic materials.

Ecological System and Biome

An **ecological system**, or ecosystem, is the community of all the living organisms in a specific area interacting with non-living factors such as temperature, sunlight, atmospheric pressure, weather patterns, wind, types of nutrients, etc. An ecosystem's development depends on the energy that passes in and out of it. The boundaries of an ecosystem depend on the use of the term, whether it refers to an ecosystem under a rock or in a valley, pond, or ocean.

A **biome** is a general ecosystem type defined by the plants and animals that live there and the local climate patterns. Examples include tropical rainforests or savannas, deserts, grasslands, deciduous forests, tundra, woodlands, and ice caps. There can be more than one type of biome within a larger climate zone. The transition area between two biomes is an ecotone, which may have characteristics of both biomes.

Erosion

Erosion is the process that breaks down matter, whether it is a rock that is broken into pebbles or mountains that are rained on until they become hills. Erosion always happens in a downhill direction. The erosion of land by weather or breaking waves is called **denudation**. **Mass wasting** is the movement of masses of dirt and rock from one place to another. This can occur in two ways: **mechanical** (such as breaking a rock with a hammer) or **chemical** (such as pouring acid on a rock to dissolve it). If the material changes color, it indicates that a break down was chemical in nature. Whatever is broken down must go somewhere, so erosion eventually builds something up. For example, an eroded mountain ends up in a river that carries the sediment towards the ocean, where it builds up and creates a wetland or delta at the mouth of the river.

Climates

Scientists have determined the following different types of **climates**:

- Polar (ice caps)
- Polar (tundra)
- Subtropical (dry summer)
- Subtropical (dry winter)
- Subtropical (humid)
- Subtropical (marine west coast)
- Subtropical (Mediterranean)
- Subtropical (wet)
- Tropical (monsoon)
- Tropical (savannah/grasslands)
- Tropical (wet)

Several factors make up and affect climates. These include:

- Temperature
- Atmospheric pressure
- The number of clouds and the amount of dust or smog
- Humidity
- Winds

The moistest and warmest of all the climates is that of the tropical rainforest. It has daily convection thunderstorms caused by the surface daytime heat and the high humidity, which combine to form thunderclouds.

Review Video: Climates
Visit mometrix.com/academy and enter code: 991320

Layers of the Earth

The earth has several distinct **layers**, each with its own properties:

- **Crust** – This is the outermost layer of the earth that is comprised of the continents and the ocean basins. It has a variable thickness (35-70 km in the continents and 5-10 km in the ocean basins) and is composed mostly of alumino-silicates.
- **Mantle** – This is about 2900 km thick, and is made up mostly of ferro-magnesium silicates. It is divided into an upper and lower mantle. Most of the internal heat of the earth is located in the mantle. Large convective cells circulate heat, and may cause plate tectonic movement.
- **Core** – This is separated into the liquid outer core and the solid inner core. The outer core is 2300 km thick (composed mostly of nickel-iron alloy), and the inner core (almost entirely iron) is 12 km thick. The earth's magnetic field is thought to be controlled by the liquid outer core.

Composition of Earth's Atmosphere

The earth's **atmosphere** is 79% nitrogen, 20% oxygen, and 1% other gases. The oxygen was originally produced almost entirely by algae-type plants. The atmosphere has four layers:

- **Troposphere** – This is the layer closest to the earth where all weather takes place. It is the region that contains rising and falling packets of air. Air pressure at sea level is 0.1 atmospheres, but the top of the troposphere is about 10% of that amount.
- **Stratosphere** – In this layer, air flow is mainly horizontal. The upper portion has a thin layer of concentrated ozone (a reactive form of oxygen) that is largely responsible for absorbing the sun's ultraviolet rays.
- **Mesosphere** – This is the coldest layer. Temperatures drop to -100°C at the top.
- **Thermosphere** – This is divided into the lower ionosphere and the higher exosphere. This layer is very thin and has many ionized atoms with a net electrical charge. The aurora and Van Allen Belts are here. This layer also absorbs the most energetic photons from the sun and reflects radio waves, enabling long distance radio communication.

Review Video: Earth's Atmosphere
Visit mometrix.com/academy and enter code: 417614

Paleontology

Paleontology is the study of prehistoric plant and animal life through the analysis of **fossil remains**. These fossils reveal the ecologies of the past and the path of evolution for both extinct and living organisms. A historical science, paleontology seeks information about the identity, origin, environment, and evolution of past organisms and what they can reveal about the past of the earth as a whole. Paleontology explains causes as opposed to conducting experiments to observe effects. It is related to the fields of biology, geology, and archaeology, and is divided into several sub-disciplines concerned with the types of fossils studied, the process of fossilization, and the ecology and climate of the past. Paleontologists also help identify the composition of the earth's rock layers by the fossils that are found, thus identifying potential sites for oil, mineral, and water extraction.

Determining the Order in Which Geologic Events Occurred Using the Rock Record

The **Law of Superposition** logically assumes that the bottom layer of a series of sedimentary layers is the oldest, unless it has been overturned or older rock has been pushed over it. In addition, since **igneous intrusions** can cut through or flow above other rocks, these other rocks are older. For example, molten rock (lava) flows out over already present, older rocks. Another guideline for the rock record is that **rock layers** are older than the folds and faults in them because the rocks must exist before they can be folded or faulted. If a rock contains **atomic nuclei**, reference tables of the half-lives of commonly used radio isotopes can be used to match the decay rate of known substances to the nuclei in a rock, and thereby determine its age. Ages of rocks can also be determined from **contact metamorphism**, the re-crystallization of pre-existing rocks due to changes in physical and chemical conditions, such as heat, pressure, and chemically active fluids that might be present in lava or polluted waters.

Matching Rocks and Geologic Events in One Place with Those of Another

Geologists physically follow rock layers from one location to another by a process called "walking the outcrop." Geologists walk along the outcropping to see where it goes and what the differences and similarities of the neighboring locations they cross are. Similar rock **types** or **patterns** of rock layers that are similar in terms of thickness, color, composition, and fossil remains tell geologists that two locations have a similar geologic history. Fossils are found all over the earth, but are from a relatively **small time period** in earth's history. Therefore, fossil evidence helps date a rock layer, regardless of where it occurs. **Volcanic ash** is a good time indicator since ash is deposited quickly over a widespread area. Matching the date of an eruption to the ash allows for a precise identification of time. Similarly, the **meteor impact** at the intersection of the Cretaceous and Tertiary Periods left a time marker. Wherever the meteor's iridium content is found, geologists are able to date rock layers.

Sequencing the Earth's Geologic History from the Fossil and Rock Record

Reference tables are used to match specimens and time periods. For example, the fossil record has been divided into time units of the earth's history. Rocks can therefore be dated by the fossils found with them. There are also reference tables for dating plate motions and mountain building events in geologic history. Since humans have been around for a relatively short period of time, **fossilized human remains** help to affix a date to a location. Some areas have missing **geologic layers** because of erosion or other factors, but reference tables specific to a region will list what is complete or missing. The theory of **uniformitarianism** assumes that geologic processes have been the same throughout history. Therefore, the way erosion or volcanic eruptions happen today is the same as the way these events happened millions of years ago because there is no reason for them to have changed. Therefore, knowledge about current events can be applied to the past to make judgments about events in the rock record.

Revealing Changes in Earth's History by the Fossil and Rock Records

Fossils can show how animal and plant life have changed or remained the same over time. For example, fossils have provided evidence of the existence of dinosaurs even though they no longer roam the earth, and have also been used to prove that certain insects have been around for hundreds of millions of years. Fossils have been used to identify four basic eras: **Proterozoic**, the age of primitive life; **Paleozoic**, the age of fishes; **Mesozoic**, the age of dinosaurs; and **Cenozoic**, the age of mammals. Most ancient forms of life have disappeared, and there are reference tables that list when this occurred. Fossil records also show the evolution of certain life forms, such as the horse from the eohippus. However, the majority of changes do not involve evolution from simple to complex forms, but rather an increase in the variety of forms.

Mountains

A **mountain** is a portion of the earth that has been raised above its surroundings by volcanic action or tectonic plate movement. Mountains are made up of igneous, metamorphic, and sedimentary rocks, and most lie along active plate boundaries. There are two major mountain systems. The **Circum-Pacific** encircles the entire Pacific Ocean, from New Guinea up across Japan and the Aleutians and down to southern South America. The **Alpine-Himalaya** stretches from northern Africa across the Alps and to the Himalayas and Indonesia. **Orogeny** is the term for the process of natural mountain formation. Therefore, physical mountains are orogens. **Folded mountains** are created through the folding of rock layers when two crustal plates come together. The Alps and Himalayas are folded mountains. The latter was formed by the collision of India with Asia. **Fault-block mountains** are created from the tension forces of plate movements. These produce faults that vertically displace one section to form a mountain. **Dome mountains** are created from magma pushing up through the earth's crust.

Volcanoes and Volcanic Mountains

Volcanoes are classified according to their activity level. An **active** volcano is in the process of erupting or building to an eruption; a dormant volcano has erupted before and may erupt again someday, but is not currently active; and an **extinct** volcano has died out volcanically and will not erupt ever again. Active volcanoes endanger plant and animal life, but lava and ash add enriching minerals to the soil. There are three types of volcanic mountains:

- **Shield volcanoes** are the largest volcanic mountains because of a repeated, viscous lava flow from small eruptions over a long period of time that cause the mountain to grow.
- **Cinder cone volcanoes**, or linear volcanoes, are small in size, but have massive explosions through linear shafts that spread cinders and ash around the vent. This results in a cone-shaped hill.
- **Composite volcanoes** get their name from the mix of lava and ash layers that build the mountain.

Subdivisions of Rock

The three major subdivisions of rock are:

- **Igneous** (magmatites) – This type is formed from the cooling of liquid magma. In the process, minerals crystallize and amalgamate. If solidification occurs deep in the earth (plutonic rock), the cooling process is slow. This allows for the formation of large crystals, giving rock a coarse-grained texture (granite). Quickly cooled magma has a glassy texture (obsidian).
- **Metamorphic** – Under conditions of high temperature and pressure within the earth's crust, rock material melts and changes structure, transitioning or metamorphosing into a new type of rock with different minerals. If the minerals appear in bands, the rock is foliated. Examples include marble (unfoliated) and slate (foliated).
- **Sedimentary** – This is the most common type of rock on earth. It is formed by sedimentation, compaction, and then cementation of many small particles of mineral, animal, or plant material. There are three types of sedimentary rocks: clastic, clay, and sand that came from disintegrated rocks; chemical (rock salt and gypsum), formed by evaporation of aqueous solutions; and biogenic (coal), formed from animal or plant remnants.

Review Video: Igneous, Sedimentary, and Metamorphic Rocks
Visit mometrix.com/academy and enter code: 689294

Glaciers

Glaciers start high in the mountains, where snow and ice accumulate inside a cirque (a small semicircular depression). The snow becomes firmly packed into masses of coarse-grained ice that are slowly pulled down a slope by gravity. Glaciers grow with large amounts of snowfall and retreat (diminish) if warm weather melts more ice than can be replaced. Glaciers once covered large areas of both the northern and southern hemispheres with mile-thick ice that carved out valleys, fjords, and other land formations. They also moved plants, animals, and rocks from one area to another. There were two types of glaciers: **valley**, which produced U-shaped erosion and sharp-peaked mountains; and **continental**, which moved over and rounded mountain tops and ridges. These glaciers existed during the ice ages, the last of which occurred from 2.5 million years ago to 12,000 years ago.

Earth Science and Weather

Layers Above the Surface of Earth

The **ozone layer**, although contained within the stratosphere, is determined by ozone (O_3) concentrations. It absorbs the majority of ultraviolet light from the Sun. The ionosphere is part of both the exosphere and the thermosphere. It is characterized by the fact that it is a plasma, a partially ionized gas in which free electrons and positive ions are attracted to each other, but are too energetic to remain fixed as a molecule. It starts at about 50 km above Earth's surface and goes to 1,000 km. It affects radio wave transmission and auroras. The ionosphere pushes against the inner edge of the Earth's magnetosphere, which is the highly magnetized, non-spherical region around the Earth. The homosphere encompasses the troposphere, stratosphere, and mesosphere. Gases in the homosphere are considered well mixed. In the heterosphere, the distance that particles can move without colliding is large. As a result, gases are stratified according to their molecular weights. Heavier gases such as oxygen and nitrogen occur near the bottom of the heterosphere, while hydrogen, the lightest element, is found at the top.

Review Video: Earth's Atmosphere
Visit mometrix.com/academy and enter code: 417614

Tropospheric Circulation

Most weather takes place in the **troposphere**. Air circulates in the atmosphere by convection and in various types of "cells." Air near the equator is warmed by the Sun and rises. Cool air rushes under it, and the higher, warmer air flows toward Earth's poles. At the poles, it cools and descends to the surface. It is now under the hot air, and flows back to the equator. Air currents coupled with ocean currents move heat around the planet, creating winds, weather, and climate. Winds can change direction with the seasons. For example, in Southeast Asia and India, summer monsoons are caused by air being heated by the Sun. This air rises, draws moisture from the ocean, and causes daily rains. In winter, the air cools, sinks, pushes the moist air away, and creates dry weather.

Common Weather Phenomena and Equipment to Measure Them

Common **atmospheric conditions** that are frequently measured are temperature, precipitation, wind, and humidity. These weather conditions are often measured at permanently fixed **weather stations** so weather data can be collected and compared over time and by region. Measurements may also be taken by ships, buoys, and underwater instruments. Measurements may also be taken under special circumstances. The measurements taken include temperature, barometric pressure, humidity, wind speed, wind direction, and precipitation. Usually, the following instruments are used: A *thermometer* is used for measuring temperature; a *barometer* is used for measuring barometric/air pressure; a *hygrometer* is used for measuring humidity; an *anemometer* is used for measuring wind speed; a *weather vane* is used for measuring wind direction; and a *rain gauge* is used for measuring precipitation.

Weather, Climate, and Meteorology

Meteorology is the study of the atmosphere, particularly as it pertains to forecasting the weather and understanding its processes. **Weather** is the condition of the atmosphere at any given moment. Most weather occurs in the troposphere and includes changing events such as clouds, storms, and temperature, as well as more extreme events such as tornadoes, hurricanes, and blizzards. **Climate**

refers to the average weather for a particular area over time, typically at least 30 years. Latitude is an indicator of climate. Changes in climate occur over long time periods.

Review Video: Climates
Visit mometrix.com/academy and enter code: 991320

Winds and Global Wind Belts

Winds are the result of air moving by convection. Masses of warm air rise, and cold air sweeps into their place. The warm air also moves, cools, and sinks. The term "prevailing wind" refers to the wind that usually blows in an area in a single direction. *Dominant winds* are the winds with the highest speeds. Belts or bands that run latitudinally and blow in a specific direction are associated with *convection cells*. *Hadley cells* are formed directly north and south of the equator. The *Farrell cells* occur at about 30° to 60°. The jet stream runs between the Farrell cells and the polar cells. At the higher and lower latitudes, the direction is easterly. At mid latitudes, the direction is westerly. From the North Pole to the south, the surface winds are Polar High Easterlies, Subpolar Low Westerlies, Subtropical High or Horse Latitudes, North-East Trade winds, Equatorial Low or Doldrums, South-East Trades, Subtropical High or Horse Latitudes, Subpolar Low Easterlies, and Polar High.

Relative Humidity, Absolute Humidity, and Dew Point Temperature

Humidity refers to water vapor contained in the air. The amount of moisture contained in air depends upon its temperature. The higher the air temperature, the more moisture it can hold. These higher levels of moisture are associated with higher humidity. **Absolute humidity** refers to the total amount of moisture air is capable of holding at a certain temperature. **Relative humidity** is the ratio of water vapor in the air compared to the amount the air is capable of holding at its current temperature. As temperature decreases, absolute humidity stays the same and relative humidity increases. A hygrometer is a device used to measure humidity. The **dew point** is the temperature at which water vapor condenses into water at a particular humidity.

Precipitation

After clouds reach the dew point, **precipitation** occurs. Precipitation can take the form of a liquid or a solid. It is known by many names, including rain, snow, ice, dew, and frost. **Liquid** forms of precipitation include rain and drizzle. Rain or drizzle that freezes on contact is known as freezing rain or freezing drizzle. **Solid or frozen** forms of precipitation include snow, ice needles or diamond dust, sleet or ice pellets, hail, and graupel or snow pellets. Virga is a form of precipitation that evaporates before reaching the ground. It usually looks like sheets or shafts falling from a cloud. The amount of rainfall is measured with a rain gauge. Intensity can be measured according to how fast precipitation is falling or by how severely it limits visibility. Precipitation plays a major role in the water cycle since it is responsible for depositing much of the Earth's fresh water.

Clouds

Clouds form when air cools and warm air is forced to give up some of its water vapor because it can no longer hold it. This vapor condenses and forms tiny droplets of water or ice crystals called clouds. Particles, or aerosols, are needed for water vapor to form water droplets. These are called **condensation nuclei**. Clouds are created by surface heating, mountains and terrain, rising air masses, and weather fronts. Clouds precipitate, returning the water they contain to Earth. Clouds can also create atmospheric optics. They can scatter light, creating colorful phenomena such as rainbows, colorful sunsets, and the green flash phenomenon.

Review Video: Clouds
Visit mometrix.com/academy and enter code: 803166

High, Middle, and Low Cloud Types

Most clouds can be classified according to the altitude of their base above Earth's surface. **High clouds** occur at altitudes between 5,000 and 13,000 meters. **Middle clouds** occur at altitudes between 2,000 and 7,000 meters. **Low clouds** occur from the Earth's surface to altitudes of 2,000 meters. Types of high clouds include cirrus (Ci), thin wispy mare's tails that consist of ice; cirrocumulus (Cc), small, pillow-like puffs that often appear in rows; and cirrostratus (Cs), thin, sheet-like clouds that often cover the entire sky. Types of middle clouds include altocumulus (Ac), gray-white clouds that consist of liquid water; and altostratus (As), grayish or blue-gray clouds that span the sky. Types of low clouds include stratus (St), gray and fog-like clouds consisting of water droplets that take up the whole sky; stratocumulus (Sc), low-lying, lumpy gray clouds; and nimbostratus (Ns), dark gray clouds with uneven bases that indicate rain or snow. Two types of clouds, cumulus (Cu) and cumulonimbus (Cb), are capable of great vertical growth. They can start at a wide range of altitudes, from the Earth's surface to altitudes of 13,000 meters.

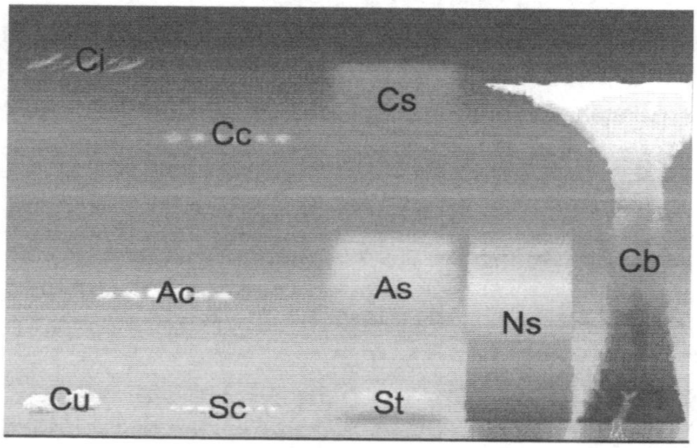

Air Masses

Air masses are large volumes of air in the troposphere of the Earth. They are categorized by their temperature and by the amount of water vapor they contain. *Arctic* and *Antarctic* air masses are cold, polar air masses are cool, and tropical and equatorial air masses are hot. Other types of air masses include *maritime* and *monsoon*, both of which are moist and unstable. There are also *continental* and *superior* air masses, which are dry. A **weather front** separates two masses of air of different densities. It is the principal cause of meteorological phenomena. Air masses are quickly and easily affected by the land they are above. They can have certain characteristics, and then develop new ones when they get blown over a different area.

Weather Fronts and Weather Maps

A **weather front** is the area between two differing masses of air that affects weather. Frontal movements are influenced by the jet stream and other high winds. Movements are determined by the type of front. Cold fronts move up to twice as fast as warm ones. It is in the turbulent frontal area that commonplace and dramatic weather events take place. This area also creates temperature changes. Weather phenomena include rain, thunderstorms, high winds, tornadoes, cloudiness, clear skies, and hurricanes. Different fronts can be plotted on weather maps using a set of designated symbols. Surface weather maps can also include symbols representing clouds, rain, temperature, air pressure, and fair weather.

Space Science

Astronomy

Astronomy is the scientific study of celestial objects and their positions, movements, and structures. *Celestial* does not refer to the Earth by itself, but does include its movement through space. Other celestial objects include the Sun, the Moon, planets, satellites, asteroids, meteors, comets, stars, galaxies, the universe, and other space phenomena. The term astronomy has its roots in the Greek words "astro" and "nomos," which means "laws of the stars."

Review Video: Astronomy
Visit mometrix.com/academy and enter code: 640556

Universe

Origin

The **universe** can be said to consist of everything and nothing. The universe contains all of space, matter, energy, and time. There are likely still phenomena that have yet to be discovered. The universe can also be thought of as nothing, since a vast portion of the known universe is empty space. It is believed that the universe is expanding. The *Big Bang theory*, which is widely accepted among astronomers, was developed to explain the origin of the universe. There are other theories regarding the origin of the universe, such as the *Steady-State theory* and the *Creationist theory*. The Big Bang theory states that all the matter in the universe was once in one place. This matter underwent a huge explosion that spread it into space. Galaxies formed from, this material and the universe is still expanding.

Structure

What can be seen of the universe is believed to be at least 93 billion light years across. To put this into perspective, the Milky Way galaxy is about 100,000 light years across. Our view of matter in the universe is that it forms into clumps which become stars, galaxies, clusters of galaxies, superclusters, and the Great Wall of galaxies. **Galaxies** consist of stars, some with planetary systems. Some estimates state that the universe is about 13 billion years old. It is not considered dense and is believed to consist of 73% dark energy, 23% cold dark matter, and 4% regular matter. Cosmology is the study of the universe. Interstellar medium (ISM) is the gas and dust in the interstellar space between a galaxy's stars.

Galaxies

Galaxies consist of stars, stellar remnants, and dark matter. **Dwarf galaxies** contain as few as 10 million stars, while giant galaxies contain as many as 1 trillion stars. Galaxies are gravitationally bound, meaning that stars, star systems, other gases, and dust orbit the galaxy's center. The Earth exists in the **Milky Way galaxy** and the nearest galaxy to ours is the **Andromeda galaxy**. Galaxies can be classified by their visual shape into elliptical, spiral, irregular, and starburst galaxies. It is estimated that there are more than 100 billion galaxies in the universe ranging from 1,000 to 100,000 parsecs in diameter. Galaxies can be megaparsecs apart. Intergalactic space consists of a gas with an average density of less than one atom per cubic meter. Galaxies are organized into clusters which form superclusters. Dark matter may account for up to 90% of the mass of galaxies. Dark matter is still not well understood.

Planets

In order of their distance from the sun (closest to furthest away), the **planets** are: Mercury, Venus, Earth, Mars, Jupiter, Saturn, Uranus, and Neptune (Pluto is now considered to be a dwarf planet). All the planets revolve around the sun, which is an average-sized star in the spiral Milky Way galaxy. They revolve in the same direction in nearly circular orbits. If the planets were viewed by looking down from the sun, they would rotate in a counter-clockwise direction. All the planets are in, or near, the same plane, called the ecliptic, and their axis of rotation is nearly perpendicular to the ecliptic. The only exception is Uranus, which is tipped on its side.

Terrestrial Planets, Jovian Planets, and Mass of Planets

The **Terrestrial Planets** are: Mercury, Venus, Earth, and Mars. These are the four planets closest to the sun. They are called terrestrial because they all have a compact, rocky surface similar to the Earth's. Venus, Earth, and Mars have significant atmospheres, but Mercury has almost no atmosphere.

The **Jovian Planets** are: Jupiter (the largest planet), Saturn, Uranus, and Neptune. They are called Jovian (Jupiter-like) because of their huge sizes in relation to that of the Earth, and because they all have a gaseous nature like Jupiter. Although gas giants, some or all of the Jovian Planets may have small, solid cores.

The sun represents 99.85% of all the matter in our solar system. Combined, the planets make up only 0.135% of the mass of the solar system, with Jupiter having twice the mass of all the other planets combined. The remaining 0.015% of the mass comes from comets, planetary satellites, asteroids, meteoroids, and interplanetary medium.

Definition of Planet

On August 24, 2006, the International Astronomical Union redefined the criteria a body must meet to be classified as a planet, stating that the following conditions must be met:

- "A planet orbits around a star and is neither a star nor a moon."
- "Its shape is spherical due to its gravity."
- "It has 'cleared' the space of its orbit."

A **dwarf planet** such as Pluto does not meet the third condition. Small solar system bodies such as asteroids and comets meet only the first condition.

Solar System

The **solar system** developed about 4.6 billion years ago out of an enormous cloud of dust and gas circling around the sun. Four rocky planets orbit relatively close to the sun. Their inside orbits are separated from the outside orbits of the four, larger gaseous planets by an asteroid belt. Pluto, some comets, and several small objects circle in the Kuiper belt outside Neptune's orbit. The Oort cloud, composed of icy space objects, encloses the planetary system like a shell.

Review Video: Solar System
Visit mometrix.com/academy and enter code: 273231

Earth's Moon

Earth's **moon** is the closest celestial body to earth. Its proximity has allowed it to be studied since the invention of the telescope. As a result, its landforms have been named after astronomers, philosophers, and other scholars. Its surface has many craters created by asteroids since it has no protective atmosphere. These dark lowlands looked like seas to early astronomers, but there is virtually no water on the moon except possibly in its polar regions. These impact craters and depressions actually contain solidified lava flows. The bright highlands were thought to be continents, and were named terrae. The rocks of the moon have been pounded by asteroids so often that there is a layer of rubble and dust called the regolith. Also, because there is no protective atmosphere, temperatures on the moon vary widely, from 265°F to -255°F.

Earth's Sun and Other Stars

A **star** begins as a cloud of hydrogen and some heavier elements drawn together by their own mass. This matter then begins to rotate. The core heats up to several million degrees Fahrenheit, which causes the hydrogen atoms to lose their shells and their nuclei to fuse. This releases enormous amounts of energy. The star then becomes stable during a stage called the **main sequence**. This is the stage our sun is in, and it will remain in this stage until its supply of hydrogen fuel runs out. Stars are not always alone like our sun, and may exist in pairs or groups. The hottest stars shine blue-white; medium-hot stars like our sun glow yellow; and cooler stars appear orange. The earth's sun is an **average star** in terms of mass, light production, and size. All stars, including our sun, have a **core** where fusion happens; a **photosphere** (surface) that produces sunspots (cool, dark areas); a red **chromosphere** that emits solar (bright) flares and shooting gases; and a **corona**, the transparent area only seen during an eclipse.

Review Video: The Sun
Visit mometrix.com/academy and enter code: 699233

Comets, Asteroids, and Meteoroids

Comets are celestial bodies composed of dust, rock, frozen gases, and ice. Invisible until they near the sun, comets emit volatile components in jets of gas and dust when exposed to the sun's heat. The **coma** is the comet's fog-like envelope that glows as it reflects sunlight and releases radiation. **Solar winds** blow a comet away from the sun and give it a tail of dust or electrically charged molecules. Each orbit of a comet causes it to lose matter until it breaks up or vaporizes into the sun.

Asteroids are irregularly-shaped boulders, usually less than 60 miles in diameter, that orbit the sun. Most are made of graphite; about 25% are silicates, or iron and nickel. Collisions or gravitational forces can cause them to fly off and possibly hit a planet.

Meteoroids are fragments of asteroids of various sizes. If they come through earth's atmosphere, they are called meteors or shooting stars. If they land on earth, they are called meteorites, and create craters on impact (the Barringer Crater in Arizona).

Fine Arts, Health, and Physical Education

Visual Arts

Creative Expression

Creativity means the ability to produce or bring into existence a work of art (music, painting, sculpture, comedy, drama, and literature) that is original and imaginative. To express something is to convey an idea, an emotion or an opinion, or to depict a direct or indirect representation of an idea, an emotion or an opinion. The idea, emotion or opinion can be shown in words, pictures, gestures, signs and symbols. A person with **creative expression** has the burning need to bring forth a unique manifestation of his or her understanding and interpretation of mankind's primal desires. A soaring music score by Beethoven, a memorable scene by Grandma Moses, a gentle poem by Emily Dickinson, a moving performance by Sir Laurence Olivier are all examples of individual creative expression by artists of uncompromising vision.

Elements of Art

There are seven basic **elements of art**: line, shape, space, texture, color, value, and form. Each has a specific function; each must be understood to truly appreciate the work of art being studied. The following definitions are composed from the *American Heritage College Dictionary*:

- **Line** is a continuous path made by a moving pen, pencil or brush that makes a real or imaginary mark in relation to a point of reference.
- **Shape** is the characteristic outline or contour of an object that is distinguished from its surroundings by its distinctive form.
- **Space** is a three-dimensional empty area with a specific outline that is reserved for a particular purpose.
- **Texture** is a surface of elements woven together that has distinctive or identifying characteristics.
- **Color** is the appearance of objects caused by different qualities of reflected light that involves hue, lightness, darkness, value and purity.
- **Value** is the quality of brightness in a particular color on a scale of white to black. Sometimes this element is grouped with color.
- **Form** is the element dealing with shape of three-dimensional figures. It is related to shape, which is made up of height and width, but also contains depth.

Use of Light and Dark in Two- and Three-Dimensional Art Forms

In western culture, the reaction to light and dark arouses strong, primitive emotions. **Light** suggests goodness, intelligence and wholeness. **Dark** expresses mystery, ignorance and evil. Contrasting these opposites in a work of art helps convey feelings and has a powerful psychological impact. Light and dark can also depict space and enhance form in two- and three-dimensional art. On a two-dimensional surface, the effects of light and shadow can be very dramatic. When light is blocked by different parts of a form and casts a shadow, the figures in a painting seem to come alive. This technique is called chiaroscuro. Light and shadow on sculpture and architecture define the form of the piece. As the contour fades away, the light grows dimmer causing changes in contrast and tonal value on the surface, which makes the object seem to swell and recede while enhancing the drama of its structural composition.

Principles of Art

In art, there are four basic **principles**: balance and harmony, proportion, unity, and variety. Each has a unique function and needs to be understood to appreciate the artist's vision whether it is shown in a painting, sculpture or a piece of architecture. The following definitions are composed from the *American Heritage College Dictionary*:

- **Balance and Harmony** is a state of equilibrium between parts that creates a pleasant arrangement in the whole and depicts a difference in dimension between opposing forces or influences.
- **Proportion** is the pleasing symmetry between objects or their parts with respect to comparative size, quantity or degree.
- **Unity** is the state of being in accord and having a continuity of purpose or action.
- **Variety**, the partner to Unity, is diversity in a collection that has specific characteristics.

Terms Associated with Color

- **Hue** — any specific color
- **Tone** — a color made by adding grey to a hue
- **Value** — the degree of light or darkness
- **Achromatic** — black, white and grays; artwork executed without color
- **Black** — the complete absence of light
- **Chroma** — the intensity, strength or purity of a color
- **Complementary Colors** — colors which appear opposite one another on a color wheel
- **Secondary colors** — orange, violet, green; each is midway between the Primaries from which it can be mixed
- **Shade** — mixing black with another color to make it darker; the opposite of shade is tint
- **Spectrum** — colors that are the result of a beam of white light that is broken by a prism into its hues
- **Tint** — the opposite of shade; combining white with a color to make it lighter

Terms Related to Positioning of Subject Matter Within a Painting

- **Background** — the part of the scene intended to be the most distant from the perspective of the viewer
- **Foreground** — the part of the scene intended to be nearest the viewer
- **Horizon** — the line where sky and earth meet; also referred to as "ground line"
- **Landscape** — a view of a section of country – applicable to outdoor scenes only
- **Middle ground** — the area between the foreground and the most distant part of a scene
- **Vertical lines** — lines that are painted straight up and down
- **Horizontal lines** — lines that are painted across the picture (90 degrees from straight up and down)
- **Point-of-view** — the angle from which the viewer is observing the work
- **Negative space** — the space behind and around an object; in two-dimensional art it is often synonymous with background
- **Overlapping** — occurs when one object partially covers another; usually done for compositional purposes
- **Design** — the arrangement of the elements of a picture

Appreciation of Visual Art

The act of **appreciating visual art** is, in its simplest form, one of simply deriving satisfaction or pleasure from observing the beauty given to an artwork by its creator. Research has shown that a capacity for appreciating (or, alternatively, creating) aesthetically pleasing art appears to be present within every individual although it does seem to vary in terms of degrees. For most people, innate abilities remain untrained or underdeveloped – not so much in terms of the possession of individual tastes and opinions or in terms of an ability to find something beautiful, but rather in an ability to recognize artistic mastery with respect to technique or style. Education can reconcile such a deficiency. Therefore, anyone can truly appreciate art, but true "art appreciation" requires some understanding of the creative process involved in production, or perhaps, some particular insight into the thoughts and feelings of the creator. Ideally, art is best appreciated when one considers both dimensions.

Wood Carving and Engraving

Wood carving is an ancient art which has changed very little in its history. The process is relatively straightforward. After selecting a suitable wood, most carving is done with a limited set of tools to create works which don't typically exhibit an abundance of fine detail. Engraving is a more refined version of carving and is sometimes a preliminary step in other artistic activities such as printmaking, where fine detail and exacting shapes are desired. Several varieties of wood can be used successfully by the engraver, although boxwood is often preferred for its favorable characteristics. The wood is sawn cross-grain, which results in a block with both a tighter grain and better shape-holding ability. Due to its exacting nature, **engraving** often requires tools similar to those used by copper and steel workers. The tools are arranged into groups such as gravers, tint tools, scorpers, spit stickers, and small chisels. A typical beginning set includes flat, round, burin and lozenge, as well as both large and small U and V cutters.

Pastels

Pastels are chemically pure pigments gently bound by gum or resin and are much softer than their harder chalk crayon cousins. Due to the nature of the pigment cohesion, durability is a primary concern when using them. The ability to correct mistakes is also severely limited. For this reason, pre-planning a work is crucial. A fairly recent addition to the arts, pastel work was pioneered mostly by French artists in the 18th century. Notable pastel artists of the era include Quentin de la Tour, Jean-Baptiste Perroneau and Jean-Baptiste Chardin. More recent artists include Odilon Redon and Mary Cassatt. Having never gained the popularity of other forms such as oils and watercolor, pastels remain one the less regarded mediums within the artistic community.

Pen and Ink

Pen and ink is one of the least demanding art forms in terms of equipment requirements. Pen and ink artists simply need the addition of virtually any kind of paper to produce their work. Historically, medieval monks employed pen and ink on prepared animal skins such as goat, sheep, calf, lamb, or kid using the quills of goose feathers. Pen use continued during the Renaissance and along with mixed media such as white highlighting, crayon and watercolors it flourished as an art form. It gained even more widespread use during the Post-Renaissance era by such artists as Rubens and Van Dyck. Hogarth is considered an exemplary penman of the 18th century while the advent of magazines and the mass production of books in the 19th century provided an outlet for notables such as Charles Keene and George du Maurier. By the 20th century, pen and ink luminaries included Matisse, Pascin and Picasso.

Elements of Sculpture Design

- **Mass** — The most influential element in sculpture, mass can have a dramatic effect upon interpretation, light reflectivity and symmetry.
- **Space** — Space in a multi-piece sculpture is an element that can be manipulated to effect interpretation by yielding clues with respect to the relationship between individual pieces.
- **Plane** — An element with two dimensions – length and width; plane thickness is typically minimized to provide the most dramatic differentiation between plane and volume.
- **Line** — Line lends an element of space to a sculpture; vertical lines belie support and strength lending a monumental quality while horizontal lines have a somewhat less dramatic effect. Convex lines can create tension while concave lines often indicate either real or implied forces.
- **Movement** — generally an implied effect; often a function of reflected light that can be altered through the manipulation of the sculpture's mass. Some sculptors, such as Alexander Calder, employ actual movement in their work through mobiles or similar effects.
- **Scale** — the relative size of the work; often a product of the manipulation of other elements such as mass.
- **Texture** — the surface quality of the work; primarily manipulated to either enhance or diminish light reflectivity and shadowing.
- **Color** — achieved through a variety of effects; can often add a sense of realism or a particular quality, such as age, to a work.

Perspective

Perspective is a system of creating the illusion of three dimensions on a two-dimensional surface. There are two basic categories of perspective – aerial and linear. **Aerial perspective** refers to atmospheric effects on objects in space and can be seen as diminishing tones for objects which are receding from view. Put simply, **linear perspective** describes a process of seeing lines on objects from various angles converge and diverge. The position from which an object is seen and drawn is called the **station point** or **point of sight**. The **horizon** is represented by the eye level or horizon line. **Ground plane** refers to the horizontal plane where the artist is standing. The **center of vision** is the point on the horizon immediately opposite the eye. **Vanishing points** occur where parallel lines converge.

Shape, Form, and Proportion

Shape is an aspect of form which constitutes the individual masses, groupings or aesthetics that the artist uses to render the overall work. It is form, combined with content, which constitutes the basis of the art work itself. **Proportion** refers to the symmetrical three-dimensionality or solidity of a work. In representational art, the intent is to create an illusion of reality by rendering a work which is convincing in form. The mathematical concept known as the "**Golden Mean**" is often employed, either purposefully or incidentally, when rendering proportion. Put simply, the "Golden Mean" is the precept that the proportion of the smaller part to the larger part of a whole is equal to that of the larger to the whole. Perhaps the most well-known demonstration of the "Golden Mean" is the 1509 Leonardo da Vinci work titled "Divine Proportion."

Protective Apparel

Protective apparel such as gloves, long sleeves, long pants and boots or shoes rather than sandals help prevent contact of chemicals with the skin. The garments should be dedicated for use in the studio or work area and washed frequently in a separate load from other laundry. If skin contact does occur, flush immediately with soapy water or other suitable cleaners. Avoid the use of solvents or bleach to clean the skin as these will often absorb and enter the blood stream where they can accumulate in internal organs. If splashes or flying debris are concerns, goggles should be worn in the work area. Ear protection is generally advised when working with noisy equipment for extended periods. Wear a properly fitted respirator or dust mask if vapors or dust are present. Refrain from wearing jewelry when working and tie long hair back to prevent it from being caught in tools and equipment. Do not work when fatigued and always wash hands before drinking, eating or smoking.

Materials to Avoid When Children Are Participating in Art Projects

Numerous materials specially designed for **children** are available commercially. Adult supervision is also advisable when children are working with art materials. All adult materials should be avoided as these may contain toxic chemicals, including solvents, thinners, shellacs, acids, alkalis, bleaches, rubber cement and permanent markers. Materials which must be sprayed such as paints, fixatives, adhesives and airbrush paints should be avoided, as should pottery glazes, copper enamels, stained glass and pastels. Also, any materials requiring solvents for clean-up such as oil paint or oil-based printmaking inks should be substituted for water-based alternatives when available. It is often best to limit the amount or quantity of material given to very young children to reduce the risk should ingestion occur. Children should also be taught to wash their hands thoroughly after working with the materials.

Local Art and Architecture

The architecture of **home construction** is one obvious place. Although many newer areas around cities lack compelling diversity and creativity in home construction, there are almost always exceptions. This is particularly true of older areas with established traditions. **Churches** are another excellent place to discover art. The relationship between religion and art is as old as most religions themselves. Christianity is certainly no exception. Modern churches frequently have collections of paintings and sculpture consistent with the beliefs of their own individual congregations. For those fortunate enough to live in Europe or in the Eastern United States, numerous older churches are accessible. Many of these are exemplary works of art in themselves. A number of **businesses**, particularly large corporations, have substantial art collections in their common areas, many of which are accessible to visitors. Shopping centers, banks, and government buildings (particularly with respect to sculpture) are often rich resources for art seekers.

Art Forms

The following definitions are taken from *The American Heritage College Dictionary*:

- A **painting** is a picture or design created in oil or water-based paint.
- **Literature** is a body of creative writing that helps define a language, period or culture.
- **Music** is sounds arranged to produce a unified composition that has melody, rhythm and timber.
- A **sculpture** is an object created by chiseling marble, molding clay or casting in metal into a real or abstract figure.
- **Theater** is dramatic or comedic literature or other such material performed by actors impersonating characters through dialogue and action.
- **Drama** is verbal literature composed of serious subject matter written specifically to be performed by actors in the theater or on television, radio or film.
- **Comedy** is humorous or satirical verbal literature depicting funny themes, situations or characters that are written to be performed by actors in the theater or on television, radio or film.

Art Terms

These definitions are from the *New York City Public Library Desk Reference*, Second Edition:

- **Carving** means to cut hard material such as stone, wood or marble to create a form.
- In **casting**, the sculptor pours plaster or molten metal into a mold and lets the substance harden into the desired form.
- A **collage** is made of separate pieces of various materials and other objects glued to a surface.
- **Drypoint** is an engraving technique that uses a sharp steel needle to create a rough edge, which produces soft, velvety lines.
- **Engraving** is the art of carving, cutting or etching a design on a wood or metal surface then adding ink so the design can be printed.
- **Etching** is the art of cutting into a metal or glass surface then bathing the surface in acid, adding ink to the plate, and printing the design.
- In architecture, a **frieze** is a horizontal band of painted or sculpted decoration usually found at the top of a wall between the molding and the cornice.
- **Lithography** is a printing process in which a stone or metal plate has been treated with an oily substance so that the desired design retains ink while the rest of the surface is treated to repel ink.
- **Modeling** is when a sculptor uses clay or wax to build up a form. Using color and light to create the illusion of a three-dimensional plane in drawing and painting is also known as modeling.
- A **polyptych** is multiple scenes hinged together. A **diptych** has two panels; a triptych has three panels.
- In architecture, when a form sticks out from the background, depending on how far it protrudes, it is known as **high relief** or **low relief** (bas-relief). In painting or drawing, if an object appears to project out from the flat surface suggesting three dimensions, it is called relief.
- **Stenciling** is the technique of applying paint or ink to forms cut out of cardboard, metal, plastic or other flat materials to create letters, numbers and other images and designs.
- A **still life** is a study of ordinary objects in an every day setting in a painting, drawing or photograph. A still life can also be created on a tabletop or in a bookcase or a shadow box.
- **Woodcutting** is the art of carving an image on a wood block then using ink or paint to print the design.

Music

Emergence of Music

Music as an artistic expression was not documented until the Middle Ages. Prior to that time, music was used as an equally contributing part of worship, poetry, and dance and served society by uniting a community to complete necessary labors, soothe mourners, express different emotions, and offer homage to a higher power. The older or ancient forms of musical expression set the foundation for the more disciplined arts of music, however, there was no musical notation for sharing these ideas until the Middle Ages. The Greeks, with their love of the lyre. established that musical foundation as surely as they did many modern theories regarding culture and philosophy. Greek musical theory introduced intervals, or relationships between pitches, using a tightened string to show how the shortening of the string to ⅔ or ¾ of the original length could change the tone when plucked.

Style of Music and Chronological Classifications of Music

The **style** of music showcases not only the time and political or spiritual mood of the period, but also the composers and the mindset of the people. Music is meant to be listened to and, as such, can be repeated, expounded upon through different media, appreciated in different ways at different times, accepted as an individualistic part of the hearer, respected as a demonstration of a culture or belief system, and touted as a societal bragging right. Music offers these different abstract feelings, but its primary purpose and people's eternal fascination with it falls back on the fact that music is created for people's enjoyment. Styles of music are usually classified into chronological sections and referred to as Renaissance, Baroque, Classical, Romantic, and Twentieth Century.

Quality of Music

Music is difficult to label as good and bad since the biggest deciding factor of the quality of music is the **listener**. Defining any **greatness** in art by comparing the positive and negative aspects limits the artistic voice of the creator and the imagination of the audience. Critics have been in the business of defining the quality of art for centuries and have often made poor calls because of their inability to accept a new style or the enduring aspect of the composer and the audience's reception of that style. For any musician to become accepted, he or she must master a particular style or technique and perform or compose with a kind of genius that inspires others. To be considered great, music must be able to stand the test of time as being an indispensable example of a kind of work for the period, country, or composer.

Symphony

As a work for an orchestra with multiple movements or multiple parts in one movement, the **symphony** contained three movements of fast-slow-fast and was named for the Italian opera *Sinfonia*. Performed with strings and winds, these musical pieces were enjoyed at private gatherings in palaces, monasteries, and residences, as well as civic functions and public concerts. The foundation for the symphony genre comes from Sammartini, whose works used the three-part movement with both strings and winds. As the Classical Period developed, the symphonic format increased to four parts or movements with an even greater transition in the third movement. After being expertly worked by Haydn, the symphony became a more celebrated style of music that allowed for greater freedom in composition and features.

Baroque Style and Classical Style

While the stylistic choices for music differ between Baroque and Classical, an integrity and depth of composition is evident in both. Music requires a certain kind of simplicity for comprehension, and the simpler styles of the **Classical Period** did not take away that complexity. While Bach may create incredible musical feats on his polyphonic style, he incorporated a lucid design in his work. The surface sounds of works by Haydn and Mozart may appear simple but are in actuality incredibly organized and conceived, using a great amount of material and genius in that simplicity. The **Baroque** composers sought to express magnificence and grandeur in their music, while the Classical composers adopted an unpretentious format of hiding deep feelings. Baroque gave us the motet and opera, but from the Classical Period came the symphony, string quartet, and sonata.

Intervals

As the basis for any discussion of melodic or harmonic relationships, the **interval** refers to the measurement from pitch to pitch. The half step or **semitone** is the smallest movement and is the distance from one key to the next in the chromatic scale, such as C to C#. The whole step or **tone** refers to a full movement in which the notes are 2 keys apart, such as from C to D. The half step and whole step act as the basis of measurement for intervallic discussions. These intervals are defined by quantity and quality. The **quantity**, or numeric value assigned to the note, is established by the musical arrangement, such as C D E F G A B. Any interval created with C and G will always be a fifth, regardless of any sharps or flats.

Scales

A **musical scale** is the sequenced arrangement of notes or pitches that are located within the octave. Both major and minor scales have seven different notes or scale degrees, and each scale degree is indicated by the Arabic number showing the position of the note as it appears in the scale. Each major scale has two similar units of four notes, or tetrachords, that are separated by a whole step where each tetrachord has two whole steps and one half step. **Minor scales** are classified as natural, harmonic, and melodic and all start with the same minor tetrachord of 1-2- b3-4 with variations occurring on degrees 6 and 7 in the upper tetrachord.

Dynamics

Dynamics is the degree of loudness or softness of a musical piece. Certain terms can indicate this degree, as well as specific abbreviations and symbols used within the music and at specific places. Dynamic marks can also indicate a change in volume or sound quality and usually suggest the character of the piece to be observed during its performance. Usually written in Italian, dynamic marks are often abbreviated and range from very soft pianissimo (pp) to mezzo piano (mp) to mezzo forte (mf) to fortissimo (ff) which is very loud. Gradual changes in volume can be represented by a < or the word **crescendo** for increasing in volume and by a > or the words **diminuendo** or **decrescendo** for decreasing in volume. These marks for the changing of volume can be several measures long or just a span of a few notes.

Tempo

The **tempo** or speed of the piece of music can be designated by specific tempo marks as well as certain Italian words that describe the speed and also the character of the piece. The words used include *grave* for very slow and serious, *largo* for broad, *lento* for slow, *adagio* for slow and with ease, *andante* for steadily moving, *moderato* for moderate, *allegretto* for fast, *allegro* for fast and cheerful, *vivace* for lively, *presto* for very fast, and *prestissimo* for as fast as possible. Other relative changes in tempo can be described with the words *ritardando*, or rit., for slowing, as well as *accelerando* for quickening and *più mosso* for faster. The tempo markings are a guide for the performance and can be interpreted differently by different conductors.

Length of Musical Notes

Songs are often written using time signatures, measures, and beats. **Time signatures** are usually displayed as a fraction, such as $\frac{4}{4}$ or $\frac{6}{8}$. The numerator describes the number of beats per **measure**. If the numerator is four, then there will be four beats per measure. The denominator describes how to count the measure. If the denominator is four, then the count uses quarter notes, whereas if it is an eight, the measure will be counted with eighth notes.

Whole Note	**Half Note**	**Quarter Note**	**Eighth Note**	**Whole Rest**	**Half Rest**	**Quarter Rest**	**Eighth Rest**
						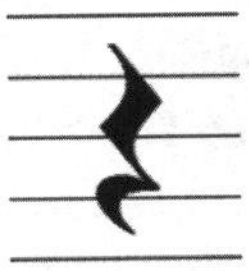	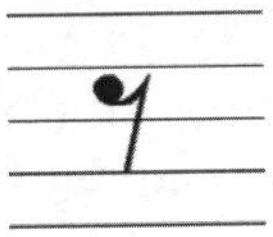
4 Beats	2 Beats	1 Beat	½ Beat	4 Beats	2 Beats	1 Beat	½ Beat

Rhythm

As the pattern of movement in a particular time, **rhythm** has referred to both the flow of a piece and the ability of the piece to maintain or uphold the pulse. Rhythm can be generally assigned to cover any aspect of music that is not related to pitch, although it has also been used as another factor for consideration with melody and harmony. As an equal partner to meter and tempo, rhythm can describe a pattern of *stresses* and *retreats* that are defined by a particular tempo or meter and are composed of hazy pitches or subtle harmonies as well as percussive bursts. For rhythm to sustain, the stresses and retreats should be frequent enough to maintain the melodic or harmonic thought and have defined articulation.

Acoustics

Acoustics refers to the study of the production and perception of sound within a particular room or area. By producing musical sound, musicians create mechanical vibrations from the stretching of strings or membranes, movement of wooden parts, and the oscillatory movement of air columns. This sound action affects the air, which carries the energy of the vibrations from the musician to the audience member. The sound is transmitted through to the brain where it is deciphered and interpreted. The perceived sound is referred to as a pure tone and has a frequency of full oscillations occurring each second. The human ear can perceive 20 to 20,000 cycles per second, or cps, and the corresponding frequency of the pure tone determines the pitch.

Music Educator's Role

Any **educator** of children is in a position to exert remarkable control and **influence** over these young lives. As such, educators are responsible in making that influence a positive one, so that the child can reach his or her fullest potential. All teachers should seek out ways to prepare for curriculum planning and designing instructions that are appropriate for the child's particular educational level. Music combines with all developmental, cognitive, language, physical, emotional, and social arenas of education and makes the music educator one of the most fundamental of teachers. Training is necessary for any teacher dealing with children; it is especially important for teachers dealing with children who are still young enough to be easily influenced. Music educators should be able to guide children in their musical experiences and encourage their progress as it occurs.

Singing and Chanting with Young Children

Young children explore their world with a different perspective than adults do, and their sense of **touch** is especially important when learning new things. Percussion and other simple instruments allow children to see and feel how an accented beat corresponds to music and the words in songs. Rhythmic songs and chants are important for children to understand the combination of sounds and beats and apply that process to their own sensory perceptions. When music educators participate in the singing or chanting, they can interact with the children, and show them how much fun moving to music and creating music can be for all ages. Through this type of exercise, children can learn how words work together and how they should sound by following the example of the music educator.

Teaching Songs to Young Children

Music educators must determine the best way to teach young children the **words** of songs, especially when those children cannot read and must learn songs by rote. The music educator can sing the same song repeatedly or incorporate different methods of participation for the children . Folk songs and nursery rhymes are easy to teach to children, since they are usually written in the limited vocal range of children and are composed of small segments. Parents may also be able to sing these songs with their children. Folk songs are usually specific to a culture or area and would probably be shared across generations. Music educators can also sing to children in order to teach them a new song that may be too complex for their abilities as yet or to show them how much fun music is.

Creative and Synchronized Movement

Movements that are associated with music and performed as dance or exercise by young children are classified as either creative movement or synchronized movement. **Creative movement** gives children a freer avenue for expression and allows them to improvise and enjoy the physical act itself. **Synchronized movement** follows an established routine and is choreographed to the rhythm and beat of the selected music. Synchronized movement helps children work as a group and realize the importance of teamwork, while creative movement allows them to freely express themselves to song. Both types of movement allow children to develop their listening skills and focus on what they are hearing. Focused listening is also considered perceptive or active listening.

Creative Movement

Creative movement involves a child's interpretation of the song without paying attention to the beat. Before a child can be expected to move freely, he or she must have a repertoire of movements already learned, and must feel comfortable choosing from that list. Before being allowed to move creatively, children should be familiar with walking, marching, running, galloping, dancing, clapping, hopping, sliding, and jumping to music. Music educators can help children expand their basis even more by suggesting **imagery exercises**, such as asking children to show how an ice cube melts or how a wind-up doll moves. Young children can also watch how older children and adults move and then attempt to duplicate those movements.

Benefits of Music Education

Combining music education with other facets of education improves the overall educational experience for children in many ways. One benefit is allowing them to learn about the use of symbols in different formats. Music education allows students to see the application of math in different subjects, learn the fulfillment of self-expression while developing creativity, and discover the fundamentals of self-image and self-discipline through music practice. Students of music education find their problem-solving skills becoming more advanced, as well as experience the intellectual satisfaction of sharing in the work required for a performance and of completing the challenge. Students do not suffer from music education and often broaden their own experiences with activities that are uplifting and wholesome.

Including Music in Curriculum

Music should be included in the **basic curriculum** for several reasons. As a topic and area of expression, music is worth learning about since it tells a lot about people and culture. Every person has the potential for musical abilities, as is evidenced in elementary classrooms, and school is the perfect place for a child to explore that possibility. By learning about music and how different voices depend on each other, students can view the interdependence of people of various backgrounds and cultures. The study of music improves other studies, especially for students who may have difficulty in some subjects. The hearing and creating of music inspires the listeners and the performers.

Increasing Focus on Music and the Arts

Music currently stands as a **sideline** to the major focus of science, math, and language regardless of the studies that show how music education can improve students' whole educational experience. An increased focus on music and the arts could motivate students to learn more in other areas, and all educational encouragement avenues should be considered for the changing student body. More researchers and educators are beginning to recognize music as a form of intellectual development along the same lines as Howard Gardner's multiple intelligence theory that encompasses linguistic, spatial, intra-personal, bodily-kinesthetic, logical-mathematical, inter-personal, naturalistic, musical, and possibly existential intelligences. These theoretical systems support the inclusion of music in the basic curriculum and argue that teaching music is only the first step to teaching all other subjects students must learn. Any learning that occurs can be fortified in other areas.

Goals of Music Education

Music educators, parents, teachers, and other adults have witnessed an **improvement** in children who participate in instrumental and choral music education and practice, not only in their musical abilities, but also in their social skills and teamwork. These children learn about *self-discipline* while improving their *self-esteem* and enhancing their *self-expression* and *creativity*. The basic foundations of learning an instrument and then mastering that instrument to play a beginner piece and eventually an advanced piece serve to instill within the child a sense of accomplishment that correlates to improved self-image and greater confidence in an ability to complete other tasks and to persevere even when those tasks appear daunting. The goal, then, of music education should be to foster a sense of purpose and self-worth in the student.

Instructing Young Children to Recognize Rhythm of Familiar Songs

Once young children have grasped the concept of reading the rhythm and are comfortable with the musical notation, the music educator should lead them in the **clapping of the beats** for songs that are familiar to them, such as "Twinkle, Twinkle Little Star." This exercise will allow children to associate their lesson on rhythm with music they know. Music educators can also clap a measure or phrase and have the children clap the same pattern back. This will involve the children in the motor skills exercise of clapping with the perceptive listening of the rhythm and the particular emphasis as it is placed on the first note or another accented note within the phrase.

Changes Technology Has Made in Music

With different inventions and increases in technology, the music of the twentieth century and modern music can be **shared** on a grander scale and in more different formats than at any time before 1900. Whereas the music of the previous centuries was expressed from one person or ensemble to another person or audience, the twentieth century saw music disseminated to larger groups of people through radio and television broadcasts, as well as through pre-recorded sessions on other media. There has also been developments in the field of electronically-produced music.

Rise and Fall of Different Types of Music Within the Past 100 Years

America has seen different **styles of musical expression** rise and fall within the past 100 years. The African-American styles of ragtime, blues, and jazz appealed to listeners, just as the folk and classical traditions of music entertained audiences years before. Western popular culture and Rock 'n' Roll have permeated musical preferences worldwide. While composers of earlier periods had to please their audience to continue creating music, the Modern composers could alienate audience members since some will listen to music because of a popular trend. The composers from non-Western countries have also affected Western composers, so that Modern music may hearken to a traditional mode but incorporate the more rhythmic pulses of monophonic Indian music. With a larger choice for musical style, modern musicians have become better able to play many different styles and have improved their own techniques and performances. This expansion has allowed for more prominent composers than any other musical period.

Instructing Young Children to Read Measures

Music is written in **measures** within the staff. To introduce young children to the concept of the measure, the music educator should have the children count the measures or sections separated by bar lines. Much of today's sheet music provides a count for the measure so that professional musicians can follow along when they are not playing or so that the conductor can call attention to a particular part of the music. Music educators can ask children to count the measures and to locate a specific measure of the music. Once children are comfortable with the basic format for musical notation, they can be instructed more effectively on how to interpret other musical notations, such as the time signature or the rhythm.

Instructing Young Children to Read Time Signatures

Music educators can show children how each measure contains a specific number of beats and how that is indicated at the beginning of the first measure with the **time signature**. Music educators can show students that the top note of the time signature tells how many beats occur in the measure and the bottom note shows which note gets one beat. The music educator can explain how a 4/4 time signature shows that there are four beats in each measure, counted as 1, 2, 3, 4. Contrasting that with a 3/4 time signature, the music educator can show that there are only three beats in each measure, and can then ask students what other time signatures would show. Eventually, music educators can show students the mathematical relationship between quarter notes and half notes, whole notes, and sixteenth notes.

Instructing Young Children to Read Rhythm

The bottom number of the **time signature** becomes important when music educators try to teach children how to read rhythm. The bottom number shows which note gets one beat. In the 4/4 time signature, the quarter note gets one beat and is counted as 1, 2, 3, 4 within the measure. A mathematical explanation of how the bottom number relates to other notes can be incorporated into the lesson, and children can see how two half notes are counted as 1, 3 while eight eighth notes are counted as 1 &, 2 &, 3&, 4&. This exercise combines a study of math with the basic fundamentals of music, and music educators can lead the children toward reading combinations of the notes and playing or clapping those rhythms.

National Music Education Standards for Instructing Children in Grades K-4

The **National Music Education Standards** as outlined for music educators instructing students in grades K-4 as they read and notate music involve the following abilities:

- Ability of each child to **read** whole, half, dotted half, quarter, and eighth notes and rests in time signatures of 2/4, 3/4, 4/4, and others
- Ability of each child to incorporate the use of a system to determine basic **pitch notation** within the treble clef as it relates to major keys
- Ability of each child to identify traditional **terms and symbols** and differentiate their meanings in regards to articulation, dynamics, and tempo while correctly interpreting these symbols during Visual and Performing Arts
- Ability of each child to incorporate the use of standard **symbols** to indicate meter, pitch, rhythm, and dynamics in easy phrases as presented by the music educator

Assisting Children in Ability to Improve Motor Skills While Improvising or Singing New Songs

As children get older, there is an increase in their vocabulary and in their ability to add experiences and movements to their personal repertoire. Music educators can assist children in their ability to improve their motor skills while improvising or singing new songs. Children between five and nine enjoy games that involve rhythm and rhyme, so jump rope rhymes or chants are a great way to show children that music can be fun and entertaining. The music educator can show children a simple or even age-specific complex rhyme or chant, and the children can add clapping or stomping as they become more familiar with the rhyme and feel comfortable enough to improvise. Such rhymes include "Teddy Bear, Teddy Bear" and "The Lady with the Alligator Purse."

Encouraging Children's Music Education at Home

To continue a child's musical education outside of school, music educators should encourage parents to involve their children in **music outings**, such as free concerts or performances in outdoor theaters where children can listen to the music as well as to the sounds of the outdoors and the audience members. Parents can even plan to attend with other families, so that the children can enjoy the outing socially as well as musically. Music educators can also help parents locate musical instructors who would be willing to provide lessons for the children. As a limited option, music educators could create a marching band take-home box for parents that includes books on the music of marching bands or even composers like John Philip Sousa, CDs of marching band songs, index cards describing how to make small instruments, and party hats to remind the parents and children that music is fun.

Instructing Children on the Concept of Rests

Music is an important skill for music educators and parents to teach, and different children will be focused on certain sounds or the volume of those sounds. **Silences** or **rests** within the music can be the most difficult to teach young children who are interested in playing or singing continuously. Based on the same concept as the whole, half, quarter and eighth note beats, rests are set up with a corresponding count and also adhere to the restrictions put in place by the time signature. Children should be introduced to the **symbols** used to indicate rests and instructed how to count each rest. When interspersing beats with rests, some music educators find that clapping the beat and then turning the palms out for the rest is an easy way to show children how the rests function in relation to the beat.

Attitude of Music Educator

Music educators should always approach any musical assignment or practice with children with the right **attitude** of patience and exploration in order for the children to get the most out of their musical experience. The best equipment and the most up-to-date books will not guarantee that children have a good experience with musical instruments and music appreciation in general, so the attitude of the music educator is paramount to the children's success. Children learn best in a classroom and musical environment that includes structure even while fostering an individualized, creative movement format of learning. Music educators should adopt a philosophy of how to introduce children to music successfully that is based on core values and life experiences.

Accommodating Children Who Are Self-Conscious

Not all children between six and nine are comfortable dancing and moving in front of other children or the music educator unless they have been doing so since they were much younger. One of the easiest ways to foster an environment of acceptability is to sing and dance **alongside** the children, so that they can see others behaving in a particular way without being ostracized or ridiculed. Music educators could also provide areas for creative movement that have higher walls or are separated and somewhat shielded from the rest of the room. The music center can include headphones so that children do not feel they are encroaching on others' quiet time for homework. Room dividers combined with rugs and drapes can also provide some basic soundproofing.

Music Classrooms

Equipment

Music classrooms for children of all ages include different types of materials that are appropriate for the development of the children. Besides large **instruments** such as pianos and large or small keyboards, the music classroom will also include rhythm instruments, percussion instruments, string instruments, Orff instruments, Montessori sound cylinders and bells, guitar, and autoharp. Optional **hardware** includes tape recorders, headphones, tapes, CDs, players, and a karaoke machine. Some music educators like to provide specific furniture for the classroom, such as containers or shelving systems for storage, tables, tents, and rocking chairs. **Music boxes** are a nice addition to smaller sections, and computer **software** may be more appropriate for older children. Music-related **pictures** can be hung around the room as well as unbreakable **mirrors** for children to watch their own movements.

Materials

Music educators may have to create simple **instruments** or may find the children are creative enough to benefit from a more hands-on experience so as to appreciate this part of the work. The **construction materials** used in a music classroom may include paper, glue, and paint, as well as rubber bands, shoe boxes, and milk cartons of different sizes. Regular **household items** such as paper or disposable plastic plates, cans with lids, plastic bottles, toilet paper tubes, mailing tubes, and wrapping paper tubes act as containers and can be filled with such items as rocks, rice, beans, sand, or seeds. The containers can be further enhanced with guitar strings, bells, or brass pipes in different lengths. Scarves and ribbons can help with movement visualization, and drum heads and sandpaper samples can introduce different textures. As always, music educators can employ whatever materials imaginable to teach children about sound.

Singing

The **voice** can be used as a musical instrument through singing or humming. With a strong link to community relations predating recorded history, **singing** has been a task of the priest, healer, actor, poet, and entertainer. Greatly popular during the Middle Ages and the Renaissance, singing became less popular with the progression of instrumental music. Vocalists were encouraged to pursue musical instruction in how to use the voice as a musical instrument and not in the folk traditions enjoyed by previous audience members. As a result, music was composed to show off the vocal ranges of singers, and it was expected that vocalists would ornament their vocal pieces the same way instrumentalists would ornament theirs. Popular music and jazz have allowed singers to develop their voices more independently than the composers of the Romantic period did.

Performing Arts

Terms Relating to Dramatic Performances

- **Acting process**—refers to the methods and materials from which an actor draws his or her ability to perform; actors should be able to verbalize the tools they use in their acting processes.
- **Affective memory**—a technique in which an actor reactivates a past experience to gain the emotional and psychological feelings associated with those events and then transferring them to a performance; used when the actor believes the character they are portraying is undergoing an event that emotionally parallels that which the actor experienced in real life.
- **Atmospheres**—defined by Michael Chekhov as the inherent energy within a specific place; actors may imagine they are in a specific location while performing in order to depict the corresponding emotions and actions that would best suit that environment, thus creating an atmosphere.
- **Character acting**—occurs when an actor must make a change to their physical person in order to perform a role; may include the use of dialect or accents that are not part of the actor's real persona or using stage makeup to create a specific facial disfigurement.

Terms Used in Theatre

- **Articulation**—the ability to clearly pronounce words while acting or performing.
- **Blocking**—developing the movements of actors on stage in relation to other actors, scenery, and props.
- **Catharsis**—the purging of an emotion, such as fear or grief, while performing on stage.
- **Concentration**—the ability of an actor to be in character through use of dialogue, attitude, voice, costume, expressions, and mannerisms.
- **Cold reading**—occurs when actors read a script for the first time.
- **Context**—the conditions or climate in which a play was written or meant to be performed.
- **Cue**—a signal that serves as an indicator of another action that is about to occur.

Externals

The elements that an actor can use in his or her environment to aid in creating specific characters are known as **externals**. An external can be a costume, a vocal change, makeup, or a set of mannerisms. For many actors, externals are the primary tool they use to create a character. By dressing or speaking in the way a character would, the actor can begin to relate to the feelings that the character would experience. Using externals to create a character is a method called **outside-in**. This means that the actor uses outside elements to cause internal changes. In order to be a character actor, one must be able to shed the restrictions of his or her everyday persona. In essence, her or she must be able to create a blank slate upon which the new character can be created.

Considerations for Costume Designers

The **costume designer's** role is very important in helping to achieve the director's vision because the costumes used should contribute to the tone and style of a production. It is important for costume designers to consult with the director in order to ensure that the costume designs will be consistent with the *theme* of the production. A costume designer must consider the *time period* in which the play is set. They must also consider the many facets of a character's *personality* and *lifestyle*, including his or her job and social status. The costumes also serve to *differentiate* and *unify* certain characters. For example, a play in which the characters are divided between servants and aristocracy should involve two distinct costuming groups. Costumes must also be practical for the actors and should allow them to move freely and change quickly.

Tools Used by Sound Technicians

In the early days of theatre, **sound** was created by any means available. For example, the sound of thunder was simulated by rolling a cannonball down a narrow trench carved into the roof of a theatre. Now, the sound of thunder can be created through the use of **digital sound equipment**. Technicians have the ability to reproduce sounds made by such things as door bells and telephones. Technicians can also reinforce these sounds through the use of amplification. The variety of technologies available in modern theatre allows for technicians to reproduce nearly any sound that might be needed for a performance. Background music and actors' voices can all be controlled through the use of speakers, microphones, and sound boards. **Sound quality** is a crucial part of any theatre experience, and a successful performance allows the audience to both see and hear the performance without distraction.

Lighting

Lighting in theatre can be used in several ways. The most basic purpose of theatre lighting is to allow the audience to see what is happening on stage. Lighting is also useful for providing depth to the stage and actors. The use of highlights and shadows, called modeling, create a three-dimensional effect. Lighting can serve an overall compositional purpose by helping to create a series of connected imagery that brings the director's *interpretation* to life. It can be used to give information about the *setting* of a play: time of day, season, and location. Light can also be used to focus the audience's attention on a particular *element* in the production. Lighting can be used to create a *mood* for a play. The proper lighting can reflect the *emotional content* of a performance, which leads to a cohesive and balanced production.

Goals for 9th-12th Grade Unit on Theatrical Presentation

Theatrical presentation involves familiarizing students with a broad range of activities that can be considered theatrical forms. Such forms include music, dance, performance, and visual arts. Students should examine the structure of each kind of dramatic form in order to determine how that particular form relates to the structure of all arts. Students should be given the opportunity to integrate their knowledge of various forms of theatre into an original performance they create themselves. Lessons should provide a means for students to study both traditional and non-traditional methods of artistic production. Lessons should also provide students with knowledge of and hands-on experience in emerging technology in theatrical productions including film, video, and computer applications.

Applying Lessons from Theatre Class to Other Subject Areas or Life Skills

In **first grade**, students can learn to cooperate in *group activities*. They also begin to understand the concept that all things in life have a beginning, a middle, and an end, just like they see in stories. In **second grade**, students learn *problem-solving skills*, which can be carried into other courses. In **third grade**, students are taught to question events and gain information through applying the *5 Ws* (who, what, when, where and why). In **fourth grade**, students learn to use acting as a tool for *understanding local history*. They also learn to work with a *team* to accomplish a specific goal. In **fifth grade**, students learn about the various *career options* available to professional actors and theatrical technicians. In **sixth grade**, students learn how theatrical skills are used in the *social sciences*, such as advertising and marketing. In **seventh grade**, students learn how the voice can be used to project *confidence* during oral presentations. In **eighth grade**, students begin to understand the various *jobs* available in theatre, and they are encouraged to research the educational requirements necessary for those jobs.

Comprehending Dance Performance by Genre

Every form of dance has signature **characteristics** that identify and define it—and that make it beautiful and distinct from all other forms. An audience member can look for these when watching particular styles of dance, and can then discern whether those characteristics are present and strongly represented. For example, **tap** exemplifies rhythm and improvisation. If choreography ignores or contradicts the rhythm in an unpleasant way, or simply repeats time steps without ever choosing to improvise movements during the breaks, it could be considered an unsuccessful representation of its form. The same methods can be applied to evaluate modern dance's expressiveness and inquiry into creative movement types, ballet's fluidity and weightlessness, and flamenco's rhythm, passion, and footwork. It should be noted, however, that working contrary to form does not necessarily make a dance "bad." Looking at form is simply a place to start when considering the elements and effects of a dance.

Eliciting Particular Feelings or Reactions

Some dances are created to elicit an **emotional response** from audiences. They may represent characters, settings, or situations about which people already have strong feelings. For example, mythological stories have always been a favorite theme across many forms of dance, as the characters are strong, their defeats disheartening, and their triumphs inspiring. Dances with a **dramatic** or **comedic** objective often borrow methods from theater, such as staging, costumes, props, and sets. These methods help set the tone for bringing forth certain feelings. In these dances, dancers often portray more emotion than usual through facial expression, gestures, and a particular kind of energy in their movements. Whereas **formalistic dances** ask audiences to focus on the "what" and "how" of a dance, **dramatic pieces** draw the viewer into the humanity of the situation. They focus on the "why" or—in **comedic pieces** portraying the absurd behavior of a character—the "who."

Importance of the Audience Member's Experience and Perspective

The performance of any **dynamic** (moving) work of art involves three essential parties: the choreographer, who creates; the dancers, who perform; and the audience member, who receives and interprets. It is important for audience members to understand that their own perspectives will color their responses to a dance every bit as much as anything the choreographer or dancers do. **Choreographers** contribute intention, knowledge, and craft. **Dancers** supply their training, focus, interpretation, and energy. **Viewers** bring their own influential elements to a dance: past experiences; a sociopolitical orientation; aesthetic preferences; and a certain degree—or lack—of knowledge about dance in general and the specific choreographer, company, or presenting institution behind the dance. As the saying goes, "We can only see what we can see." Differing combinations of the viewer characteristics mentioned above create a different version of the dance for every viewer, shaping perception more strongly than any choreographic intention.

Design Elements in Formalistic Dance Pieces

A **choreographer** may create a dance to explore the relationship between floor patterns and the directions dancers face, or to explore patterns in time created by combining long delays and short bursts of movement. The choreographer might even include "what happens if" scenarios that are based on chance. In these dances, the **space** is quite visible in varying shapes made by bodies and the movements themselves, as well as levels, planes, facings, directions, and floor patterns in which the dancers move. **Time** can also be measured in the speed, duration, rhythms, arrangement, and sequencing of the movements. Choreographers can also explore **dynamics** by varying the weight put into the movements and the energy and timing with which the dancers approach, maintain, and release movements. Although **abstract dances** do not specifically aim to evoke viewers' emotions, they may still do so—and will certainly create impressions and elicit reactions of some kind.

Questions to Gain Greater Insight into a Dance

Many viewers leave a dance performance asking one main **question**: "What was that all about?" However, there are other questions audience members can ask and answer for themselves or other spectators that are slightly smaller in scope and more likely to conjure up bits of understanding. These include: Did a clear message come through in the dance? What was that message? Did the dance tell a story, express feelings, solve a puzzle, comment on a situation, or just look pretty? Were there repeated movements or series that were easy to identify? Did specific images catch your attention? What images caught your attention, and what were they likely meant to express? What might the choreographer's intentions have been? What was the choreographer trying to say? Did the dance say it clearly? How did you feel after the dance? Can you distill the description of that feeling down to one sentence? Can you express that feeling using a single word?

Cultural Context of a Body of Work or Particular Dance

Cultural context—the time, place, cultural climate, and artistic influences surrounding artists and their work—can provide a strong set of clues to a viewer trying to analyze a dance or canon of work, and can be understood by using several methods. Comparing and contrasting a dance with other dances from the **same time period**—whether works made by the choreographer in question or several different choreographers—can give a clear "snapshot" of a certain era, especially if it is or was defined by particular historical or political events. Comparing and contrasting a dance with other forms of art from the same time period can provide an even clearer picture of the cultural climate of the time. Comparing and contrasting a dance with **earlier works** by the same choreographer can illustrate the development of the artist's canon throughout his or her career.

Using Imagery to Improve Technique

Imagery connects the unfamiliar with the familiar, allowing a dancer to understand and feel the movement being performed. Following are some examples of imagery that could be used to improve technique, and their desired effects:

- **To improve balance**: The image of sand slowly falling and accumulating (as in an hourglass) to fill up a standing leg
- **To prolong lift in a leap**: The image of a gazelle leaping and remaining suspended for a second before landing
- **To achieve deeper abdominal contraction**: The image of a snail curling deep into its spiraling shell
- **To sharpen angular movement and shapes**: The image of skyscrapers that are full of hard lines and acute angles
- **To soften tension in port de bras**: The image of a soft blanket gently gliding over the skin, or of gentle waves washing the arms
- **To accelerate attack in an assemblé**: The image of stepping on a dollar bill before someone else gets it
- **To better employ plié in preparation for jumps:** The image of a floor made out of springs

Classical Ballet

Classical ballet technique revolves around a dancer's lifted, contracted torso. To provide stability, strength in the core muscles of the body is needed. The limbs are elevated from the core. Arms are typically extended away from the body in "airy" postures. The legs perform movements in a position rotated or "turned out" from the hips, requiring flexibility in the muscles of the hips and legs. Balances are often held upon the tips of the toes, known as "en pointe." The majority of movement is done in **upright positions**—balanced, locomoting upon, or jumping/leaping and landing upon the feet. This requires both flexibility and strength in the legs and feet. Movement is largely directed away from the floor, as the ballet dancer continually strives to create the illusion of weightlessness and effortlessness. The ultimate visual goal is elevation and elongation of the "lines" of the body, and of movement.

Modern Dance

Although **modern dance** shares some features with ballet, it was largely a response to—and rebellion against—ballet. It took shape under a banner of individual exploration into natural, instinctive, expressive movement styles, and has developed ever since into its own always-evolving entity that encompasses as many styles of movement as there are dancers. Movement philosophies prevalent in modern dance are: an emphasis on coordinating movement with the breath; a focus on shifting the weight freely across the feet, hands, shoulders, pelvis, spine, or any other body part that touches the floor; the use of an articulated spine and the limbs; a focus on working with the floor and the force of gravity; and an intention to explore or express a personal, intellectual, emotional, design, philosophical, or other concept through movement.

Terminology and Form in Modern Dance

Modern dance emphasizes the finding of an **individual, personally authentic movement style** over the codification of form and structure. Individual styles are often informed by the specific focus of a dancer's creative exploration and the needs of the physical body. Modern dance has **no standardized terminology**, so even though it uses many standard terms from its predecessor, ballet (plié, tendu, and battement, for example), these are augmented by countless other movement words that range from basic commands (bend, contract, and swing, for instance) to terms specific to each teacher's movement philosophy. Modern dance classes do not share a universally codified structure or sequence, although, like ballet classes, they begin with warm-up movements. Instead of being performed at a barre, however, they are usually performed at center, sometimes beginning from a supine position on the floor. From warm-ups, classes then progress through a series of increasingly demanding movements before finishing with the learning and performing of a choreographic combination.

Floor Work

Because of modern dance's emphasis on **groundedness**, a connection to the floor, and a working cooperation with gravity—as well as its openness to experimentation—the modern form of dance involves more **floor work** than other forms of dance, such as ballet or tap. In these forms, dancers usually stand on their feet. Floor work can be done while kneeling, crouching, on hands and knees, sitting, or lying on the floor. Combinations of these positions can also be used. Movements can include crawling, rolling, scooting, dragging, slithering, etc. Often, movements at this level can express ideas of earth, gravity, weight, debasement, filth, ugliness, evil, disadvantage, poverty, sadness, or dejection, among others. Floor work also supports the modern ethos by affording opportunities to use **unconventional body parts** for balance, locomotion, and pivoting (as in shoulder stands, dragging the prone body forward with the elbows, or spinning on one sitz bone), as well as to invert the body in unfamiliar orientations.

Social Dance and Other Traditional Dance Throughout the World

"**Folk dance**" is a catch-all term for any traditional dance participated in communally by non-professionals. Worldwide, these dances can be placed into two main categories: religious dance and social dance. Both are an effective way of transmitting culture and reinforcing a people's communal values and experiences.

Religious dances reflect a people's spiritual beliefs. They include storytelling dances to transfer knowledge, medicine dances for healing or protection, imitation dances (mimicking important animals or events), commemorative dances demarcating annual events (solstices, harvests, animal migrations, etc.) or personal landmarks in individuals' lives (birth, initiation, marriage, death, etc.), and dances to achieve a spiritual connection with deities.

Social dances are primarily for recreation and community. They include work dances (mimicking movements of a particular kind of labor); courtship dances (less prevalent in cultures that impose strict limitations on contact between the sexes); war dances to prepare, motivate, or intimidate before battle; and communal dances to enhance cooperation.

Social dance is, by definition, communal dance. It is created for the purpose of affirming a community's shared knowledge, culture, and experiences. The dance steps, as well as the music, costumes, and other accompanying traditions, are handed down from one generation to the next through observation and participation, rather than via a rigid scholastic format.

To best facilitate this informal learning, traditional dance steps are usually simple and somewhat natural. In many cases, steps are based on movements used in the work and daily lives of the people and their ancestors, and so are already familiar to the people learning them. Possible examples of familiar movements are fishermen pulling nets and farmers planting seeds.

Often, steps are rhythmic and feature set foot patterns, as rhythm and patterns are both easy devices for categorizing and recalling information. Most importantly, dances are taught in a fun, social environment, which motivates dancers to learn the dance steps, remember them, and look forward to performing them.

Health

Health

Quite simply, **health** is the state of being sound in mind, body, and spirit. According to the World Health Organization, health is not only the absence of disease, but the presence of physical, mental, and social well-being. When assessing an individual's health, a professional is likely to examine him or her from a physical, psychological, spiritual, social, intellectual, or environmental standpoint. Although every individual has his or her own standard of health, it is common for people to recognize the following characteristics as healthy: an optimistic outlook in life, the ability to relax, a supportive home life, a clean environment, a satisfying job, freedom from pain and illness, and the energy necessary to enjoy life.

Wellness

Health professionals refer to the highest state of health as **wellness**. Wellness has a number of definitions: it may mean enjoying life, working towards a defined purpose, or deliberately taking the steps necessary to avoid disease and maximize health. Wellness is different from health in that it means actively *enhancing* health, not just *maintaining* good health. Total wellness depends on psychological, physical, and social factors. In the general model for wellness, all of these factors combine to produce the individual's complete level of wellness. Indeed, part of the reason why health professionals promote the idea of wellness is to show people that all the areas of their lives depend on one another.

Psychological Health

In order to achieve **psychological health**, you must have an accurate and favorable impression of yourself. Having healthy **self-esteem** does not mean overestimating your talents and value; it means feeling good about your role in life and expecting that you will have the personal resources to deal with any adversity. A person who has a reasonable concept of themselves will be able to tolerate the faults of others, based upon the knowledge gained from self-reflection. Part of establishing a realistic but positive view of the world is accepting that there are many things that you will be unable to change in life, and that rather than making yourself miserable about them, you can direct your attention to those things that are under your control.

Vital Signs

Every individual should be able to identify the **vital signs** and know how to measure them. The four common measures considered to be vital signs are body temperature, blood pressure, pulse rate, and respiration rate. **Body temperature** can be taken with a thermometer and should register between 96º and 99.9º Fahrenheit, depending on the time of day and sex (women tend to have slightly higher temperatures). Measuring **blood pressure** requires some equipment; a normal blood pressure is between 120/70 and 140/90, depending on age and sex. A normal **pulse rate** is about 72 beats per minute. A normal **respiration rate** is between 15 to 20 breaths a minute.

Health Education as Community Service

In a general sense, all of health education can be seen as **community service**. By teaching positive health behaviors and promoting good health to students, health teachers are improving the **quality of life** for everyone in the community. More specifically, though, the Center for Disease Control has recommended that health educators use their special training to improve health through work outside of school. Many health educators participate in fundraising for health charities, give speeches on health related topics, or work in the community to generate enthusiasm for exercise and nutrition. According to the Code of Ethics for health educators, it is imperative for those with knowledge and skills to advance positive health behaviors whenever possible and, thus, help their community.

Gender Differences

Science has documented that men and women not only have differences in appearance but actually **think** and **sense** in different ways. In most cases, women have stronger senses of hearing, smell, and taste, while men tend to have better vision. Men tend to be stronger, though women often have better fine motor skills. Brain scans have displayed significant differences in the areas of the brain that are more active in men and women. Science has not yet determined whether these differences are entirely physiological or whether upbringing and environment contribute. Most scientists believe that a combination of nature and nurture create the **differences between the genders**.

Smog

Smog is the informal name given to the combination of smoke, gases, and fog that accumulates in major industrial or metropolitan areas. Most smog is created by motor vehicles, wood-burning stoves, industrial factories, and electric utilities plants. **Gray smog**, which is mainly sulfur dioxide, is common in the eastern United States because of the high concentration of industry. This kind of smog acts like cigarette smoke on the lungs, impairing the ability of the cilia to expel particulates. **Brown smog** comes from automobiles and is mainly composed of nitrogen dioxide. Ozone, one of the other components of brown smog, can impair the immune system. Automobiles are also known to produce carbon monoxide, which diminishes the ability of the red blood cells to carry oxygen.

Skeletal System

The **skeletal system** is composed of about 200 bones which, along with the attached ligaments and tendons, create a protective and supportive network for the body's muscles and soft tissues. There are two main components of the skeletal system: the axial skeleton and the appendicular skeleton. The **axial skeleton** includes the skull, spine, ribs, and sternum; the **appendicular skeleton** includes the pelvis, shoulders, and the various arm and leg bones attached to these. There are few differences between the male and female skeleton: the bones of a male tend to be a bit larger and heavier than those of the female, who will have a wider pelvic cavity. The skeleton does not move, but it is pulled in various directions by the muscles.

Review Video: Skeletal System
Visit mometrix.com/academy and enter code: 256447

Water

A person should drink 7 to 10 average sized glasses of **water** daily. Water is probably the most important substance a person can consume. Water carries nutrients throughout the body and regulates body temperature. Water lubricates joints, aids digestion, and helps speed waste matter out of the body. Losing even 5% of the body's water causes immediate physical symptoms, like dizziness, fatigue, and headache; losing 15% of the body's water can be fatal. The normal daily loss is between 64 and 80 ounces of water a day, which is equal to about 9 large glasses of water. Many fruits and vegetables contain helpful water, but people should still consume the recommended amount of water each day. People who are active, live at a high altitude, or travel a great deal should be sure to drink even more water.

Fat

Fats are divided into two main categories: saturated and unsaturated. **Saturated fats** are mostly found in meat, lard, butter, coconut, and palm oil. Doctors consider these fats to be the most hazardous to health because they increase the risk of heart disease and certain kinds of cancer.

Unsaturated fats include sunflower oil, corn oil, olive oil, and canola oil. The last two oils are called **monounsaturated fats** and are particularly good for the body because they lower cholesterol. Recent research has concluded that the most harmful kinds of fats are **trans fats**, which are formed when liquid vegetable oil is processed to make table spreads and cooking fats. Trans fats have been consistently shown to create buildup in arteries, a process which can impair heart health.

Relationship Between Cholesterol and Fat

Many fats can increase **cholesterol**, a substance in the body which has consistently been linked with **heart disease**. Cholesterol has many positive uses in the body, like helping the liver operate and helping to form many hormones, but if cholesterol becomes too abundant, it can build up in the arteries and impede the flow of blood. Research has shown that **saturated fats** cause a more significant buildup of cholesterol than unsaturated fats or other foods that contain cholesterol. In order to minimize cholesterol in the diet, individuals should cut back on fats altogether, but especially limit their intake of saturated fats. Monounsaturated fats, like canola and olive oil, are a good, low-cholesterol source of fat.

Fiber

Whole grains, fruits, and vegetables are all excellent sources of **fiber**. Fiber can be either insoluble or soluble. **Insoluble fibers** (cellulose and lignin, for example) speed digestion and can reduce the risk of colon cancer and heart disease. Wheat and corn bran, leafy vegetables, and fruit and vegetable skins are all great sources of insoluble fiber. **Soluble fibers** (pectins and gums, for example) lower cholesterol levels and help manage the level of blood sugar. They can be found in the pulp of fruits and in vegetables, oats, beans, and barley. Doctors warn that most Americans do not eat nearly enough fiber. However, increasing fiber in your diet should be done gradually, as a sudden increase in fiber can result in bloating, cramps, and diarrhea.

Alcoholism

The National Council on Alcoholism and Drug Dependence considers **alcoholism** as a disease that is influenced by social, environmental, and genetic factors. The common features of alcoholism are the inability to control consumption, continued drinking despite negative consequences, and distorted thinking patterns (like irrational denial). It is important to note that alcoholism is not simply the result of a weak will but is a **physiological state** that requires medical treatment so that it can be controlled. Many individuals may have a problem with alcoholism but not realize it if they are still functioning well overall and only drink in social situations. Alcoholics tend to be those who, even when they aren't drinking, place an undue amount of psychological emphasis on alcohol.

Drug Abuse

A **drug** is any chemical substance that changes the way a person acts or feels. Drugs may affect a person's mental, physical, or emotional state. Though many drugs are taken to improve the condition of the body or to remedy personal problems, drugs can also undermine health by distorting a person's mind and weakening a person's body. According to the World Health Organization, **drug abuse** is any excessive drug use that is not approved by the medical profession. The use of some drugs in any quantity is considered abuse; other drugs must be taken in large quantities before they are considered to have been abused. There are health risks involved with the use of any drug, legal or illegal, insofar as they introduce a foreign substance into the balanced system of physical health.

Pollution

Many people do not consider **pollution** a personal health issue, but polluted air and water can affect every aspect of a person's life. Scientists define pollution as any change in the air, soil, or water that impairs its ability to host life. Most pollution is the byproduct of human acts. Some of the common health problems associated with pollution are nasal discharge, eye irritation, constricted air passages, birth defects, nausea, coughing, and cancer. Environmental agents that change the DNA of living cells are called **mutagens**, and they can lead to the development of cancer. Pollutants that can pass through the placenta of a woman and cause damage to an unborn child are called **teratogens**.

Safety of Our Water Supply

Even though Americans have generally been able to rely on the **water supply**, in recent years some concerns have been raised about the prevalence of potentially dangerous chemicals in water. **Fluoride**, which has greatly improved dental health by strengthening teeth since it was added to the water supply, may be damaging to bone strength if it is consumed in great volume. **Chlorine**, which is often added to water to kill bacteria, may increase the risk of bladder cancer. One of the most dangerous chemicals that can affect water is **lead**, which is known to leach from pipes and enter the drinking supply. High amounts of lead in the body can cause serious damage to the brain and heart.

Cancer

Every **cancer** has some characteristics in common with other cancers, but it may be more or less treatable depending on its particular nature. The most common forms of cancer are carcinoma, sarcoma, leukemia, and lymphoma. **Carcinoma** is the most common kind of cancer; it originates in the cells that line the internal organs and the outside of the body. **Sarcomas** are those cancers that develop in the connective and supportive tissues of the body, namely bones, muscles, and blood vessels. **Leukemias** are cancers that originate in the blood-creating parts of the body: the spleen, bone marrow, and the lymph nodes). **Lymphomas** are cancers that originate in the cells of the lymph system where impurities are filtered out.

Tobacco and Other Carcinogens

By now, most Americans should be aware that the risk of developing cancer is increased more by **cigarette smoking** than by any other single behavior. Not only do cigarettes lead to lung cancer, but they also lead to cancer of the mouth, pharynx, larynx, esophagus, pancreas, and bladder. The risk of developing cancer is not limited to cigarettes: pipes, smokeless tobacco, and cigars all put a person at risk. **Second-hand smoke** has a similar effect; scientists have shown that individuals who are exposed to environmental smoke for more than 3 hours a day are three times more likely to develop cancer than those not exposed. In addition to tobacco, other acknowledged carcinogens are asbestos, dark hair dye, nickel, and vinyl chloride. Individuals should always try to make certain their living and working spaces are well ventilated to reduce the harmful substances in the air.

Obesity

Obesity is a condition of the body where an individual has increased his or her own body weight significantly beyond what is normally considered healthy, usually by excessive eating. Obesity occurs because the individual takes in more food than his or her body can actually use, and the excess food is stored as fat. Overeating is the primary cause of obesity, but obesity can also be tied to family history, genetic factors, stress and lack of sleep, various illnesses and conditions, and many other causes. An individual who is obese is at a significantly higher risk for certain health problems, including problems with the heart, stomach, muscles, lungs, skin, nervous system, and many other areas of the body. The best way to treat obesity is through a **well-balanced diet** that eliminates excessive food intake and a **rigorous exercise program**. In extreme cases, individuals may also use medication or even surgery to help lower their weight.

Improving Health by Setting Goals

Individuals who are most likely to make positive permanent changes in their health set **realistic goals** along the way. When setting goals, individuals should identify what resources (time, money, and effort) are available to achieve them. Individuals should also identify the potential barriers to success and consider ways to minimize or remove these problems. It is always better to set a number of small, attainable goals rather than big goals that may be difficult to achieve.

Physical Fitness

Physical fitness is the body's ability to perform all of its tasks and still have some reserve energy in case of an emergency. People who are physically fit can meet all of their daily physical needs, have a realistic and positive image of themselves, and are working to protect themselves against future health problems. Physical fitness has three main components: *flexibility*, *cardiovascular fitness*, and *muscular strength* or endurance. Some other factors, like agility and balance, are also often considered when assessing physical fitness. The benefits of pursuing physical fitness throughout life are not only physical but mental and emotional; regular exercise is proven to reduce the risk of disease and increase life expectancy.

Flexibility

A person's **flexibility** is his or her *range of motion* around particular joints. An individual's flexibility will vary according to age, gender, and posture. Some individuals may be less flexible because of bone spurs, and some individuals may be less flexible because they are overweight. Typically, an individual's flexibility will increase through childhood until adolescence, at which point joint mobility slows and diminishes for the rest of the individual's life. Muscles and the connective tissue around them (tendons and ligaments) will contract and become tighter if they are not used to their potential. Lack of flexibility can lead to a buildup of tension in the muscles and can increase the risk of injury during exercise.

Benefits of Regular Exercise

Maintaining physical fitness has a number of advantages besides improving personal appearance. It has been shown time and again that habitual **exercise** is the best way to prevent coronary death. In fact, individuals who don't exercise are twice as likely as active individuals to die of a heart attack. Exercise makes the lungs more efficient, as they are able to take in more oxygen and make better use of it. This provides the body with more available energy. Exercise also benefits the bones. Individuals who do not exercise are more likely to have weak or brittle bones, and they are more prone to osteoporosis, in which bones lose their mineral density and become dangerously soft.

The benefits of **regular exercise** are both physical and mental. It is well documented that frequent exercise improves a person's mood, increases energy, focus, and alertness, and reduces anxiety. In fact, long workouts cause the release of mood-elevating chemicals called **endorphins** into the brain. Exercise also reduces the risk of disease. By aiding in the proper digestion, exercise reduces the risk of colon and rectal cancers. Studies have also indicated that women who exercise are less likely to develop breast cancer. Finally, exercise is beneficial because it helps people lose weight and keep it off. The body's **metabolism** remains elevated for a prolonged period after exercise, which means food is processed more quickly and efficiently. In addition, regular exercise helps suppress the appetite.

Nutrition and Exercise

For most people, the balanced diet depicted in the USDA's **MyPlate** supplys all the nutrients the body needs to maintain a program of physical fitness. However, individuals who are seriously testing their endurance by exercising for periods of more than an hour at a time will need to increase their intake of **complex carbohydrates**, which keep the level of blood sugar stable and increase the amount of available glycogen. Contrary to popular thought, heavy workouts do not require a diet high in protein, and in fact, consuming too much protein can put a severe strain on the kidneys and liver. Similarly, most health experts discourage the use of dietary supplements and body-building foods unless under supervision because these products can easily result in nutritional imbalances.

Water as an Important Component of Exercise

Water is the most important thing for a person to consume before, during, and after exercise. On hot days, active people can sweat up to a quart of water. If you become **dehydrated**, your heart will have a difficult time providing oxygen and nutrients to muscles. Even sports drinks cannot provide the hydrating effect of cool water because the sodium, sugar, and potassium in them delay their absorption into the body. Salt tablets should be avoided as well; they are potentially dangerous and unnecessary. Although people do lose a bit of sodium when they sweat, this is more than offset by the huge amount of salt in the average American diet.

First-Aid

Since it is necessary to act fast when an **emergency** happens, it is a good idea to think ahead and have a **plan** in place. If you are in a public place, you may want to begin by shouting for help to see if a doctor is available. Someone should immediately dial 911. Do not attempt any resuscitation techniques unless you are trained. If you have a car and it is appropriate, you should immediately take the victim to the nearest hospital. Furthermore, every home should have some basic first-aid supplies. A good first-aid kit will include bandages, sterile gauze pads, scissors, adhesive tape, calamine lotion, cotton balls, thermometer, ipecac syrup (to induce vomiting), a sharp needle, and safety pins.

Physical Addiction to Smoking

Nicotine is consistently shown to be far more **addictive** than alcohol; whereas only one in ten users of alcohol will eventually become alcoholics, approximately eight of ten heavy smokers will attempt and fail to quit. The method that nicotine uses is similar to that of other addictive substances: it creates an immediate positive feeling when taken, it will cause painful withdrawal symptoms if it is not taken, and it stimulates powerful cravings in the user even after it is removed from the system. Nicotine addiction can become so strong that a heavy smoker will experience withdrawal symptoms a mere two hours after smoking. Persistent tobacco use will also lead to an increased tolerance for nicotine, and so the user will have to consume more and more to achieve the pleasure or avoid the pain.

Avoiding Alcohol Abuse

There are a few guidelines students should know so that they can avoid chronic **alcohol abuse**. First, never use alcohol as a medicine or as a way to escape personal problems. Always drink slowly, and if possible, alternate alcoholic and non-alcoholic beverages. It is a good idea to eat both before and during drinking so that less alcohol rushes into the bloodstream. Drinking should never be the primary reason for a social function, though individuals should try to avoid drinking alone, as well. At a party, it is a good idea to avoid mixed drinks, as it is often difficult to tell just how much alcohol they contain. Finally, and most importantly, every person should have the self-control to say "no" to a drink without feeling guilty or rude.

Psychological and Physical Dependence on Drugs

A **psychological dependence on drugs** may begin as a craving for the pleasurable feelings or relief from anxiety that the drug provides. However, this craving can soon turn into a dependency on the drug in order to perform normal mental operations. A **physical dependency**, on the other hand, is said to occur when the individual requires increasing amounts of the drug to get the desired effect. Many drugs, like marijuana or hallucinogens, do not cause withdrawal symptoms; others, like heroin or cocaine, may be extremely painful to stop using. Individuals with a severe chemical dependency will eventually use a drug like this simply to avoid experiencing the effects of withdrawal. Typically, an individual with a severe dependency will try to stop many times without success.

Appetite

The feeling of **hunger** can be caused by up to 12 different hormones and areas of the brain. There is even some speculation that the size of an individual's fat cells may cause him or her to feel hungry. **Appetite** is the physiological desire to eat, and though it is thought to be the body's means of avoiding failure, it can also be stimulated when the body does not really need food. Humans tend to stop eating when they reach the point of **satiety**, in which they are no longer hungry and feel full. Scientists have advanced the set-point theory of appetite, which contends that each individual has an internal system that is geared to regulate hunger and satiety so as to keep body fat at a certain rate.

Relationship Between Exercise and Weight Loss

Despite the appeal of quick solutions to obesity, **exercise** remains the best way to reduce weight and maintain weight loss. Many people think that increasing exercise will make them want to eat more; in actuality, frequent exercise tends to reduce the appetite, and since it raises the rate of metabolism, it also helps keep weight off. There are numerous other advantages to exercise in regard to weight; exercise burns off fat reserves and increases muscle mass. Since muscle tends to use calories more quickly than fat, this means it will be more difficult for the individual to put on pounds of fat. In study after study, individuals who exercise regularly are shown to be more likely to lose weight and keep it off.

Digestive System

The **digestive system** is composed of organs that convert food into energy. This process begins with the teeth, which grind food into small particles that are easy to digest. Food is then carried through the pharynx (throat) and esophagus to the stomach. In the stomach, it is partially digested by strong acids and enzymes. From there, food passes through the small and large intestines, the rectum, and out through the anus. On this journey, it will be mixed with numerous chemicals so that it can be absorbed into the blood and lymph system. Some food will be converted into immediate energy, and some will be stored for future use; whatever cannot be used by the body will be expelled as waste.

Review Video: Gastrointestinal System
Visit mometrix.com/academy and enter code: 378740

Muscular System

The **muscles** of the body are attached to the skeleton by tendons and other connective tissues. Muscles exert force and move the bones of the body by converting chemical energy into contractions. Every muscular act is the result of some muscle growing shorter. The muscles themselves are composed of millions of tiny proteins. Muscles are stimulated by nerves that link them to the brain and spinal cord. There are three types of muscles: **cardiac muscles** are found only in the heart and pump the blood through the body, **smooth muscles** surround or are part of internal organs, **skeletal muscles** are those a person controls voluntarily. Skeletal muscles are the most common tissue in the body, accounting for between 25 and 40% of body weight.

> **Review Video: Muscular System**
> Visit mometrix.com/academy and enter code: 967216

ENDOCRINE SYSTEM

The **endocrine system** creates and secretes the hormones that accomplish a wide variety of tasks in the body. The endocrine system is made up of glands. These glands produce chemicals that regulate metabolism, growth, and sexual development. Glands release hormones directly into the bloodstream, where they are then directed to the various organs and tissues of the body. The endocrine system is generally considered to include the pituitary, thyroid, parathyroid, and adrenal glands, as well as the pancreas, ovaries, and testes. The endocrine system regulates its level of hormone production by monitoring the activity of hormones; when it senses that a certain hormone is active, it reduces or stops production of that hormone.

> **Review Video: Endocrine System**
> Visit mometrix.com/academy and enter code: 678939

CIRCULATORY SYSTEM

The **circulatory system** is composed of the heart, the blood vessels, and the blood. This system circulates the blood throughout the body, giving nutrients and other essential materials to the body cells and removing waste products. **Arteries** carry blood away from the heart, and **veins** carry blood back to the heart. Within body tissues, tiny **capillaries** distribute blood to the various body cells. The heart takes oxygenated blood from the lungs and distributes it to the body; when blood comes back bearing carbon dioxide, the heart sends it to the lungs to be expelled. Other organs not always considered to be a part of this system (for instance, the kidneys and spleen) help to remove some impurities from the blood.

HORMONE SYSTEM

Hormones are the chemicals that motivate the body to do certain things. They are produced in the organs that make up the endocrine system. With the exception of the sex organs, males and females have identical endocrine systems. The actions of the hormones are determined by the **hypothalamus**, an area of the brain about the size of a pea. The hypothalamus sends messages to the pituitary gland, which is directly beneath it. The **pituitary gland** turns on and off the various glands that produce hormones. Hormones, once released, are carried to their targets by the bloodstream, at which point they motivate cells and organs to action. Hormones can influence the way a person looks, feels, behaves, and matures.

COMMUNICABLE AND NON-COMMUNICABLE DISEASES

Communicable diseases are those that are caused by microorganisms and can be transferred from one infected person or animal to a previously uninfected person or animal. Although some diseases are passed on by direct contact with an infected individual, many can be spread through close proximity: airborne bacteria or viruses account for most communication of disease. Some examples of communicable disease are measles, smallpox, influenza, and scarlet fever. Some communicable diseases require specific circumstances for transmission; for instance, tetanus requires the presence of infected soil or dirt. Any disease that cannot be transferred from one person or animal to another is considered non-communicable.

Infectious and Non-Infectious Diseases

Infectious diseases are those that are caused by a virus, bacterium, or parasite. Infectious diseases are distinguished from non-infectious diseases in that they stem from biological causes, rather than from physical or chemical causes (as in the case of burns or poisoning). An infectious disease will always have an **agent** (something that has the disease and spreads it to others) and a **vector** (a way of transmitting the disease). In the case of malaria, for instance, a parasite contains the disease, and it is introduced to the body when a mosquito carrying it places it in the bloodstream. The vector of an infectious disease does not need to be biological; many diseases are transmitted through water, for example.

Viruses

Viruses are the smallest of the pathogens, but they are also the most difficult to destroy. Viruses consist of a small bit of nucleic acid (either DNA or RNA) inside a coating of protein. Viruses are unable to reproduce by themselves, so they infest the reproductive systems of cells already in the body and command them to make new viral cells. These new cells are then sent to other parts of the body. Some of the most common viruses are influenza, herpes, hepatitis, and papilloma. It is difficult to treat viruses without also damaging the cells that they are using. Antibiotics, for instance, have no effect on viruses. Special antiviral drugs must be taken, and even these do not entirely eliminate the presence of the virus.

Bacteria

Bacteria are simple, one-celled organisms and are the most common microorganism and pathogen. Most bacteria do not cause disease; in fact, many bacteria are important to body processes. Bacteria can harm the body when they release enzymes that actually digest other body cells or when they produce toxins. Since bacteria are quite different from the normal body cell, they can usually be effectively treated with antibiotics. However, not just any antibiotic can be used to treat every bacterial infection; a doctor must determine the particular strain of bacteria that is causing the problem before he or she writes a prescription. Over time, bacteria may become resistant to antibiotics, so it is best not to take too much of this effective treatment.

Immune System

The body uses a number of different weapons to try to defeat infections. Most obviously, the **skin** repels most invaders. Many substances produced by the body (like mucus, saliva, and tears) also fight against infection. When these methods are ineffective, however, the immune system goes to work. The **immune system** consists of parts of the lymphatic system, like the spleen, thymus gland, and lymph nodes, and vessels called lymphatics that work to filter impurities out of the body. The *spleen* is where antibodies are made, as well as the place where old red blood cells are disposed. The *thymus gland* fortifies white blood cells with the ability to find and destroy invaders. The *lymph nodes* filter out bacteria and other pathogens.

Review Video: Immune System
Visit mometrix.com/academy and enter code: 622899

Basic Immune Response

Whenever an **antigen**, or infecting substance, enters the body, the **immune system** immediately goes to work to defeat it. To begin with, the **T cells** fight the antigen, assisted by **macrophages** (cells that scavenge for foreign or weakened cells). While this battle is raging, the **B cells** create **antibodies** to join in. Many pathogens will be transported to the **lymph nodes**, where a reserve store of antibodies will eliminate them. It is for this reason that the lymph nodes often become swollen during cold and flu season. If the antigens find some success, the body will rush a greater blood supply to the infected area, enriching the supply of oxygen and nutrients. In the event that the pathogens are able to contaminate the blood stream, the infection becomes systemic and much more dangerous.

ALLERGIES

An **allergy** is a hypersensitivity or overreaction to some substance in a person's environment or diet; it is the most common kind of immune disorder. There are many different symptoms of an **allergic reaction**, but the most common are sneezing, hives, eye irritation, vomiting, and nasal congestion. In some extreme cases, the person may collapse and even die. Allergic triggers, or **allergens**, can be anything from peanuts to pollen, from insect bites to mold. Although there is no way to reverse or eliminate a personal allergy, science has made progress in treating the allergic reaction. These days, it is possible to be treated for an allergic reaction without becoming drowsy or sluggish.

IMMUNIZATIONS

Despite the overwhelming evidence supporting the use of **immunization** in preventing potentially life-threatening diseases, many Americans still neglect to get the basic immunizations. At present, the American Academy of Pediatrics recommends that every child be immunized against measles, mumps, smallpox, rubella, diphtheria, tetanus, and hepatitis B. Some vaccinations will need to be repeated on a certain schedule. Basically, a vaccination is the intentional introduction of a small amount of an antigen into the body. This stimulates the immune system to learn how to fight that particular antigen. There are certain vaccinations that a pregnant woman should not get, and a person should never be vaccinated if he or she is sick.

COMMON COLD

The **common cold** is one of the most pesky and irritating of viruses, though it is rarely a great risk to long-term health. One reason the cold is so difficult to fight is that there are over 200 varieties of the virus, so the body is never able to develop a comprehensive immunity. The cold virus is typically spread through the air or through contact. There is no completely effective medical treatment, either. Indeed, doctors warn that taking aspirin and acetaminophen may actually suppress the antibodies that the body needs to fight the infection and may therefore contribute to some symptoms. There is also no conclusive evidence to support taking vitamin C in large doses. Antihistamines, which many people credit with relieving the symptoms of the common cold, may make the user drowsy.

CANCER

Cancer is the uncontrolled growth and spread throughout the body of abnormal cells. Cancer cells, unlike the regular cells of the body, do not follow the instructions encoded in the body's DNA. Instead, these cells reproduce themselves quickly, creating neoplasms, or tumors. A **tumor** may be either benign, when it is not considered dangerous, or malignant (cancerous). Unless they are stopped, cancer cells continue to grow, crowding out normal cells in a process called infiltration. Cancer cells can also **metastasize**, or spread to other parts of the body by entering the bloodstream or lymphatic system. The gradual overtaking of the body by these cancer cells will eventually make it impossible to sustain human life.

Hygiene

Importance

Besides helping you maintain an attractive appearance, **hygiene** is essential for keeping you healthy and free of disease. The body is usually covered with a certain amount of bacteria, but if this number is allowed to grow too high, you may place yourself at risk for disease. Individuals who fail to regularly wash their hair are more likely to have head lice, and those who fail to properly clean their genitals are more susceptible to urinary tract infections. Good hygiene also reduces an individual's contagiousness when sick. Hygiene is especially important when dealing with **food**: failing to wash everything involved in the preparation of a meal can result in the spread of bacterial infections like E. coli and hepatitis A.

Basic Personal Hygiene Practices

To stay clean and reduce the risk of disease, students should practice **daily basic hygiene**. Everyone should wash their hair and body daily and should wash their hands more frequently than that. Teeth should be brushed between one and three times daily. Always wash hands before eating, avoid spitting or nose-picking, and cover your mouth when sneezing. Try to avoid coming into contact with any bodily fluids, and keep your clothes and living space clean. Finally, avoid putting your fingers in your mouth, and try not to touch any animals before eating.

Similarities Between Basic Food Preparation and Medical Hygiene

There are a few basic **hygiene habits** that every individual should practice when preparing food or performing basic medical procedures. Always clean off the areas where food will be prepared, and wash your hands after touching any uncooked foods. Do not use the same tools to prepare different foods. Always refrigerate foods before and after they are used. Label stored food to indicate when it was produced. Dispose of any uneaten food that cannot be stored. When performing basic medical procedures, always use sterile bandages and any necessary protective clothing, like masks, gloves, or eyewear. Always make sure any medical waste, like used bandages, is disposed of securely.

USDA Dietary Guidelines

Inception to the Early 1990s

The United States Department of Agriculture began issuing **nutrition guidelines** in 1894, and in 1943 the department began promoting the Basic 7 food groups. In 1956, Basic 7 was replaced with the Basic Four food groups. These were fruits and vegetables, cereals and breads, milk, and meat. Basic Four lasted until 1992, when it was replaced with the **Food Pyramid**, which divided food into six groups: 1) Bread, cereal, rice, pasta 2) Fruit 3) Vegetables 4) Meat, poultry, fish, dry beans, eggs, nuts 5) Milk, yogurt, cheese 6) Fats, oils, sweets. The Food Pyramid also provided recommendations for the number of daily servings from each group.

USDA's MyPlate

The **USDA's Food Pyramid** was heavily criticized for being vague and confusing, and in 2011 it was replaced with **MyPlate**. MyPlate is much easier to understand, as it consists of a picture of a dinner plate divided into four sections, visually illustrating how our daily diet should be distributed among the various food groups. Vegetables and grains each take up 30% of the plate, while fruits and proteins each constitute 20% of the plate. There is also a representation of a cup, marked Dairy, alongside the plate. The idea behind MyPlate is that it's much easier for people to grasp the idea that half of a meal should consist of fruits and vegetables than it is for them to understand serving sizes for all the different kinds of foods they eat on a regular basis.

Most experts consider MyPlate to be a great improvement over the Food Pyramid, but it has still come under criticism from some quarters. Many believe too much emphasis is placed on protein, and some say the dairy recommendation should be eliminated altogether. The Harvard School of Public Health created its own **Healthy Eating Plate** to address what it sees as shortcomings in MyPlate. Harvard's guide adds healthy plant-based oils to the mix, stresses whole grains instead of merely grains, recommends drinking water or unsweetened coffee or tea instead of milk, and adds a reminder that physical activity is important.

Importance of Self-Image in Relationships

One of the most important determinants of how an individual forms relationships with others may be how that individual **perceives him or herself**. If an individual feels unlovable, it may be impossible for him or her to seek affection from others. If a person has confidence in him or herself, he or she should be able to develop honest and open relationships with others. Though the phrase is a bit clichéd, it is nevertheless true that a person cannot love another without loving him or herself. Sadly, studies have shown that individuals who have a negative opinion of themselves tend to establish relationships with people who treat them poorly and thus reinforce their negative self-image.

Fair Play

Fair play is the term used to describe the goal of sportsmanship in physical education. Fair play includes following rules, displaying etiquette, helping others, including everyone, sharing equipment, playing safely, persevering, working collaboratively, and winning without cheating. It also teaches students how to win without gloating or putting down their competitors. Creating an environment of fair play allows physical education to promote physicality while remaining inclusive and sensitive to the needs of all learners.

Conflict Resolution

It is inevitable in life that everyone will come into **conflict** with some difficult individuals. Many people persistently spar with others because they have a **personality disorder** based on low self-esteem or illness. For the most part, you will not be close enough to an individual to try and change them in any permanent way. Therefore, in most cases of conflict, health professionals recommend acknowledging the other person's viewpoint and then finding a way to either avoid or circumvent that person. If **confrontation** is necessary, you should state your feelings honestly and politely. If possible, try to avoid making confrontations personal. Sometimes it helps to have a third party mediate an especially contentious dispute.

Effects of Siblings

Siblings (brothers and sisters) can be almost as important as parents in helping children develop models for their future relationships. **Sibling rivalry**, for example, can have damaging consequences in other relationships if it is taken too far. Likewise, children who feel they were appreciated by their parents less than their brothers or sisters may go through life expecting to be taken for granted. Typically, people grow more distant from their siblings during adolescence, as each tries to assert his or her own independence. Later in life, though, people report much stronger relationships with their brothers and sisters. Siblings may not be as close as friends for some, but they nevertheless occupy a unique and prized place in people's lives.

Typical State Educational Standards for Physical Education Classes

A typical state standard in **physical education** is for students to understand the rules for a variety of physical activities, including games and sports. Some examples of the kinds of **benchmarks** that a state education department might specify for this standard are, for third grade: to identify the rules and procedures in specified physical activities, including games. The benchmarks for fifth grade are: to demonstrate that they understand the rules that must be followed when participating in specified physical activities, including games. Example benchmarks for high school grades are: to demonstrate the rules in complex versions of at least two different categories of movement forms in individual activities, dual activities, cardiorespiratory and aerobic lifetime activities, outdoor activities, team sports, aquatics, self-defense, yoga, martial arts, dance, and strength training and conditioning. For a standard of identifying the rules, procedures, and etiquette in a specified game or physical activity, a typical benchmark for fifth grade might be to demonstrate and explain the rules, procedures, and etiquette to follow when participating in physical activities or games; for eighth grade, to apply safe, effective rules, procedures, and etiquette for specific activities or games; and for high school, to analyze and apply the safe, effective rules, procedures, and etiquette for specific activities or games.

Physical Education

Assessing Personal Fitness

Personal fitness is particular to the individual. Some people may be considered fit when they can run for a mile without stopping, while others may be athletic enough to accomplish that feat without really being in shape. Most people will acquire a sense of their own fitness only after spending a great deal of time exercising, setting fitness goals, and working to achieve them. However, those who want more objective data on their physical condition may submit to **testing** at a sports medicine laboratory. There, they will have their muscular and cardiovascular endurance measured on a treadmill, their body fat measured in a submersion tank, and their flexibility tested through a variety of trials.

Cardiovascular Fitness

An individual's **cardiovascular fitness** is the ability of his or her heart to pump blood through the body at the necessary rate. Proper cardiovascular fitness can be achieved through **aerobic exercise**: that is, any activity during which the amount of oxygen taken into the body is equal to or more than the amount the body is using. Jogging, walking, or riding a bike are all examples of aerobic activity. The heart also gets an excellent workout during **anaerobic exercise**, in which the body takes in less oxygen than it needs to maintain the activity. Sprinting or swimming fast can be anaerobic exercises, if they leave the person breathless. **Nonaerobic exercise**, like bowling or golf, does not challenge the heart and lungs and therefore will not improve cardiovascular fitness.

Muscle Strength and Endurance

Developing **healthy muscles** is not simply a matter of lifting the heaviest possible object. The ability to use your muscles over and over without getting tired is also an important part of physical fitness. Developing muscular strength and endurance will help make body tissue firmer and more resilient. Well-maintained muscles tend to work more efficiently, and they can withstand more strain. Furthermore, muscular development aids in circulation, causing the whole body to absorb and make use of nutrients in the blood more quickly. Strength and endurance training has also been shown to be one of the most effective ways to lose weight, as developed muscles burn more calories than does fat.

Importance of Exercising Muscles

Muscles are in a constant state of **change**. If muscles are not used, they will atrophy and weaken; on the other hand, if they are regularly exercised, they will grow stronger and possibly larger. Muscles are best exercised when they are **overloaded** or asked to do more than they usually do. When you are training your muscles, you will need to gradually increase the amount of the weight or the number of repetitions to ensure that your muscles are always receiving a challenge. Many fitness professionals contend that a good muscular workout will be somewhat painful because muscles can only be developed by exceeding their normal requirements. However, not every kind of pain is profitable for a muscular workout, and individuals should be careful to distinguish muscular fatigue from injury, particularly when they are lifting heavy loads.

Physical Education

The meaning of the phrase "**physical education**" may seem obvious at first glance, but it is quite possible for individuals to have very distinct ideas of what physical education entails. Physical education, by most accounts, is composed of **exercise** (the use of the body), **play** (the action generated by the exertion of the body), **games** (competitions of any kind), **leisure** (freedom from the responsibilities of work), **recreation** (any activity that refreshes the mind and body after work), **sport** (physical activities performed for pleasure or achievement), and **athletics** (organized, competitive activities). So, a general definition of physical education might be that it is the process whereby an individual improves his or her physical, mental, and social skill through physical activity.

Warming Up and Cooling Down in Exercise

There are important reasons for warming up before and cooling down after exercise. For one thing, performance is always enhanced by **warming up**. Muscles tend to work more effectively when their temperature has been slightly raised; they are also more resistant to strains and tears at a higher temperature. Warming up directs the blood to working muscles and gives the heart time to adjust to the increased demands of the muscles. Warming up also stimulates the secretion of synovial fluid into the joints, which makes them less likely to suffer wear and tear. Warming up should include slow stretching and low-impact cardiovascular exercise. **Cooling down** is important for easing the body's transition to a normal resting condition. Stretching and slowly decreasing cardiovascular workload aids the heart in its readjustment.

Physical Education as Recreation Versus Competition

One of the perennial issues facing physical educators is whether activities should be promoted as forms of recreation or as competition. If **competition** is to be the dominant feature, then activities must have explicit rules, a formal way of keeping score, and identifiable winners and losers. When students are taught activities for competition, the emphasis will be on practicing specific skills, and avoiding mistakes as much as possible. When sports are taught as **recreation**, participation is the most important factor for students. Each student should get an equal amount of experience and performance time, regardless of his or her skill level. Although score is typically not kept in strictly recreational activities, students may receive certificates for good sportsmanship or diligent participation.

Aerobic Fitness

A **minimum of aerobic fitness** has been achieved when you are able to exercise three times a week at 65% of your maximum heart rate. The easiest means of achieving this level of fitness is by running for 30 minutes three or four times a week. **Moderate aerobic fitness** is achieved by exercising four or more times a week for at least 30 minutes at a heart rate that is 75% or more of maximum. This level of aerobic fitness is appropriate for athletes who are seeking to play vigorous sports like football or tennis. **Maximum aerobic fitness** can only be achieved by working close to maximum heart rate several times a week and by exercising vigorously almost every day. In order to achieve this level of fitness, you must consistently work beyond your anaerobic threshold. A good way to do this is having interval training or brief, high-intensity workouts.

Lymphatic System

The **lymphatic system** is connected to the cardiovascular system through a network of capillaries. The lymphatic system filters out organisms that cause disease, controls the production of disease-fighting antibodies, and produces white blood cells. The lymphatic system also prevents body tissues from swelling by draining fluids from them. Two of the most important areas in this system are the right lymphatic duct and the thoracic duct. The **right lymphatic duct** moves the immunity-bolstering lymph fluid through the top half of the body, while the **thoracic duct** moves lymph throughout the lower half. The spleen, thymus, and lymph nodes all generate and store the chemicals which form lymph and which are essential to protecting the body from disease.

Nervous System

The **nervous system** collects information for the body and indicates what the body should do to survive in the present conditions. For instance, it is the nervous system that administers a bad feeling when the body is cold, and then sends a more positive message when a person warms up. These important messages are sent by the nerves, which vary in size and cover the entire body. The **central nervous system** is composed of the brain and spinal cord, and the peripheral nervous system is composed of the rest of the body, including those organs which a person does not voluntarily control. The **peripheral nervous system** is divided into *sympathetic* and *parasympathetic systems*, which counterbalance one another to allow for smooth function.

Cartilage

The areas of bones that are close to joints are covered in a shiny connective tissue known as **cartilage**. Cartilage supports the joint structure and protects the fragile bone tissue underneath. Cartilage is susceptible to injury because it is subject to gravitational pressure as well as pressure born of joint movement itself. Long-term stress to cartilage can result in rheumatoid arthritis and osteoarthritis. There are no blood vessels in cartilage; nutrients are delivered by the synovial fluid, and from nearby blood vessels. Cartilage contains a huge number of spongy fibers because it needs to absorb a great deal of shock. Especially resilient cartilage, known as **fibrocartilage**, is found between the vertebrae and in the knees, among other places.

Ligaments

Ligaments are dense bundles of fibers running parallel to one another from one bone in a joint to another. Ligaments are a part of the joint capsule, although they may also connect to other nearby bones that are not part of the joint. Ligaments are not like muscles; they cannot contract. Instead, ligaments passively strengthen and support the joints by absorbing some of the tension of movement. Ligaments do contain nerve cells which are sensitive to position and speed of movement, and so ligaments can hurt. One function of this pain is to alert the person to an unnatural or dangerous movement of the joint. Ligaments may also be strained or ruptured if they are placed under unnecessary or violent stress.

Muscle Tissue

Muscle tissue is made up of bundles of fibers which are held in position and separated by various partitions. These partitions range from large (deep fascia, epimysium) to small (perimysium, endomysium), and often extend beyond the length of the muscle and form tendons connecting to a bone. Each muscle cell is extremely long and has a large amount of nuclei. Every muscle cell contains a number of smaller units called **sarcomeres**; these contain thick filaments of the protein myosin and thin filaments of the protein actin. Muscle tissue contracts when a nerve stimulates the muscle and the thin filaments compress within the sarcomere, causing a general muscle contraction.

Gross Motor Skills

The three types of fundamental **gross motor skills** include locomotor, balance, and ball skills. **Locomotor skills** involve movement from place to place, such as running, jumping, skipping, or hopping. Teachers can help improve these skills by organizing relay races or obstacle courses for students to compete in. The second type of gross motor skill, **balance**, involves movement where the body remains in place, such as bending, stretching, or twisting. These skills can be improved by providing opportunities for yoga or basic calisthenics. The third gross motor skill, **ball skills**, describes a student's ability to throw, catch, kick, or manipulate a ball or similar item. These skills can be improved by providing opportunities to partake in sports such as softball, kickball, or bowling. With younger students, equipment such as beanbags or balloons could be substituted.

TExES Practice Test

English Language Arts and Reading

1. *Sea* and *see*, *fair* and *fare*, are called:

a. Homophones
b. Antonyms
c. Homographs
d. Twin words

2. In preparation for writing a paper, a class has been instructed to skim a number of Internet and print documents. They are being asked to:

a. Read the documents several times, skimming to a deeper level of understanding each time
b. Read the documents quickly, identifying those that offer the most specific information
c. Read the documents quickly, looking for key words in order to gather the basic premise of each
d. Read the documents carefully, looking for those that offer the most in-depth information

3. Which of the following is the best definition of information literacy?

a. It is the set of skills required for reading and comprehending different information.
b. It is the cognitive skill set necessary to amass a comprehensive base of knowledge.
c. It is the skill set required for the finding, retrieval, analysis, and use of information.
d. It is the set of skills necessary for effectively communicating information to others.

4. Which of the following choices describes the best introduction to a unit on oral traditions from around the world?

a. Introducing games that practice new sight words, encoding words based on phonics rules, and answering short comprehension questions.
b. Setting up video-conferencing with a school in Asia so that students can communicate with children from other countries.
c. Inviting a guest speaker from a nearby Native American group to demonstrate oral story-telling to the class.
d. Creating a slide show presentation about various types of oral cultures and traditions and characteristics of each.

5. A syllable must contain:

a. A vowel
b. A consonant
c. Both a vowel and a consonant
d. A meaning

6. Where does a prefix appear in a word?

a. at the beginning
b. at the end
c. in the middle
d. any place

7. According to MLA guidelines for writing research papers, which of the following is correct regarding citations of web sources if you cannot immediately see the name of a source's author?

a. Assume the author is not named, as this is a common occurrence on the Web.
b. Do not name an agency or corporation as the author if it is the sponsor of the source.
c. Author names are often on websites but need additional searching to discover.
d. It is not permissible to cite the book or article title in lieu of an author's name.

8. A student says, "We learned that knowledge and understanding of language is important." This is an example of an error in which of these?

a. Phonology
b. Semantics
c. Syntax
d. Pragmatics

9. The purpose of corrective feedback is:

a. To provide students with methods for explaining to the teacher or classmates what a passage was about
b. To correct an error in reading a student has made, specifically clarifying where and how the error was made so that the student can avoid similar errors in the future
c. To provide a mental framework that will help the student correctly organize new information
d. To remind students that error is essential in order to truly understand and that it is not something to be ashamed of

10. A third grader knows he needs to write from left to right and from top to bottom on the page. He knows what sounds are associated with specific letters. He can recognize individual letters and can hear word families. He correctly identifies prefixes, suffixes, and homonyms, and his reading comprehension is very good. However, when he is asked to write, he becomes very upset. He has trouble holding a pencil, his letters are very primitively executed, and his written work is not legible. He most likely has:

a. Dysgraphia
b. Dyslexia
c. Dyspraxia
d. Nonverbal learning disorder

11. Which statement is correct regarding the relationship of your audience profile to the decisions you make in completing a writing assignment?

a. How much time you spend on research is unrelated to your audience.
b. Your audience does not influence how much information you include.
c. The writing style, tone, and wording you use depend on your audience.
d. How you organize information depends on structure, not on audience.

12. When creating an outline, it is important to use

a. prepositions.
b. progressivism.
c. abbreviation.
d. subordination.

13. Of the following sentences, which one appeals to emotion?

a. It is dangerous to use a cell phone while driving because you steer one-handed.
b. Statistics of greater accident risk show cell phone use while driving is dangerous.
c. It is really stupid to use a cell phone when you drive because it is so dangerous.
d. Many state laws ban cell phone use when driving due to data on more accidents.

14. Examples of onomatopoeia are:

a. Sink, drink, mink, link
b. Their, there, they're
c. Drip, chirp, splash, giggle
d. Think, in, thin, ink

15. Which of the following exercises would be the most appropriate tool for helping students evaluate the effectiveness of their own spoken messages?

a. Discuss written and oral assignments in class before completing them. Once the assignments are completed, the teacher meets individually with each student to discuss the content and effectiveness of each student's work.
b. Instruct students to present oral reports in class, which are then "graded" by classmates. A score of 1-10 is assigned based on students' perception of the reports' clarity. The student's average score determines his report's effectiveness.
c. Ask each student to prepare an oral report and a content quiz that highlights the report's main idea. The student then uses classmates' scores on the reviews to determine his report's effectiveness.
d. Put students into groups of three. Two students complete a role-playing assignment based on prompts provided by the teacher. The third student gives constructive feedback on how the other two can refine and clarify their speech.

16. When teaching students relationships between sounds and letters and between letters and words, what practices should teachers best follow?

a. Use a variety of instructional techniques, but including only the auditory and visual modes
b. Incorporate multisensory modalities within a variety of instructional strategies and materials
c. Always adhere to the same exact instructional method and materials to ensure consistency
d. Introduce similar-looking letters and similar-sounding phonemes together for discrimination

17. Dr. Jenks is working with a group of high school students. They are about to read a science book about fossils. Before they begin, she writes the words *stromatolites, fossiliferous,* and *eocene* on the board. She explains the meaning of each word. These words are examples of:

a. Academic words
b. Alliteration
c. Content-specific words
d. Ionization

18. An understanding of the meanings of prefixes and suffixes such as *dis, mis, un, re, able,* and *ment* are important for:

a. Reading comprehension
b. Word recognition
c. Vocabulary building
d. Reading fluency

19. If a student were asked to use a similar word to describe someone who was happy, he or she would use

a. an antonym.
b. a homonym.
c. a synonym.
d. an euphemism.

20. Among the following, which is NOT a common academic standard for kindergarten students in decoding and identifying words?

a. Showing knowledge that letter sequences correspond to phoneme sequences
b. Understanding that word sounds and meanings change along with word letters
c. Decoding monosyllabic words using initial and final consonant and vowel sounds
d. Matching letters to consonant sounds; reading simple, monosyllabic sight words

21. When you have a writing assignment, which of the following is true about your reader audience?

a. You need not identify the audience because it is the assigning teacher.
b. You should consider how your readers are likely to use what you write.
c. You should know your writing purpose more than a reader's purposes.
d. You are overthinking to wonder about readers' likely attitude/reaction.

22. Silent reading fluency can best be assessed by:

a. Having the student retell or summarize the material to determine how much was understood
b. Giving a written test that covers plot, theme, character development, sequence of events, rising action, climax, falling action, and outcome. A student must test at a 95% accuracy rate to be considered fluent at silent reading
c. Giving a three-minute Test of Silent Contextual Reading Fluency four times a year. The student is presented with text in which spaces between words and all punctuation have been removed. The student must divide one word from another with slash marks, as in the following example: The/little/sailboat/bobbed/so/far/in/the/distance/it/looked/like/a/toy. The more words a student accurately separates, the higher her silent reading fluency score
d. Silent reading fluency cannot be assessed. It is a private act between the reader and the text and does not invite critique

23. Homonyms such as *bare* and *bear* are similar in sound yet have different meanings. What would a teacher suggest a student do to avoid misusing these words?

a. Memorize the definitions of the difficult words.
b. Check a dictionary or thesaurus to verify a word's usage.
c. Avoid encountering difficult words.
d. Ignore being precise in the definition.

24. According to the English Language Arts and Reading TEKS, which of the following are students in grades 1-3 expected to do?

a. Regularly read materials at the independent level, i.e., text containing 1 in 10 or fewer difficult words
b. Select text to read independently using author knowledge, difficulty estimation, and personal interest
c. Regularly read materials at the instructional level, i.e., text containing 1 in 20 or fewer difficult words
d. Read aloud from unfamiliar texts fluently, i.e., with accuracy, phrasing, expression, and punctuation

25. A student is able to apply strategies to comprehend the meanings of unfamiliar words; can supply definitions for words with several meanings such as *crucial, criticism,* and *witness*; and is able to reflect on her background knowledge in order to decipher a word's meaning. These features of effective reading belong to which category?

a. Word recognition
b. Vocabulary
c. Content
d. Comprehension

26. Which type of nonverbal message deals with belonging, control, respect, or disapproval?

a. Emotive messages
b. Relational messages
c. Relationship messages
d. Interpersonal messages

27. Which of the following gives an example of a fallacy of inconsistency?

a. "There are exceptions to all general statements."
b. "Please pass me; my parents will be upset if I fail."
c. "He is guilty: there is no evidence he is innocent."
d. "Have you stopped cheating on your assignments?"

28. Which of the following correctly represents the sequence of stages or steps in the writing process?

a. Prewriting, drafting, revising, editing, publishing
b. Prewriting, drafting, editing, publishing, revising
c. Prewriting, editing, drafting, revising, publishing
d. Prewriting, drafting, editing, revising, publishing

29. Arthur writes a paper. One classmate identifies ideas and words that resonated with her when she read it. Another describes how reading the paper changed his thinking. A third asks Arthur some questions about what he meant by certain statements in the paper. A fourth suggests a portion of the paper that needs more supporting information. This description is most typical of...

a. A portfolio assessment.
b. A holistic scoring.
c. A scoring rubric.
d. A peer review.

30. In the model known in reading instruction as the Three Cueing Systems, which of these relate most to how sounds are used to communicate meaning?

a. Syntactic cues
b. Semantic cues
c. Phonological cues
d. Pragmatic cues

31. Which text should a teacher choose in order to practice the skills of previewing and reviewing information?

a. A poem
b. A chapter from the students' science class textbook
c. A library book of each student's own choosing
d. A short story from language arts class

32. In preparation for writing a paper, a high school class has been instructed to skim a number of Internet and print documents. They are being asked to:

a. Read the documents several times, skimming to a deeper level of understanding each time
b. Read the documents quickly, identifying those that offer the most specific information
c. Read the documents quickly, looking for key words in order to gather the basic premise of each
d. Read the documents carefully, looking for those that offer the most in-depth information

33. *Bi, re,* and *un* are:

a. Suffixes, appearing at the beginning of base words to change their meaning
b. Suffixes, appearing at the end of base words to enhance their meaning
c. Prefixes, appearing at the beginning of base words to emphasize their meaning
d. Prefixes, appearing at the beginning of base words to change their meanings

34. Some experts maintain that teaching reading comprehension entails not just the application of skills, but the process of actively constructing meaning. They describe this process as *interactive*, *strategic,* and *adaptable*. Which of the following best defines the *interactive* aspect of this process?

a. The process involves the text, the reader, and the context in which reading occurs.
b. The process involves readers' using a variety of strategies in constructing meaning.
c. The process involves readers' changing their strategies to read different text types.
d. The process involves changing strategies according to different reasons for reading.

35. At the beginning of each month, Mr. Yi has Jade read a page or two from a book she hasn't seen before. He notes the total number of words in the section and also notes the number of times she leaves out or misreads a word. If Jade reads the passage with less than 3% error, Mr. Yi is satisfied that Jade is:

a. Reading with full comprehension
b. Probably bored and should try a more difficult book
c. Reading at her independent reading level
d. Comfortable with the syntactical meaning

36. Which of the following students may need extra instruction and evaluation with respect to oral language skills?

a. Rosa: whose first language is Spanish. Rosa speaks with a distinct accent and can be difficult to understand when speaking about a new or unfamiliar topic.
b. Greer: who avoids oral assignments when possible. He avoids speaking up in class and only responds when called upon.
c. Ashley: who often has trouble answering questions in class. Her responses are often off-topic. She also struggles with oral presentations, seeming to present a string of unrelated facts.
d. Brett: who frequently becomes loud and disruptive whenever group work is assigned. He often becomes involved in heated discussions with classmates when discussing ideas.

37. Which of the following is most accurate regarding writing style?

a. The kind of diction you use does not affect style.
b. You add style later to give your writing personality.
c. Style is unrelated to your control of your content.
d. Your purpose for writing guides your writing style.

38. Editing involves:

a. Correcting surface features such as sentence fragments, spelling, and punctuation
b. Fine-tuning the underlying structure of the piece to make the theme stand out
c. Reconsidering ideas, adding or subtracting information, and changing the underlying structure
d. Adding illustrations, charts, and other useful addenda

39. A teacher wants to work on her students' listening comprehension in addition to their reading comprehension since she understands that the skills are interrelated. She has a series of short stories that she thinks the students will enjoy. Which of the following would be the best supplement to typical written comprehension exercises?

a. Preview the content and then read the stories aloud to the students. Assess listening comprehension through verbal and written questions.
b. Ask the students to choose one story each to read aloud to a small group. Encourage the students to discuss what they have learned afterward.
c. Assign each student a story to read and require them to write a report on it. Each student should then present his or her report based on what he or she has learned to the class.
d. Have the students read stories aloud to the class, and create mock tests based upon the main ideas which they identify.

40. A teacher has a student in her class who is not very motivated to write because he finds it difficult. She observes he has a highly visual learning style, does not like reading books but loves graphic novels, and has considerable artistic drawing talent and interest. Which of the following instructional strategies would best address his individual needs, strengths, and interests?

a. Giving him audio recordings to accompany and guide his writing homework
b. Letting him complete all assignments by drawing pictures instead of writing
c. Having him draw the pictures and write accompanying text in graphic novels
d. Providing and assigning him to view animated videos on the topic of writing

41. A reading teacher feels that some of his strategies aren't effective. He has asked a specialist to observe him and make suggestions as to how he can improve. The reading specialist should suggest that first:

a. The teacher set up a video camera and record several sessions with different students for the specialist to review. The presence of an observer changes the outcome; if the specialist is in the room, it will negatively affect the students' ability to read
b. The teacher reflects on his strategies himself. Which seem to work? Which don't? Can the teacher figure out why? It's always best to encourage teachers to find their own solutions so that they can handle future issues themselves
c. They meet to discuss areas the teacher is most concerned about and decide on the teacher's goals
d. The specialist should arrive unannounced to observe the teacher interacting with students. This will prevent the teacher from unconsciously over-preparing

42. Which of the following is an example of a portmanteau?

a. Fax
b. Brunch
c. Babysitter
d. Saxophone

43. Which of the following MOST accurately summarizes the relationship between reading fluency and reading comprehension?

a. As students develop greater reading comprehension, their reading fluency also improves.
b. When students develop greater reading fluency, their reading comprehension improves.
c. The relationship between reading fluency and reading comprehension is a reciprocal one.
d. Reading fluency and reading comprehension are two separate, mainly unrelated skill sets.

44. To determine the subject matter of a section within a text chapter, what should the teacher tell the student to do?

a. Read the section heading
b. Read the chapter glossary
c. Read the index in the text
d. Read through the section

45. A class is reading *A Wrinkle in Time*. The teacher asks students to write a short paper explaining the story's resolution. She is asking them to locate and discuss the story's:

a. Outcome
b. Highest or most dramatic moment
c. Plot
d. Lowest point

Mathematics

1. Determine the number of diagonals of a dodecagon.

a. 12
b. 24
c. 54
d. 108

2. A dress is marked down by 20% and placed on a clearance rack, on which is posted a sign reading, "Take an extra 25% off already reduced merchandise." What fraction of the original price is the final sale price of the dress?

a. $\frac{9}{20}$
b. $\frac{11}{20}$
c. $\frac{2}{5}$
d. $\frac{3}{5}$

3. Aaron goes on a run every morning down the straight country road that he lives on. The graph below shows Aaron's distance from home at times throughout his morning run. Which of the following statements is (are) true?

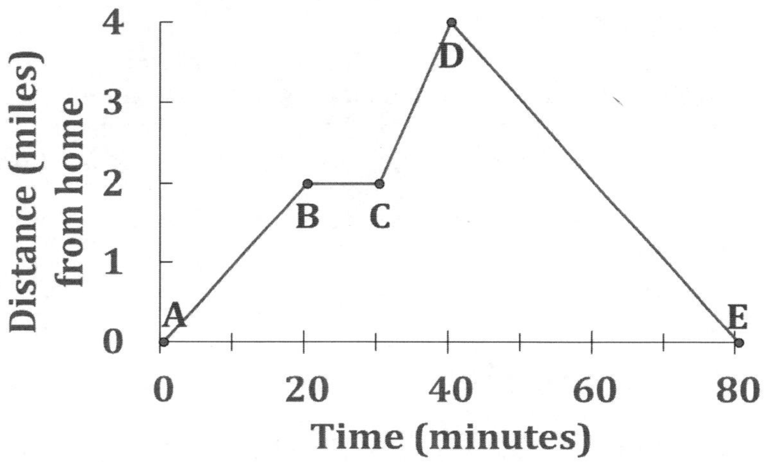

I. Aaron's average running speed was 6 mph.
II. Aaron's running speed from point A to point B was the same as from point D to E.
III. Aaron ran a total distance of four miles.

a. I only
b. II only
c. I and II
d. I, II, and III

4. If a, b, and c are even integers and $3a^2 + 9b^3 = c$, which of these is the largest number which must be factor of c?

a. 2
b. 3
c. 6
d. 12

5. Solve $\frac{x-2}{x-1} = \frac{x-1}{x+1} + \frac{2}{x-1}$.

a. $x = 2$
b. $x = -5$
c. $x = 1$
d. No solution

6. How can an EC teacher best facilitate children's development of math communication and literacy?

a. By asking the children questions
b. By observing children's behaviors
c. By lecturing to model language use
d. By having children write about math

7. If the midpoint of a line segment graphed on the xy-coordinate plane is $(3, -1)$ and the slope of the line segment is -2, which of these is a possible endpoint of the line segment?

a. $(-1,1)$
b. $(0, -5)$
c. $(7,1)$
d. $(5, -5)$

8. 320 students are surveyed. 120 of the students like only Dallas. 150 of the students like only Houston. 48 of the students like neither city. How many students like Dallas *and* Houston?

a. 2
b. 3
c. 4
d. 5

9. What is the educational purpose of having students measure the length of an object, such as their desk or table, with non-standard measuring units smaller than the object, such as crayons?

a. Measuring with small units is easier for young children
b. Children cannot read the markings on a standard ruler or yard stick
c. Students learn to measure something larger than a unit with repetitive use of that unit
d. Students will later be able to transfer measurements from meters to yards

10. Which of the following statements is true?

a. A number is divisible by 6 if the number is divisible by both 2 and 3.
b. A number is divisible by 4 if the sum of all digits is divisible by 8.
c. A number is divisible by 3 if the last digit is divisible by 3.
d. A number is divisible by 7 if the sum of the last two digits is divisible by 7.

11. A dress is marked down 45%. The cost, after taxes, is $39.95. If the tax rate is 8.75%, what was the original price of the dress?

a. $45.74
b. $58.61
c. $66.79
d. $72.31

12. Which of the following represents an inversely proportional relationship?

a. $y = 3x$
b. $y = \frac{1}{3}x$
c. $y = \frac{3}{x}$
d. $y = 3x^2$

13. Of the following, which is/are NOT an example(s) of math manipulatives?

a. Tangrams for shape recognition
b. Large magnetic number boards
c. Printed mathematical formulas
d. Play money, toy cash registers

14. Of the following, which is prerequisite for young children to understand before they can engage in accurately estimating basic measurements of quantities?

a. Knowledge of math vocabulary words indicating estimation
b. Knowledge of how to make predictions that are appropriate
c. Knowledge of how to achieve estimates that are reasonable
d. Knowledge of what relative quantities and comparisons are

15. Eric has a beach ball with a radius of 9 inches. He is planning to wrap the ball with wrapping paper. Which of the following is the best estimate for the number of square feet of wrapping paper he will need?

a. 4.08
b. 5.12
c. 7.07
d. 8.14

16. Which of the following transformations has been applied to ΔABC?

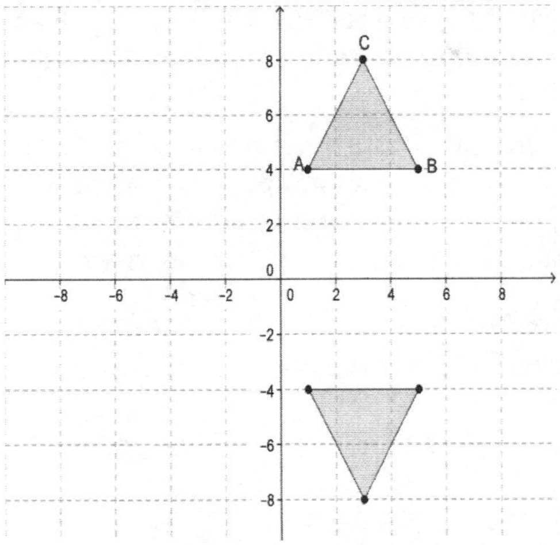

a. translation
b. rotation of 90 degrees
c. reflection
d. dilation

17. Kayla rolls a die and tosses a coin. What is the probability she gets an even number and heads?

a. $\frac{1}{6}$
b. $\frac{1}{4}$
c. $\frac{1}{3}$
d. 1

18. Mrs. Miller is teaching a unit on numbers and operations with her sixth-grade class. At the beginning of class, she asks the students to work in groups to sketch a Venn diagram to classify whole numbers, integers, and rational numbers on a white board. Which of the following types of assessments has the teacher used?

a. Summative assessment
b. Formative assessment
c. Formal assessment
d. Informal assessment

19. Which of the following learning goals is most appropriate for a fourth-grade unit on geometry and measurement?

a. The students will be able to use a protractor to determine the approximate measures of angles in degrees to the nearest whole number.
b. The students will be able to describe the process for graphing ordered pairs of numbers in the first quadrant of the coordinate plane.
c. The students will be able to determine the volume of a rectangular prism with whole number side lengths in problems related to the number of layers times the number of unit cubes in the area of the base.
d. The students will be able to classify two-dimensional figures in a hierarchy of sets and subsets using graphic organizers based on their attributes and properties.

20. Sophia is at the market buying fruit for her family of four. Kiwifruit is only sold in packages of three. If Sophia would like each family member to have the same number of kiwifruits, which of the following approaches can Sophia use to determine the fewest number of kiwifruits she should buy?

a. Sophia needs to determine the greatest common multiple of 3 and 4.
b. Sophia needs to determine the least common multiple of 3 and 4.
c. Sophia needs to determine the least common divisor of 3 and 4.
d. Sophia needs to determine the greatest common divisor of 3 and 4.

21. A 6th grade math teacher is introducing the concept of positive and negative numbers to a group of students. Which of the following models would be the most effective when introducing this concept?

a. Fraction strips
b. Venn diagrams
c. Shaded regions
d. Number lines

22. Which of the following problems demonstrates the associative property of multiplication?

a. $2(3 + 4) = 2(3) + 2(4)$
b. $(3 \times 6) \times 2 = (4 \times 3) \times 3$
c. $(2 \times 3) \times 4 = 2 \times (3 \times 4)$
d. $6 \times 4 = 4 \times 6$

23. Which of the following formulas may be used to represent the sequence 8, 13, 18, 23, 28, ...?

a. $a_n = 5n + 3$
b. $a_n = n + 5$
c. $a_n = n + 8$
d. $a_n = 5n + 8$

24. Which of the following best describes an isosceles triangle?

a. A triangle with no sides of equal measurement and one obtuse angle
b. A triangle with three sides of equal measurement
c. A triangle with two sides of equal measurement and two acute angles
d. A triangle with one right angle and two non-congruent acute angles

25. Mr. Amad draws a line with a slope of $-\frac{2}{3}$ on the white board through three points. Which of the sets could possibly be these three points?

a. $(-6, -2), (-7, -4), (-8, -6)$
b. $(-4, 7), (-8, 13), (-6, 10)$
c. $(-3, -1), (-6, 1), (0, -3)$
d. $(-2, -3), (-1, -3), (0\ -3)$

26. Given this stem and leaf plot, what are the mean and median?

Stem	Leaf
1	6 8
2	0 1
3	4
4	5 9

a. Mean = 28 and median = 20
b. Mean = 29 and median = 20
c. Mean = 29 and median = 21
d. Mean = 28 and median = 21

27. The 6th grade teachers at Washington Elementary School are doing a collaborative unit on cherry trees. Miss Wilson's math classes are making histograms summarizing the heights of black cherry trees located at a local fruit orchard. How many of the trees at this local orchard are 73 feet tall?

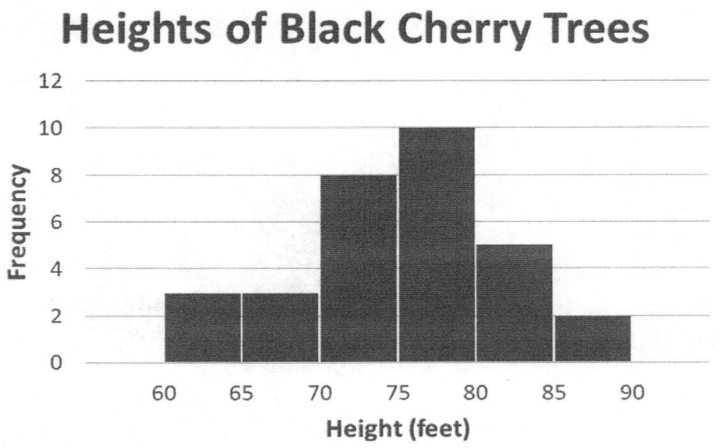

a. 8
b. That information cannot be obtained from this graph
c. 9
d. 17

28. Which of these is true about having an awareness of patterns and relationships in the real world?

a. Our understanding the basic structure of things is uninformed by it.
b. It helps us understand series of events, but not predict future ones.
c. It is unrelated to our basic feeling of confidence in the environment.
d. It increases our self-efficacy about interacting with our environment.

29. Mrs. Vories, a fifth-grade teacher, asks her class to use compatible numbers to help her determine approximately how many chicken nuggets she needs to buy for a school-wide party. The school has 589 students and each student will be served nine nuggets. Which student correctly applied the concept of compatible numbers?

a. Madison estimates: $500 \times 10 = 5{,}000$ nuggets
b. Audrey estimates: $600 \times 5 = 3{,}000$ nuggets
c. Ian estimates: $600 \times 10 = 6{,}000$ nuggets
d. Andrew estimates: $500 \times 5 = 2{,}500$ nuggets

30. The table below shows the average amount of rainfall Houston receives during the summer and autumn months.

Month	Amount of Rainfall (in inches)
June	5.35
July	3.18
August	3.83
September	4.33
October	4.5
November	4.19

What percentage of rainfall received during this timeframe, is received during the month of October?

a. 13.5%
b. 15.1%
c. 16.9%
d. 17.7%

31. A can has a radius of 1.5 inches and a height of 3 inches. Which of the following best represents the volume of the can?

a. 17.2 in^3
b. 19.4 in^3
c. 21.2 in^3
d. 23.4 in^3

32. What is the area of the shaded region in the figure shown below?

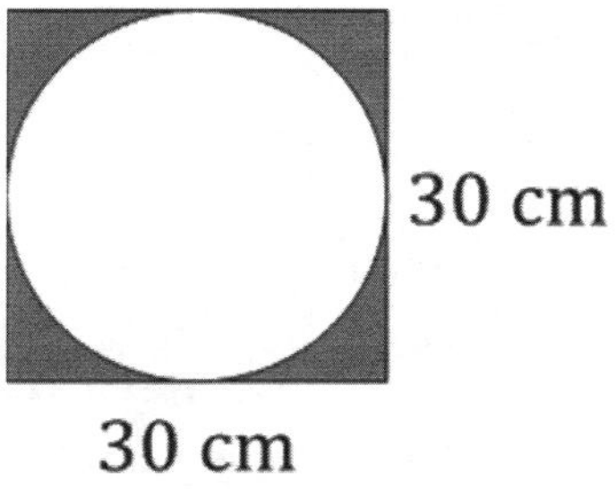

a. 177 cm^2
b. 181 cm^2
c. 187 cm^2
d. 193 cm^2

33. What is the perimeter of the trapezoid graphed below?

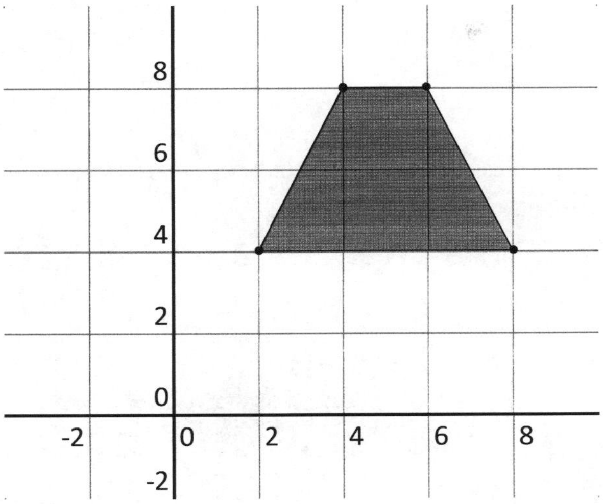

a. $4 + \sqrt{10}$
b. $8 + 4\sqrt{5}$
c. $4 + 2\sqrt{5}$
d. $8 + 2\sqrt{22}$

34. The vertices of a polygon are $(2, 3)$, $(8, 1)$, $(6, -5)$, and $(0, -3)$. Which of the following describes the polygon most specifically?

a. Parallelogram
b. Rhombus
c. Rectangle
d. Square

35. $A = \{5, 9, 2, 3, -1, 8\}$ and $B = \{2, 0, 4, 5, 6, 8\}$. What is $A \cap B$?

a. $\{5, 2, 8\}$
b. $\{-1, 0, 2, 3, 4, 5, 6, 8, 9\}$
c. $\emptyset$
d. $\{5, 8\}$

36. In a pack of 20 jelly beans, there are two licorice- and four cinnamon-flavored jelly beans. What is the probability of choosing a licorice jelly bean followed by a cinnamon jelly bean?

a. $\frac{2}{5}$
b. $\frac{8}{20}$
c. $\frac{2}{95}$
d. $\frac{1}{50}$

37. Amy saves $450 every 3 months. How much does she save after 3 years?

a. $4,800
b. $5,200
c. $5,400
d. $5,800

38. The box-and-whisker plot displays student test scores by class period. Use the data to answer the following question:

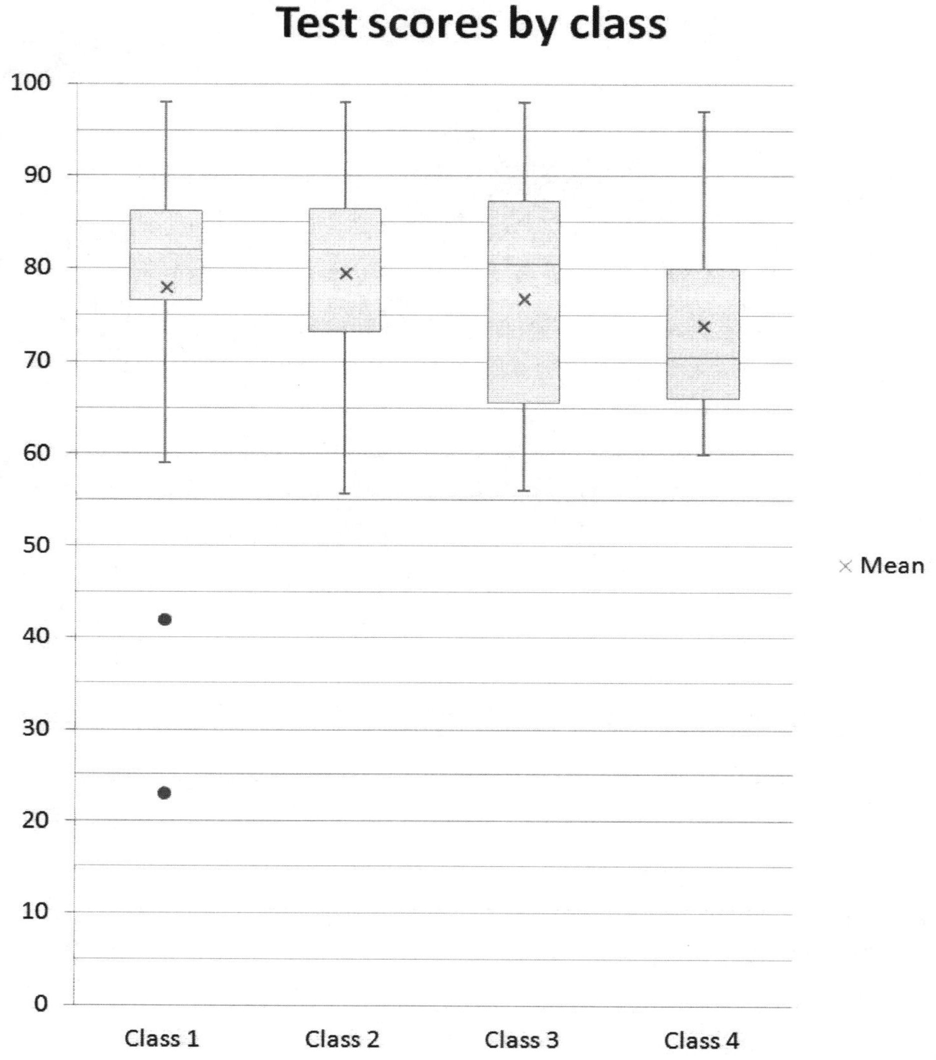

What is the probability that a student chosen at random from class 2 made above a 73 on this test?

a. 0.25
b. 0.5
c. 0.6
d. 0.75

39. Given that x is a prime number and the greatest common factor of x and y is greater than 1, compare the two quantities.

Quantity A	Quantity B
y	the least common multiple of x and y

a. Quantity A is greater.
b. Quantity B is greater.
c. The two quantities are the same.
d. The relationship cannot be determined from the given information.

40. If 1" on a map represents 60 ft, how many yards apart are two points if the distance between the points on the map is 10"?

a. 1800
b. 600
c. 200
d. 2

Social Studies

1. Emily West, a multiracial woman, who was captured by Santa Anna prior to the battle of San Jacinto and thought to have contributed to the Texans victory, is associated with which of the following symbols of Texas:

a. The Lone Star
b. The Yellow Rose
c. The Blue Lacy
d. The Bluebonnet

2. During the decolonization of the Cold War years, which of the following events occurred chronologically latest?

a. The Eastern Bloc and Satellite states became independent from the Soviet Union
b. Canada became totally independent from British Parliament via the Canada Act
c. The Bahamas, in the Caribbean, became independent from the United Kingdom
d. The Algerian War ended, and Algeria became independent from France

3. The Yellow River Valley began to emerge as a cultural center during the:

a. Shang Dynasty
b. Neolithic Era
c. Xia Dynasty
d. Paleolithic Era

4. How long can members of the Federal Judiciary serve?

a. Four years
b. Eight years
c. For life
d. Six years

5. Which of the following questions would most likely be asked by a historian concerned with the philosophy of history?

a. What issues shaped the writing of Plato's Republic?
b. Should history be measured by changes in individual lives or by larger political trends?
c. Why were the religions of Shinto and Buddhism able to merge in Japan?
d. Should historians study modern primitive cultures as a means of learning about past civilizations?

6. Which of the following statements is *not* true about the Gilded Age in America?

a. The Gilded Age was the era of the "robber barons" in the business world
b. The Gilded Age got its name from the excesses of the wealthy upper-class
c. The Gilded Age had philanthropy Carnegie called the "Gospel of Wealth"
d. The Gilded Age is a term whose origins have not been identified clearly

7. Which of the following exemplifies the multiplier effect of large cities?

a. The presence of specialized equipment for an industry attracts even more business.
b. The large population lowers the price of goods.
c. Public transportation means more people can commute to work.
d. A local newspaper can afford to give away the Sunday edition.

8. Which invention had a major role in communication during the Civil War?

a. Morse Code
b. Telephone
c. Radio
d. Computer

9. Thai food has become increasingly popular in the United States, though it is prepared in slightly different ways here. This is an example of

a. Cultural divergence.
b. Assimilation.
c. Cultural convergence.
d. Acculturation.

10. The idea that the purpose of the American colonies was to provide Great Britain with raw materials and a market for its goods is an expression of:

a. Free trade.
b. Most favored nation status.
c. Mercantilism.
d. Laissez-faire capitalism.

11. During the early Medieval period in Europe, before the 5th century, where were the main centers of literacy found?

a. They were in the homes of the wealthy
b. They were in the churches and monasteries
c. They were in the local artisan and craft guilds
d. There were no centers of literacy

12. How must inferior courts interpret the law?

a. According to the Supreme Court's interpretation
b. According to the Constitution
c. However they choose
d. According to the political climate

13. Which entity in American government is the closest to direct democracy?

a. The Electoral College
b. The House of Representatives
c. Committees within the Senate
d. The Supreme Court

14. Power divided between local and central branches of government is a definition of what term?

a. Bicameralism
b. Checks and balances
c. Legislative oversight
d. Federalism

15. In social sciences, reification is best understood as:

a. using qualitative data instead of quantitative data.
b. treating an abstraction as a concrete thing.
c. the use of heuristic devices.
d. mistaking subjectivity for objectivity.

16. Which of the following will result if two nations use the theory of comparative advantage when making decisions of which goods to produce and trade?

a. Each nation will make all of their own goods
b. Both nations will specialize in the production of the same specific goods
c. Each nation will specialize in the production of different specific goods
d. Neither nation will trade with one another

17. The presidential veto of legislation passed by Congress illustrates which principal in American government?

a. Checks and balances
b. Federal regulation
c. Freedom of speech
d. Separation of church and state

18. Which of the following statements is an opinion?

a. The Congressional Black Caucus began in 1969.
b. The CBC is often referred to as Congress's conscience.
c. Every year for two decades, the CBC has proposed a national budget.
d. Apartheid was the worst political system of the twentieth century.

19. To be President of the United States, one must meet these three requirements:

a. The President must be college educated, at least 30 years old, and a natural citizen
b. The President must be a natural citizen, have lived in the U.S. for 14 years, and have a college education
c. The President must be a natural citizen, be at least 35 years old, and have lived in the U.S. for 14 years
d. The President must be at least 30 years old, be a natural citizen, and have lived in the U.S. for 14 years

20. Which of the following is most likely to benefit from inflation?

a. A bond investor who owns fixed-rate bonds
b. A retired widow with no income other than fixed Social Security payments
c. A person who has taken out a fixed-rate loan
d. A local bank who has loaned money out at fixed rate

21. After the Civil War, urban populations increased. This growth was likely due to:

a. An increased reliance on agriculture
b. The Industrial Revolution
c. Prohibition
d. Slavery persisting in some areas

22. Assume a society has a given production possibilities frontier (PPF) representing the production of cheese and butter. Which of the following would cause the PPF to move outward?

a. The invention of a new machine that makes cheese more efficiently
b. An increase in the production of butter
c. An increase in the production of cheese
d. A decrease in the production of cheese and butter

23. The Trail of Tears was:

a. The forced removal of British soldiers after the American Revolution
b. The forced evacuation of Cherokee peoples into Oklahoma
c. The forced evacuation of freed slaves from the South after the Civil War
d. The tears of Betsy Ross while she sewed the first American flag

24. What is the main reason that tropical regions near the Equator tend to experience relatively constant year-round temperatures?

a. They are usually located near the ocean
b. The angle at which sunlight hits them remains relatively constant throughout the year
c. They are located along the "Ring of Fire"
d. They do not have seasons

25. Which of the following is *not* correct regarding assumptions of mercantilism?

a. The money and the wealth of a nation are identical properties
b. In order to prosper, a nation should try to increase its imports
c. In order to prosper, a nation should try to increase its exports
d. Economic protectionism by national governments is advisable

26. What does the data in this table most directly describe?

Inputs	1	2	3	4
Output	20	50	80	100

a. The Law of Diminishing Marginal Returns
b. Law of Increasing Opportunity Cost
c. Law of Demand
d. Consumer surplus

27. Congressional elections are held every ____________ years.

a. Four
b. Two
c. Six
d. Three

28. All else being equal, which of the following locations is likely to have the coolest climate?

a. A city located at 6,000 feet above sea level
b. A city located at 500 feet above sea level
c. A city that receives less than 10 inches of precipitation per year
d. A city that receives more than 50 inches of precipitation per year

29. The Erie Canal is 363 miles long and connects which body of water to Lake Erie?

a. The Mississippi River
b. The Hudson River
c. The Susquehanna River
d. The Lehigh River

30. As used in geographical maps, which of the following is a synonym for the term *latitude?*

a. Longitude
b. Parallel
c. Meridian
d. Coordinate

31. What is the main difference between a primary election and a caucus?

a. A primary election is privately run by political parties, and a caucus is held by local governments
b. Caucuses are always held on the same day, but the dates of state primaries vary
c. A caucus is privately run by political parties, and a primary is an indirect election run by state and local governments
d. Primary elections are all held on the same date, but the dates of caucuses vary

32. Which of the following statements is not true of daily life for the average European in the 1500s?

a. Life was not significantly different from the medieval era.
b. The majority of people worked in agriculture.
c. Life expectancy was short.
d. Most people were literate, due to well-financed public education programs.

33. Which of the following conquistadores unwittingly gave smallpox to the indigenous peoples and destroyed the Aztec empire in Mexico?

a. Balboa
b. Ponce de Leon
c. Cortes
d. De Vaca

34. An action's opportunity cost is best explained in terms of:

a. the minimum amount a business must borrow for the action.
b. the opportunities given up in order to pursue that action.
c. the percentage of one's overall budget that the action requires.
d. the cost of a long-term action adjusted for inflation.

Question 35 refers to the following chart:

Jail Inmates by Sex and Race

Year	1990	1995	2000	2005
Male	365,821	448,000	543,120	646,807
Female	37,198	51,300	70,414	93,963
Juveniles	2,301	7,800	7,613	6,759
White	169,600	203,300	260,500	331,000
Black	172,300	220,600	256,300	290,500
Hispanic	58,100	74,400	94,100	111,900

[Source: U.S. Dept. of Justice; does not include federal or state prisons.]

35. Based on the chart, which of the following statements is NOT accurate?

a. Fewer women than men are incarcerated in each year sampled.
b. The rate of jail incarceration rose for every subgroup of prisoner.
c. In 2000 and in 2005, more whites were incarcerated in jails than any other race.
d. Rate of Hispanic jailing has steadily increased over the fifteen years represented.

36. What is true regarding survey findings about family differences among American socioeconomic and racial groups?

a. Cultural and demographic factors influence disagreement styles more than parental stress does.
b. Low-socioeconomic young children have no more development/behavior problems than others.
c. Data have shown more violence in African-American families, then in Latino, then White families.
d. Socioeconomically disadvantaged children have more problems and receive more help for these.

37. A researcher is collecting data for her study on parenting. She hypothesized that countries where mothers carry their infants on their person have children who have more secure attachments as toddlers. Which method would be the most helpful in collecting data for this study?

a. Interviewing parents in the United States about their methods of carrying babies.
b. Determining methods of carrying babies and studying the toddlers in several countries.
c. Researching popular methods of carrying infants on the internet.
d. Collecting data on the number of strollers sold in several countries.

38. Which of the following is *not* one of the core demographic variables?

a. Fertility
b. Diversity
c. Mortality
d. Migration

39. How did Egypt's geographical features most contribute to the stability of ancient Egyptian culture?

a. The Nile River regularly and predictably flooded, irrigating crops.
b. The expanse of the Nile River prevented Egyptians from settling elsewhere.
c. The Valley of the Kings divided Upper Egypt from Lower Egypt.
d. The Mediterranean Sea enabled contact between Egyptians and other ancient peoples.

40. Though the incorporation into the United State was favored by the majority of the Texas population when it became independent of Mexico in 1836, Texas was not annexed until the end of 1845. Which of the following was <u>not</u> a reason for the delay?

a. Both major political parties feared that adding another slave state to the union would upset the volatile balance between pro-slavery and anti-slavery American factions.
b. American politicians were afraid of triggering a war with Mexico, which did not want to recognize the independence of its former territory.
c. The British government was suspected of trying to intervene in Texas affairs and arrange the emancipation of its slaves.
d. The southern and western borders of Texas were not well defined. There was uncertainty as to what exact land area the United States was annexing.

Science

1. Scientists often form hypotheses based on particular observations. Which of the following is NOT true of a good hypothesis?

a. A good hypothesis is complex.
b. A good hypothesis is testable.
c. A good hypothesis is logical.
d. A good hypothesis predicts future events.

2. What will happen to light waves as they hit a convex lens?

a. They will be refracted and converge.
b. They will be refracted and diverge.
c. They will be reflected and converge.
d. They will be reflected and diverge.

3. Which of the following animal structures is not paired to its correct function?

a. Muscle System – controls movement through three types of muscle tissue
b. Nervous System – controls sensory responses by carrying impulses away from and toward the cell body
c. Digestive System – breaks down food for absorption into the blood stream where it is delivered to cells for respiration
d. Circulatory System – exchanges gasses with the environment by delivering oxygen to the bloodstream and releasing carbon dioxide

4. Why would it be ethical for local and state governments to conduct a risk-benefit analysis in making decisions about city planning and development?

a. Governments must know what the benefits of a new development are for people and the economy in order to persuade opponents and the public who are against it.
b. Knowledge of the environmental risks and benefits to humans is required for gaining building permits.
c. The benefits to people and the economy must outweigh the risks to determine whether their decision to build is fair.
d. The benefits to people and the economy can be used to ignore the risks associated with any new development.

5. After a science laboratory exercise, some solutions remain unused and are left over. What should be done with these solutions?

a. Dispose of the solutions according to local disposal procedures.
b. Empty the solutions into the sink and rinse with warm water and soap.
c. Ensure the solutions are secured in closed containers and throw away.
d. Store the solutions in a secured, dry place for later use.

6. A dihybrid cross is made between the dominant genes for Brown eyes (B) and Blonde hair (S), and the recessive genes for blue eyes (b) and red hair (s). What fraction of offspring would have the genotype BbSs in the F2 generation?

a. 1/16
b. 3/16
c. 4/16
d. 9/16

7. Which of the following is a source of nonrenewable energy?

a. Solar power
b. Wind power
c. Wood
d. Coal

8. What laboratory practice can increase the accuracy of a measurement?

a. repeating the measurement several times
b. calibrating the equipment each time you use it
c. using metric measuring devices
d. following SDS information

9. Which biome features scrubby plants and small evergreen trees and also has a hot, dry summer followed by a wetter winter?

a. Taiga
b. Coniferous forest
c. Chaparral
d. Savanna

10. A gas is held in a closed container and held at constant temperature. What is the effect of increasing the volume of the container by 3 times?

a. The pressure is tripled.
b. The pressure increases by one-third.
c. The pressure decreases to one-third.
d. The pressure remains constant.

11. Which of the following terms describes an intrusion of magma injected between two layers of sedimentary rock, forcing the overlying strata upward to create a dome-like form?

a. Sill
b. Dike
c. Laccolith
d. Caldera

12. Which of the following is needed for an experiment to be considered successful?

a. a reasonable hypothesis
b. a well-written lab report
c. data that others can reproduce
d. computer-aided statistical analysis

13. Which of the following statements about heat transfer is NOT true?

a. As the energy of a system changes, its thermal energy must change or work must be done.
b. Heat transfer from a warmer object to a cooler object can occur spontaneously.
c. Heat transfer can never occur from a cooler object to a warmer object.
d. If two objects reach the same temperature, energy is no longer available for work.

14. Repetition is important to scientific inquiry because

a. It is the only way to prove that an experiment is valid
b. It adds to the number of statistics supporting the concept
c. It assists the scientist in determining which data to consider
d. It requires many groups of investigators working on a project

15. The precision of a number of data points refers to:

a. How accurate the data is
b. How many errors the data contains
c. How close the data points are to the mean of the data
d. How close the actual data is to the predicted result

16. The most recently formed parts of the Earth's crust can be found at:

a. Subduction zones.
b. Compressional boundaries.
c. Extensional boundaries.
d. Mid-ocean ridges.

17. Which type of nuclear process features atomic nuclei splitting apart to form smaller nuclei?

a. Fission
b. Fusion
c. Decay
d. Ionization

18. If you were testing the effectiveness of a cream that reduced the signs of wrinkles around women's eyes, which of the following would be a good control group?

a. Rats with no wrinkles
b. A group of women with no wrinkles around their eyes who are given the cream
c. A group of women with wrinkles who are given a harmless cream that has no effect
d. A group of women with wrinkles around their eyes

19. What drives weather systems to move west to east in the mid-latitudes?

a. The prevailing westerlies
b. The prevailing easterlies
c. The trade winds
d. The doldrums

20. How are organisms, such as snakes, cacti, and coyotes, able to survive in harsh desert conditions?

a. Over thousands of years, these organisms have developed adaptations to survive in arid climates
b. These organisms migrate out of the desert during the summer months, only living in the desert for a portion of the year
c. Snakes, cacti, and coyotes work together to find sources of food and water
d. Snakes, cacti, and coyotes are all aquatic species that live in ponds and rivers during the hot day

21. In which of the following scenarios is work not applied to the object?

a. Mario moves a book from the floor to the top shelf.
b. A book drops off the shelf and falls to the floor.
c. Mario pushes a box of books across the room.
d. Mario balances a book on his head.

22. Which of the following ethical questions regarding biotechnology would be answered and regulated by the FDA (the Food and Drug Administration)?

a. Should the packaging of meat products that come from cloned animals be labeled?
b. Should nitrate or sulfate fertilizers be added to oil spills to assist the decomposition of crude oil by bacteria?
c. Should parents be allowed to genetically alter an embryo by choosing its physical characteristics?
d. Should cells or components of cells be used to create industrially useful products?

23. Which of the following is considered a non-renewable resource?

a. Glass
b. Wood
c. Cattle
d. Soil

24. The stream of charged particles that escape the Sun's gravitational pull is best described by which of the following terms?

a. Solar wind
b. Solar flare
c. Solar radiation
d. Sunspots

25. According to Ohm's Law, how are voltage and current related in an electrical circuit?

a. Voltage and current are inversely proportional to one another.
b. Voltage and current are directly proportional to one another.
c. Voltage acts to oppose the current along an electrical circuit.
d. Voltage acts to decrease the current along an electrical circuit.

26. Where are the reproductive organs of a plant?

a. Style
b. Stigma
c. Flowers
d. Sepals

27. What is the definition of work?

a. the amount of energy used to accomplish a job
b. the force used to move a mass over a distance
c. the amount of energy used per unit of time
d. energy stored in an object due to its position

28. Which of the following is a solute?

a. Salt in a mixture of salt and pepper
b. Air in mixture of ash and air
c. Water in a mixture of salt and water
d. Sugar in a mixture of sugar and water

29. What causes the motion of glaciers?

a. Gravity
b. Erosion
c. Wind
d. Temperature change

30. Students are planning to assemble and operate a small gasoline engine. Which safety concern should have the highest priority?

a. An open fuel tank could release sickening fumes.
b. Fingers could be injured if caught in the gears.
c. Spilled liquids may cause a short in the starter.
d. The exhaust fumes require adequate ventilation.

31. What part of a plant system responds to stimuli by releasing water via transpiration, except during adverse conditions like a drought when it closes up to prevent the plant from dehydration?

a. Pith
b. Stomata
c. Guard cells
d. Sepals

32. The electrolysis of water is an example of ____.

a. an adiabatic process
b. a chemical change
c. a synthesis reaction
d. reverse osmosis

33. When using a light microscope, how is the total magnification determined?

a. By multiplying the ocular lens power times the objective being used.
b. By looking at the objective you are using only.
c. By looking at the ocular lens power only.
d. By multiplying the objective you are using times two.

34. What effect does science have on technology?

a. Science verifies what technology discovers
b. Technology often results from scientific discoveries
c. Science has no effect on technology; each is independent of the other
d. Scientific progress is dependent on technology

35. What steps should precede drawing a conclusion about a hypothesis?

a. Testing, observing, and recording data
b. Communicating the hypothesis to others
c. Comparing data with data of other groups
d. Writing the results so they can be replicated

36. Which of the following are required by all typical organisms in order to survive?

a. Water, cells, shelter, and space
b. Food, water, cellular growth, nurturing
c. Food, water, sunlight, and air
d. Air, shelter, space, and companionship

37. The amount of potential energy an object has depends on all of the following except its

a. mass.
b. height above ground.
c. gravitational attraction.
d. temperature.

38. Which of the following molecules is thought to have acted as the first enzyme in early life on earth?

a. Protein
b. RNA
c. DNA
d. Triglycerides

39. In a food chain, where does energy go after the secondary consumer dies?

a. Back to the Sun
b. To the producers
c. Into the air becoming wind
d. To decomposers

40. When you walk barefoot on a hot sidewalk, what process is primarily responsible for heat transfer from the sidewalk to your foot?

a. Conduction
b. Convection
c. Radiation
d. None of the above.

41. A long nail is heated at one end. After a few seconds, the other end of the nail becomes equally hot. What type of heat transfer does this represent?

a. Radiation
b. Conduction
c. Convection
d. Entropy

42. What other planet in the solar system experiences a greenhouse effect similar to that observed on Earth?

a. Mercury
b. Venus
c. Neptune
d. Saturn

43. Which of the following is an example of a trace fossil?

a. A mouse jaw
b. A footprint
c. A shark tooth
d. A cast of a skull

44. When two tectonic plates are moving laterally in opposing directions, this is called a:

a. Transforml boundary.
b. Compressional boundary.
c. Oppositional boundary.
d. Lateral boundary.

45. The energy radiated by stars is produced by:

a. Neutronicity.
b. Nuclear fusion.
c. Nuclear fission.
d. Gravitational confinement.

Fine Arts, Health and Physical Education

1. Which of the following artistic elements is most commonly used to create the illusion of depth in a painting?

a. Balance
b. Line
c. Contrast
d. Symmetry

2. A rubric would not be an appropriate evaluation tool for which of the following types of student activities?

a. A summative assessment with multiple-choice questions
b. A project in which students write a report and deliver a presentation about a famous work of art
c. A summative assessment in which students create a portfolio demonstrating their mastery of various photographic techniques
d. A formative assessment in which students write a brief paragraph analyzing an artist's use of the elements of composition

3. Which of the following tempos is played between 120 and 168 beats per minute?

a. Presto
b. Moderato
c. Allegro
d. Largo

4. Ms. Franklin is teaching a second-grade class a lesson on ceramics. The most appropriate activity for students at this grade level would be

a. making pinch pots and coil pots.
b. throwing pots using a pottery wheel.
c. making and attaching handles to pots.
d. glazing pots using a kiln.

5. In printmaking, a stone plate would be used to produce a(n)

a. linocut.
b. lithograph.
c. etching.
d. screen print.

6. A photograph of a small child standing alone in an empty room would have

a. asymmetrical composition.
b. symmetrical composition.
c. artistic unity.
d. lots of negative space.

7. Which of the following terms refers to the relative lightness or darkness of color in a painting?

a. Hue
b. Intensity
c. Value
d. Texture

8. Which of the following composers is most strongly associated with the Romantic Period?

a. Johann Sebastian Bach
b. Maurice Ravel
c. Aaron Copeland
d. Johannes Brahms

9. Cajun music of Louisiana traces its roots back to which European culture?

a. French
b. Dutch
c. Flemish
d. Portuguese

10. Which of the following is the most important aspect of writing or choosing a script for a third-grade classroom?

a. There needs to be a lesson learned at the end of the story
b. The script must be appropriate for both the performer(s) and the audience
c. The script must not call for expensive props
d. The dialogue must not contain offensive language

11. Analyzing each character in a script, studying biographical information, and understanding each characters' strengths and weaknesses are important aspects of:

a. Developing character relationships
b. Script analysis
c. Plot development
d. Psychological dissection

12. Which of the following BEST describes the relation between oxygen and muscles in aerobic exercise?

a. Slow twitch muscle delivers oxygen to the heart.
b. Slow twitch muscle takes oxygen from the blood.
c. Fast twitch muscle delivers oxygen to the heart.
d. Fast twitch muscle takes oxygen from the blood.

13. What is a common accompanying pattern in which chords are played note-by-note successively instead of simultaneously?

a. Arpeggio
b. Scales
c. Blocked chord
d. Ostinato

14. Visual literacy can best be described as the

a. ability to communicate through images and comprehend the messages contained in images.
b. ability to construct three-dimensional images.
c. incorporation of literary text into works of art.
d. incorporation of art into literary texts.

15. An important script element that appears in all capital letters and tells the reader about the current scene setting is known as what?

a. Slug line
b. Header
c. Scene description
d. Theme

16. Which of the following activities is most likely to increase cardiovascular endurance?

a. cross-country running
b. volleyball
c. weight training
d. rock climbing

17. A diet that includes over 20 grams of fiber daily:

a. may interfere with the effective absorption of essential vitamins and minerals.
b. is likely to increase the concentration of cholesterol in the blood.
c. helps prevent constipation and lowers the risk of digestive disorders.
d. is useful in treating irritable bowel syndrome.

18. Before they can be used by the body as fuel, complex carbohydrates must be converted into

a. glucose.
b. amino acids.
c. lipids.
d. folic acid.

19. In order for a director to get an idea of a performer's capabilities and talent, he might ask the performer to read a script he or she has never seen before. This is called:

a. Blind reading
b. Preliminary reading
c. Sight reading
d. Cold reading

20. The most efficient way for young people to increase their strength and endurance is by:

a. playing sports such as volleyball and basketball.
b. making weight training a part of their daily exercise regimen.
c. lifting heavy weights with few repetitions.
d. lifting moderately heavy weights with many repetitions.

21. With respect to actor placement onstage, the term "upstage" means what?

a. The actor is toward the back of the stage, away from the audience
b. The actor is positioned at the front of the stage, close to the audience
c. The actor is exactly at the center of the stage
d. The actor is standing on an X on the stage that was put in place by the director

22. Which of the following is LEAST likely to trigger an asthma attack?

a. Stress
b. Moderate exercise
c. Pollen
d. Tobacco smoke

23. The best defense against the common cold is to:

a. stay warm and dry.
b. drink eight glasses of water daily.
c. wash hands frequently.
d. take daily supplements of zinc and vitamin C.

24. The main dietary sources of saturated fat are:

a. meat and dairy products.
b. fish and poultry.
c. fruits and vegetables.
d. nuts and beans.

25. A contusion is:

a. a bruise usually caused by a jarring blow.
b. a torn or stretched muscle or tendon.
c. an injury to a ligament.
d. a blow to the skull that alters mental functioning.

Use the information below to answer Question 26:

You and your best friend are walking through a park and you find a diamond ring. You want to find the ring's rightful owner, but your friend insists on selling the ring for extra spending money.

26. A fourth-grade drama teacher instructs two of her students to act out the above scenario using improvisation. This exercise is intended to aid in the class's comprehension of which of the following components of drama?

a. Conflict
b. Climax
c. Foreshadowing
d. Role reversal

27. Which form of drama, also known as creative drama, involves an instructor guiding participants to first imitate actual experiences and then reflect upon them?

a. Product-centered drama
b. Process-centered drama
c. Natural-state drama
d. Method acting

28. A complete exercise program incorporates both aerobic and anaerobic activities. Which of the following is an example of anaerobic exercise?

a. Soccer
b. Strength training
c. Swimming
d. Bicycling

29. When encountering a difficult passage, how do musicians most effectively practice that passage?

a. Playing it as fast as possible
b. Studying it away from the instrument
c. Playing it slowly and thoughtfully
d. Playing the sections before and after

30. According to the American Academy of Pediatrics, how many young people experience symptoms of depression at some time during adolescence?

a. Nearly all
b. As many as one in thirteen
c. About 3%
d. About one in a hundred

31. In order to for a pigment to reach the desired consistency for fluid painting, with which of the following should it not be combined?

a. Turpentine
b. Fresco
c. A tempera
d. An oil medium

32. Which of the following is not one of the primary elements of art?

a. Dimension
b. Unity
c. Texture
d. Space

33. Which of the following factors in motor development is most likely to be affected by motor development itself?

a. family attitudes
b. poor nutrition
c. self-confidence
d. societal perceptions

34. The black church heavily influenced which of the following musical genres through improvisation, storytelling, and call and response?

a. Metal
b. Latin
c. Grunge
d. Blues

35. Which of the following is true about teaching in order to develop motor skills?

a. Activities for developing motor skills should vary in order to retain student interest.
b. It is best to use the same activity until all the students have mastered a basic skill.
c. Motor skills develop best when students engage in free and unstructured play.
d. Challenging skills are best taught by using them in structured game situations.

36. Which of the following is NOT a component of the non-specific immune mechanism?

a. skin
b. inflammatory response
c. neutrophils
d. antibodies

37. What is the difference between 3/4 time and 6/8 time, by definition?

a. There is no difference.
b. 3/4 time uses three beats per measure, while 6/8 time uses six beats per measure.
c. In 3/4 time the quarter note acts as the one beat unit, while in 6/8 time the eighth note acts as the one beat unit.
d. 3/4 time uses a quicker tempo.

38. How does physical exercise improve a person's mental abilities?

a. It does not.
b. It causes greater blood flow to the brain.
c. It lowers cholesterol.
d. It causes the brain to release endorphins.

39. What is the relative difference in frequency between these two notes?

a. 1:1
b. 2:1
c. 4:1
d. 8:1

40. Which of the following activities is most likely to help develop cardiovascular endurance?

a. running for 15 minutes five times a week
b. playing racquetball 20 minutes three times a week
c. bowling for 15 minutes five times a week
d. playing baseball 20 minutes three times a week

Answers and Explanations

English Language Arts and Reading

1. A: Homophones. Homophones are a type of homonym that sound alike but are spelled differently and have different meanings. Other examples are *two, to,* and *too; their, they're,* and *there.*

2. C: Read the documents quickly, looking for key words in order to gather the basic premise of each. Skimming allows a reader to quickly gain a broad understanding of a piece of writing in order to determine if a more thorough reading is warranted. Skimming allows students who are researching a topic on the Internet or in print to consider a substantial body of information in order to select only that of particular relevance.

3. C: According to the Association of College and Research Libraries, Information Literacy is the set of skills that an individual must have for finding, retrieving, analyzing, and using information. It is required not just for reading and understanding information (A). Information Literacy does not mean learning and retaining a lot of information (B), or only sharing it with others (D), but rather knowing how to find information one does not already have and how to evaluate that information critically for its quality and apply it judiciously to meet one's purposes.

4. C: Oral language is a vital aspect of any language arts instruction. Often, the first concepts of language are transmitted via oral and auditory processes. The first Americans also possessed a rich oral culture in which stories and histories were passed down through generations via storytelling. Inviting a guest speaker who is part of this culture helps students understand more about cultures in their world, as well as the value of oral language and storytelling. This introduction gives students a relevant personal experience with which to connect what they will be learning in class.

5. A: A vowel. A syllable is a minimal sound unit arranged around a vowel. For example, *academic* has four syllables: *a/ca/dem/ic.* It is possible for a syllable to be a single vowel, as in the above example. It is not possible for a syllable to be a single consonant.

6. A: Prefixes appear at the beginning of words, while suffixes appear at the end of words.

7. C: On the internet, it often occurs that the name of the author of an article or book is actually provided but is not obviously visible at first glance. Web sources frequently include the author's name, but on another page of the same site, such as the website's home page; or in a tiny font at the very end of the web page, rather than in a more conspicuous location. In such cases, students doing online research may have to search more thoroughly than usual to find the author's name. Therefore, they should not immediately assume the author is not named (A). Also, many Web sources are sponsored by government agencies or private corporations and do not give individual author names. In these cases, the research paper *should* cite the agency or corporation name as author (B). Finally, it is much more common for online sources to omit an author's name than it is in print sources. In these cases, it is both permitted and advised by the MLA to cite the article or book title instead (D).

8. C: The example has an error in subject-verb agreement, which is a component of syntax (sentence structure and word order). Phonology (A) involves recognition and production of speech sounds and phonemes, including differentiation, segmentation, and blending. Semantics (B) involves the meanings of words. Pragmatics (D) involves the social use of language to communicate and meet one's needs.

9. B: To correct an error in reading a student has made, specifically clarifying where and how the error was made so that the student can avoid similar errors in the future. A reading teacher offers corrective feedback to a student in order to explain why a particular error in reading is, in fact, an error. Corrective feedback is specific; it locates where and how the student went astray so that similar errors can be avoided in future reading.

10. A: Dysgraphia. Dysgraphic individuals have difficulty with the physical act of writing. They find holding and manipulating a pencil problematic. Their letters are primitively formed, and their handwriting is illegible.

11. C: The kind of audience for whom you are writing, as well as your purpose for writing, will determine what style, tone, and wording you choose. Knowing who your audience is will enable you to select writing strategies, a style and tone, and specific word choices that will be most understandable and appealing to your readers. Knowing the type of audience will also dictate how much time to spend on research (A). Some readers will expect more supporting evidence while others will be bored or overwhelmed by it. Similarly, you will want to include more or less information depending on who will be reading what you write (B). And while the structure of your piece does inform how you organize your information, you should also vary your organization according to who will read it (D).

12. D: There are four main components to an effective outline. Subordination means that the information in the heading is more general, while the subheadings are more specific. For example:

I. Visit and Evaluate College Websites

A. Note important statistic

B. Look for interesting classes

The other three components of an effective outline include parallelism, coordination, and division.

13. C: This sentence appeals to the reader's emotions by stating simply that it is dangerous and "really stupid" to use a cell phone while driving; it does not provide any evidence or logic to support the statement. Steering one-handed makes driving more dangerous is a logical, common-sense argument. Supporting evidence such as statistics of greater accident risk is an appeal to logic. Citing the fact that many state laws ban cell phone use while driving supports the idea that it is dangerous and also refers to data on more accidents from doing so, also appealing to logic rather than emotion.

14. C: *Drip, chirp, splash, giggle.* Onomatopoeia refers to words that sound like what they represent.

15. C: Each answer can be an effective tool in teaching students to build oral language skills. The question makes clear that the objective is to help students evaluate their own oral language skills, which will assist them in both spoken and written assignments. The only answer choice that involves the student himself evaluating his message is choice C. When the student prepares a review/quiz based upon important information, he or she will be more able to speak specifically to that information. When classmates complete the review, the student can identify any patterns in the questions' answers that give clues as to how well those main ideas were communicated. In this way, the student can evaluate how effective the oral presentation was, without relying on classmates or the teacher.

16. B: Teachers should apply a variety of instructional techniques to enable students with different strengths, needs, and learning styles to understand sound-letter and letter-word relationships, but they should not restrict the instructional modalities to auditory and visual (A) simply because sounds are auditory and letters are visual. Multisensory modalities (B) are more effective because different students use different senses to learn; redundancy is necessary for learning; and input to multiple senses affords a more multidimensional learning experience, promoting comprehension and retention. While some aspects of this instruction should be consistent (e.g., starting with high-frequency letters and with phonemes children can produce more easily), sticking to only one method and set of materials (C) prevents using variety to reach all students. Visually similar letters and auditorily similar phonemes should *not* be introduced together (D) before students can discriminate among them; teachers should begin with more obvious differences.

17. C: Content-specific words. Because these words are specific to paleontology, it's unlikely the students know their meanings. Without understanding what these words mean, the students would not be able to understand the content of the passage they were about to read.

18. A: Reading comprehension. Prefixes and suffixes change the meanings of the root word to which they are attached. A student who understands that *un* means "not" will be able to decipher the meanings of words such as *unwanted, unhappy,* or *unreasonable.*

19. C: A synonym is a word that has a similar meaning. A n antonym is a word that means the opposite. A homonym is a word that sounds the same but has different spelling and meaning. A euphemism is an inoffensive word used in place of an offensive word.

20. C: Decoding monosyllabic words by referring to the initial and final consonant, short vowel, and long vowel sounds represented by their letters is a common academic standard for 1st-grade students. Typical academic standards for kindergarten students include demonstrating knowledge of letter-sound correspondences (A); understanding the alphabetic principle (B); matching letters to their corresponding consonant (and short vowel) sounds; and reading simple, monosyllabic sight words (D), i.e., high-frequency words.

21. B: For any writing assignment, you should first target an audience, perform an audience analysis, and develop an audience profile to determine what you should include in and omit from your writing. Even though the assigning teacher may be the only one to read your writing, you should not assume he or she is your main audience (A) because the teacher may expect you to write for other readers. In addition to first knowing your purpose for writing before beginning, you should also consider what purpose your writing will meet for your readers (C) and how they are likely to use it. Considering your audience's attitudes toward what you will write and their likely reactions to it is also important to shaping your writing and is NOT overthinking (D).

22. C: Giving a three-minute Test of Silent Contextual Reading Fluency four times a year. The student is presented with text in which spaces between words and all punctuation have been removed. The student must divide one word from another with slash marks, as in the following example: *The/little/sailboat/bobbed/so/far/in/the/distance/it/looked/like/a/toy*. The more words a student accurately separates, the higher her silent reading fluency score. Silent reading fluency can be monitored over time by giving the Test of Silent Contextual Reading Fluency (TSCRF) four times a year. A similar assessment tool is the Test of Silent Word Reading Fluency (TOSWRF), in which words of increasing complexity are given as a single, undifferentiated, and unpunctuated strand. As with the TSCRF, three minutes are given for the student to separate each word from the next. *Itwillcannotschoolbecomeagendaconsistentphilosophysuperfluous* is an example of such a strand.

23. B: Checking a dictionary or thesaurus is correct. In cases of words that sound alike but have different meanings, checking a dictionary or thesaurus will ensure correct usage of a word.

24. B: Standards expect 1st- to 3rd-graders to read materials regularly that are at the independent level, which they define as text where approximately 1 in 20 words or fewer are difficult for the student—not 1 in 10 (A). Students are also expected to select text to read independently, informed by their knowledge of authors, text genres and types; their estimation of text difficulty levels; and their personal interest (B). They should also read text regularly that is at the instructional level, which they define as including no more than 1 in 10 words the reader finds difficult—not 1 in 20 (C). Finally, standards expect students to read aloud fluently from familiar texts, not unfamiliar ones (D).

25. B: Vocabulary. Strategizing in order to understand the meaning of a word, knowing multiple meanings of a single word, and applying background knowledge to glean a word's meaning are all ways in which an effective reader enhances vocabulary. Other skills include an awareness of word parts and word origins, the ability to apply word meanings in a variety of content areas, and a delight in learning the meanings of unfamiliar words.

26. B: Relational messages, as opposed to content messages, are concerned with the relationship between a speaker and a recipient rather than with the overt subject of the communication. They may convey belonging, respect, or disapproval, among other things. They are frequently largely or entirely nonverbal; because of this, they may be supported with verbal feedback to confirm them. The content of the message, "Should I come over after work?" is a logistical request. If a speaker leans forward to touch a recipient who is weeping, the relational message is "Do you need my support?" The recipient might respond with a nod and a grateful look, or might clarify the speaker's offer by saying, "I won't be good company, but you can come."

27. A: A fallacy of inconsistency exists in a statement that contradicts itself or defeats itself. Saying there are exceptions to all general statements is itself a general statement; therefore, according to the content, this statement must also have an exception, implying there are NOT exceptions to all general statements. Choice B is an example of a fallacy of irrelevance: passing or failing is determined by course performance, so asking to pass because parents will be upset if one fails is an irrelevant reason for appealing to a teacher for a passing grade. Choice C is an example of a fallacy of insufficiency: a statement is made with insufficient evidence to support it. A lack of evidence of innocence is not enough to prove one is guilty because there could also be an equal lack of evidence of guilt. Choice D is an example of a fallacy of inappropriate presumption: asking someone if s/he has stopped cheating presumes that s/he has cheated in the past. The person being asked this question cannot answer either "yes" or "no" without confirming that s/he has indeed been cheating. If the person being asked has not been cheating, then the person asking the question is making a false assumption.

28. A: After prewriting (planning, visualizing, brainstorming), the correct sequence of steps in the writing process are drafting, in which the writer takes the material generated during prewriting work and makes it into sentences and paragraphs; revising, where the writer explores any changes that would improve the quality of the writing; editing, in which the writer examines his or her writing for factual and mechanical (grammar, spelling, punctuation) errors and correcting them; and publishing, when the writer finally shares what he or she has written with others who will read it and give feedback.

29. D: This description is most typical of the process of peer review. Classmates read Arthur's paper and then they identify values in it, describe it, ask questions about it, and suggest points for revision. These are types of helpful feedback identified by experts on writing and collaborative writing. The other choices, however, are not typically collaborative. For a portfolio assessment (A), the teacher collects finished work products from a student over time, eventually assembling a portfolio of work. This affords a more authentic assessment using richer, more multidimensional, and more visual and tactile products for assessment instead of using only standardized test scores for assessment. Holistic scoring (B) is a method of scoring a piece of writing for overall quality (evaluating general elements such as focus, organization, support, and conventions) rather than being overly concerned with any individual aspect of writing. A scoring rubric (C) is a guide that gives examples of the levels of typical characteristics in a piece of writing that correspond to each available score (for example, scores from 1-5).

30. C: Phonological cues are based on the speech sounds in words and their alphabetic representations in print. Readers can identify words by knowing sound-to-letter correspondences. Syntactic cues (A) are based on how words are arranged and ordered to create meaningful phrases, clauses, and sentences. Semantic cues (B) are based on the meanings of morphemes and words and how they combine to create additional meanings. Pragmatic cues (D) are based on the readers' purposes for reading and their understanding of how textual structures function in the texts that they read.

31. B: Previewing and reviewing are skills that assist in learning detailed or large amounts of information. Using these concepts, students learn skills such as skimming and outlining to get an idea of what the text is about before actually reading it. After reading, the students learn to review the information they learned and compare it to their initial previews. This method is particularly helpful when individuals are reading in order to learn new information, as they would be when reading their science texts.

32. C: Read the documents quickly, looking for key words in order to gather the basic premise of each. Skimming allows a reader to quickly gain a broad understanding of a piece of writing in order to determine if a more thorough reading is warranted. Skimming allows students who are researching a topic on the Internet or in print to consider a substantial body of information in order to select only that of particular relevance.

33. D: Prefixes, appearing at the beginning of base words to change their meanings. Suffixes appear at the end of words. Prefixes are attached to the beginning of words to change their meanings. *Un+happy, bi+monthly,* and *re+examine* are prefixes that, by definition, change the meanings of the words to which they are attached.

34. A: The process of actively constructing meaning from reading is interactive, in that it involves the text itself, the person reading it, and the setting in which the reading is done: the reader interacts with the text, and the text interacts with the reader by affecting him/her; the context of reading interacts with the text and the reader by affecting them both; and the reader interacts with the reading context as well as with the text. Choice B is a better definition of the *strategic* aspect of the process. Choices C and D are better definitions of the *adaptable* aspect of the process.

35. C: Reading at her independent reading level. When reading independently, students are at the correct level if they read with at least 97% accuracy.

36. C: Oral language skills can be distinguished from specific speech characteristics exhibited by some children. Many students like Rosa, whose first language is not English, will speak with an accent and may be less clear when speaking about a topic that is unfamiliar. In fact, even those who are not English Language Learners may exhibit difficulty speaking on new topics. Greer may avoid oral assignments or speaking in class for a number of reasons, such as self-consciousness. This student could be helped by evaluating oral language skills in a one-on-one environment or by introducing peer scaffolding to help reduce anxiety. Brett's demeanor in group assignments may also be due to social characteristics rather than oral skills; it would be important to evaluate his skills in various contexts. Ashley, however, shows marked problems communicating orally both in class discussion and in prepared assignments. She would benefit from specific instruction related to presenting ideas orally.

37. D: Knowing your purpose for writing means knowing what you want to achieve with the content of your writing, and knowing this will determine your writing style. Your choice of words and how formal or informal your writing is—your diction—*does* affect your style (A). Diction and tone should be consistent in your writing style and should reflect vocabulary and writing patterns that suit your writing purpose best. Style is not added later to give writing personality (B). It develops from your purpose for writing, or what you want to accomplish with your writing. Style *is* directly related to your control of the content (C) of your writing.

38. A: Correcting surface features such as sentence fragments, spelling, and punctuation. Editing is the final step in the writing process. The writer has already decided the ideas or events are in proper order, have been sufficiently described, and are clear. Now the writer turns his or her attention to surface features, "scrubbing" errors in spelling, punctuation, and syntax from the writing.

39. A: In choice A, the teacher guides previewing of information to show students how to put themselves in the right frame of mind to listen carefully for meaning. Students are then able to listen in a guided way based upon the previewing. By varying the type of comprehension assessment, the teacher will get a better understanding of what the students learned. Choice B is a good exercise but does not provide for direct instruction by the teacher or a particularly skilled student. In Choice C, students are focusing more on reading comprehension than listening since they must read the story to themselves and then write a report. There is then no way to gauge what they have learned. Choice D would be useful but does not include teacher-guided previewing, which is very helpful in building comprehension.

40. C: Because this student loves reading graphic novels and has both talent and enjoyment in drawing, having him create his own graphic novels is a good way to motivate him to write by using his visual style, ability, and interest to access writing activity. Giving audio recordings (A) to a highly visual student is not as appropriate to his strengths and interests. Letting him substitute drawing pictures for all writing assignments (B) would address his strengths and interests, but not his needs for learning to write. Having him watch animated videos about writing (D) would suit his visual learning style, but would not give him the actual writing practice he needs.

41. C: They meet to discuss areas the teacher is most concerned about and decide on the teacher's goals. In order to best achieve goals, those goals must be understood and established.

42. B: The word "brunch" is a blend of "breakfast" and "lunch". Blends of two or more words are known as portmanteau words. (*Portmanteau* is a French word meaning a suitcase.) "Fax" (A) is an example of clipping, or shortening a word, from its original "facsimile." "Babysitter" (C) is an example of compounding, or combining two or more words into one. "Saxophone" (D) is an example of proper noun transfer: A Belgian family that built musical instruments had the last name of Sax, and this wind instrument was named after them. These represent some of the ways that new words have entered—and still do enter—the English language.

43. C: Researchers and educators have found that reading fluency and reading comprehension are closely linked: the more fluently a student can read, the more able the student's brain is to process the meaning of text. For example, developing automaticity of word identification enhances comprehension. Conversely, the better a student can understand the text, the more fluently s/he can read it. Therefore, while choices A and B are both true, each represents only half of the relationship whereas choice C indicates the relationship's mutual nature; and choice D is incorrect as reading fluency and reading comprehension are interrelated components in deriving meaning from text and not separate.

44. A: Students need to know why and how to use text features to inform their reading. Reading headings above sections within chapters (A) help students determine the main subject matter of each section. Reading the glossary for a chapter (B) gives students definitions of terms used in the chapter. Reading the index in a text (C) is a way to locate page numbers of references to subjects or authors in the text. Whether they will be reading the entire section or not, students need not read through the whole thing (D) only to determine its subject matter when its heading will typically indicate this. Headings inform students of topics in advance if they will be reading the section; if they are doing research or choosing what to read, headings can help them decide.

45. A: Outcome. Story action can be analyzed in terms of rising action, story climax, falling action, and resolution. Rising action consists of those events that occur before and lead up to the story's most dramatic moment, or climax. The climax occurs toward the end of the book, but rarely, if ever, right at the end. Following the climax, the consequences of that dramatic moment are termed "falling action." The story reaches the resolution with the outcome of the falling action.

Mathematics

1. C: One strategy is to draw polygons with fewer sides and look for a pattern in the number of the polygons' diagonals.

Polygon	Sides	Diagonals	Δ Diagonals
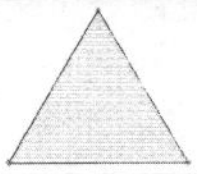	3	0	-
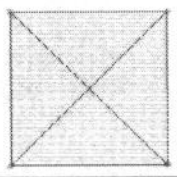	4	2	2
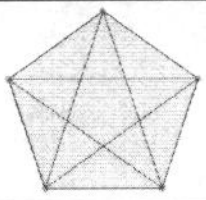	5	5	3
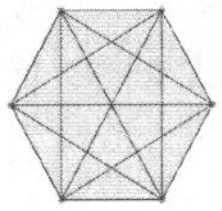	6	9	4

A quadrilateral has two more diagonals than a triangle, a pentagon has three more diagonals than a quadrilateral, and a hexagon has four more diagonals than a pentagon. Continue this pattern to find that a dodecagon has 54 diagonals.

2. D: When the dress is marked down by 20%, the cost of the dress is 80% of its original price; thus, the reduced price of the dress can be written as $\frac{80}{100}x$, or $\frac{4}{5}x$, where x is the original price. When discounted an extra 25%, the dress costs 75% of the reduced price, or $\frac{75}{100}\left(\frac{4}{5}x\right)$, or $\frac{3}{4}\left(\frac{4}{5}x\right)$, which simplifies to $\frac{3}{5}x$. So the final price of the dress is three-fifths of the original price.

3. C: Aaron ran four miles from home and then back again, so he ran a total of eight miles. Therefore, statement III is false. Statements I and II, however, are both true. Since Aaron ran eight miles in eighty minutes, he ran an average of one mile every ten minutes, or six miles per hour; he ran two miles from point A to B in 20 minutes and four miles from D to E in 40 minutes, so his running speed between both sets of points was the same.

4. D: Since a and b are even integers, each can be expressed as the product of 2 and an integer. So, if we write $a = 2x$ and $b = 2y$, $3(2x)^2 + 9(2y)^3 = c$.

$$3(4x^2) + 9(8y^3) = c$$
$$12x^2 + 72y^3 = c$$
$$12(x^2 + 6y^3) = c$$

Since c is the product of 12 and some other integer, 12 must be a factor of c. Incidentally, the numbers 2, 3, and 6 must also be factors of c since each is also a factor of 12.

5. B: Notice that choice C cannot be correct since $x \neq 1$. ($x = 1$ results in a zero in the denominator.)

$$\frac{x-2}{x-1} = \frac{x-1}{x+1} + \frac{2}{x-1}$$
$$\frac{x-4}{x-1} = \frac{x-1}{x+1}$$
$$(x+1)(x-4) = (x-1)(x-1)$$
$$x^2 - 3x - 4 = x^2 - 2x + 1$$
$$-5 = x$$

6. A: EC teachers can learn much about how young children are learning new mathematical concepts through observing their behaviors (B); but to help them develop math communication, realize the linguistic functions of math, and develop overall literacy, teachers must also elicit spoken expressions from children about their own knowledge and thought processes. They can do this by asking children questions (e.g., "What shape is this? How about this one? How are these shapes different? Why/how do you think they are different?" etc.). They can then use children's responses to elicit additional expressions from them. While teachers can certainly model language use for children (C) in their speech, including conversations, discussions, directions, and lessons, lecturing (C) is not the best method, especially with young children. Assigning writing about math (D) supports children's reading and writing development and supports literacy too, but is not a substitute for questioning and eliciting further responses.

7. D: The point $(5, -5)$ lies on the line which has a slope of -2 and which passes through $(3, -1)$. If $(5, -5)$ is one of the endpoints of the line, the other would be $(1,3)$.

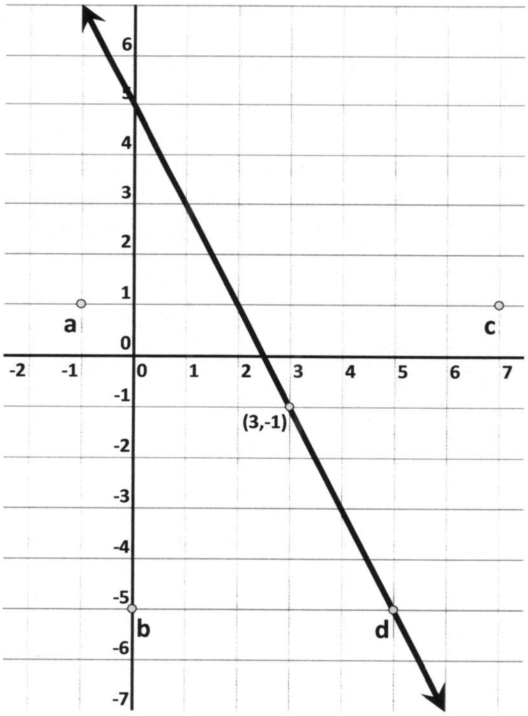

8. A: A Venn diagram such as the one shown below may be drawn to assist in finding the answer.

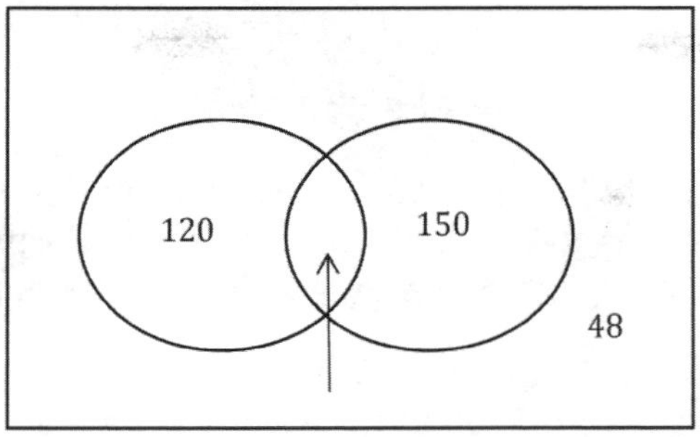

Since the set contains 320 total people, the solution is equal to $320 - (120 + 150 + 48)$ or 2 people.

9. C: This exercise is a way to lay the foundation for measuring techniques and spatial awareness.

10. A: If a number is divisible by 2 and 3, it is also divisible by the lowest common multiple of these two factors. The lowest common multiple of 2 and 3 is their product, 6.

11. C: The original price may be modeled by the equation, $(x - 0.45x) + 0.0875(x - 0.45x) = 39.95$, which simplifies to $0.598125x = 39.95$. Dividing each side of the equation by the coefficient of x gives $x \approx 66.79$.

12. C: An inversely proportional relationship is written in the form $\boldsymbol{y} = \frac{\boldsymbol{k}}{\boldsymbol{x}}$, thus the equation $\boldsymbol{y} = \frac{\boldsymbol{3}}{\boldsymbol{x}}$ shows that y is inversely proportional to x.

13. C: Printed mathematical formulas are an example of abstract mathematical concepts presented abstractly. Young children cannot access such concepts in abstract presentations. However, they can learn to understand abstract concepts when they are presented using concrete manipulatives like tangrams for shape recognition (A), or for reproducing and designing patterns, solving spatial problems, etc.; large, magnetized numbers and number boards (B) for doing math computations concretely; play money and toy cash registers (D) for monetary numerical activities; linking cubes, color tiles; and many other math manipulatives, which are available for teachers/schools to purchase, and/or which teachers can create in homemade versions using common found objects.

14. D: To be able to make accurate estimates of quantities, children must first understand relative and comparative concepts such as bigger than, smaller than, more of, less of, etc. The process of estimating numbers and amounts in lieu of actual exact measurements helps young children to *learn* math vocabulary words (A) like *around, about, more than, less than,* etc., rather than vice versa. By practicing estimation, children also learn how to make predictions appropriately (B) and attain reasonable estimates (C), rather than the other way around.

15. C: The surface area of a sphere may be calculated using the formula $SA = 4\pi r^2$. Substituting 9 for r gives $SA = 4\pi(9)^2$, which simplifies to $SA \approx 1017.36$. So the surface area of the ball is approximately 1017.36 square inches. There are twelve inches in a foot, so there are $12^2 = 144$ square inches in a square foot. In order to convert this measurement to square feet, then, the following proportion may be written and solved for x: $\frac{1}{144} = \frac{x}{1017.36}$. So $x \approx 7.07$. He needs approximately 7.07 square feet of wrapping paper.

16. C: The original triangle was reflected across the x-axis. When reflecting across the x-axis, the x-values of each point remain the same, but the y-values of the points will be opposites.

$$(1,4) \to (1,-4), \qquad (5,4) \to (5,-4), \qquad (3,8) \to (3,-8)$$

17. B: The probability may be written as $P(E \text{ and } H) = P(E) \times P(H)$. Substituting the probability of each event gives $(E \text{ and } H) = \frac{1}{2} \times \frac{1}{2}$, which simplifies to $\frac{1}{4}$.

18. B: This is a formative assessment because she is assessing students while she is still teaching the unit. Summative assessments are given at the end of the unit. Formal assessments are usually a quizzes or tests. Informal assessments include asking individual students questions.

19. A: Choice A is correct because standards for fourth grade state that students will be able to use a protractor to determine the approximate measures of angles in degrees to the nearest whole number. Choices B, C, and D are stated in the standards for fifth grade.

20. B: Sophia needs to find multiples of 3 (3, 6, 9, 12, 15...) and multiples of 4 (4, 8, 12, 16,...) and find the least common multiple between them, which is 12. The greatest common divisor of 3 and 4 is 1. The least common divisor between two numbers is always 1. The greatest common multiple can never be determined.

21. D: Number lines can help students understand the concepts of positive and negative numbers. Fraction strips are most commonly used with fractions. Venn diagrams are commonly used when comparing groups. Shaded regions are commonly used with fractions or percentages.

22. C: The associative property of multiplication states that when three or more numbers are multiplied, the product is the same regardless of the way in which the numbers are grouped. Choice C shows that the product of 2, 3, and 4 is the same with two different groupings of the factors. Choice A demonstrates the distributive property. Choice B shows grouping, but the factors are different. Choice D demonstrates the commutative property of multiplication.

23. A: The sum of 3 and the product of each term number and 5 equals the term value. For example, for term number 4, the value of 23 is equal to $5(4) + 3$, or 23.**24. C:** Triangles can be classified as scalene, isosceles, or equilateral. Scalene triangles have no equal side measurements and no equal angle measurements. Isosceles triangles have two sides of equal measurement and two angles of equal measurement. Equilateral triangles have three sides of equal measurement and three angles of equal measurement. A right triangle is isosceles only if its two acute angles are congruent.

25. C: The slope of a line can be found from any two points by the formula $slope = \frac{y_2-y_1}{x_2-x_1}$. A quick sketch of the point in choice C reveals a line with a negative slope. Substituting the last two points into the formula yields $slope = \frac{-3\ -1}{0-(-6)}$ which reduces to $\frac{-4}{6}$ or $\frac{-2}{3}$. The points in choice A form a line with a positive slope. The points in choice B form a line with a negative slope of $\frac{-3}{2}$. The points in choice D form a horizontal line.

26. C: The mean is the average of the data and can be found by dividing the sum of the data by the number of data: $\frac{16+18+20+21+34+45+49}{7} = 29$. The median is the middle data point when the data are ranked numerically. The median is 21.

27. B: The histogram only shows that there are eight trees between 70 and 75 feet tall. It does not show the individual heights of the trees. That information cannot be obtained from this graph

28. D: Being aware that patterns (regular repetitions) and relationships (associations between/among things) exist in the world affords us greater self-efficacy about our interacting with the environment, as well as increasing our sense of confidence in the environment itself (C). This awareness not only helps us to understand sequences of events; it moreover enables us to predict the next event in the series before it occurs (B). Having an awareness of patterns and relationships in things also informs our understanding of the basic structure of those things (A).

29. C: The number 589 can be estimated to be 600. The number 9 can be estimated to be 10. The number of chicken nuggets is approximately 600×10, which is 6,000 nuggets.

30. D: The total rainfall is 25.38 inches. Thus, the ratio $\frac{4.5}{25.38}$, represents the percentage of rainfall received during October. $\frac{4.5}{25.38} \approx 0.177$ or 17.7%.

31. C: The volume of a cylinder may be calculated using the formula $V = \pi r^2 h$, where r represents the radius and h represents the height. Substituting 1.5 for r and 3 for h gives $V = \pi(1.5)^2(3)$, which simplifies to $V \approx 21.2$.

32. D: The area of the square is equal to $(30)^2$, or 900 square centimeters. The area of the circle is equal to $\pi(15)^2$, or approximately 707 square centimeters. The area of the shaded region is equal to the difference of the area of the square and the area of the circle, or $900 \text{ cm}^2 - 707 \text{ cm}^2$, which equals 193 cm^2. So, the area of the shaded region is about 193 cm^2.

33. B: The perimeter is equal to the sum of the lengths of the two bases, 2 and 6 units, and the diagonal distances of the other two sides. Using the distance formula, each side length may be represented as $d = \sqrt{20} = 2\sqrt{5}$. Thus, the sum of the two sides is equal to $2\sqrt{20}$, or $4\sqrt{5}$. The whole perimeter is equal to $8 + 4\sqrt{5}$.

34. D: Since all of the answer choices are parallelograms, determine whether the parallelogram is also a rhombus or a rectangle or both. One way to do this is by examining the parallelogram's diagonals. If the parallelogram's diagonals are perpendicular, then the parallelogram is a rhombus. If the parallelogram's diagonals are congruent, then the parallelogram is a rectangle. If a parallelogram is both a rhombus and a rectangle, then it is a square. A plot of the quadrilateral would be:

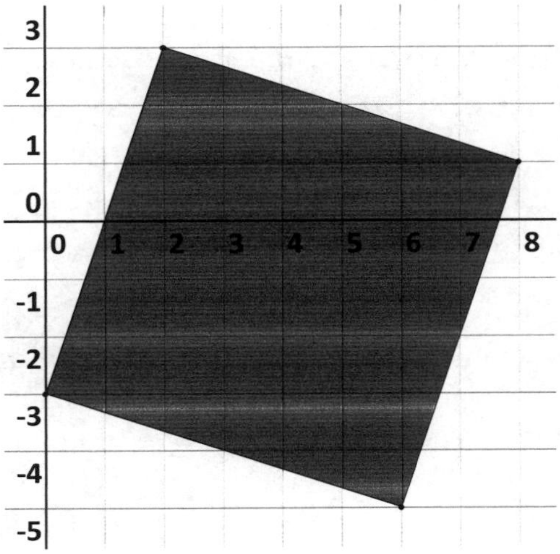

To determine whether the diagonals are perpendicular, find the slopes of the diagonals of the quadrilateral:

Diagonal 1: $\frac{6-2}{-5-3} = \frac{4}{-8} = -\frac{1}{2}$

Diagonal 2: $\frac{0-8}{-3-1} = -\frac{8}{-4} = 2$

The diagonals have opposite inverse slopes and are therefore perpendicular. Thus, the parallelogram is a rhombus.

To determine whether the diagonals are congruent, find the lengths of the diagonals of the quadrilateral:

Diagonal 1: $\sqrt{(6-2)^2 + (-5-3)^2} = \sqrt{(4)^2 + (-8)^2} = \sqrt{16+64} = \sqrt{80} = 4\sqrt{5}$

Diagonal 2: $\sqrt{(0-8)^2 + (-3-1)\text{^}2} = \sqrt{(-8)^2 + (-4)\text{^}2} = \sqrt{64+16} = \sqrt{80} = 4\sqrt{5}$

The diagonals are congruent, so the parallelogram is a rectangle.

Since the polygon is a rhombus and a rectangle, it is also a square.

35. A:$A \cap B$ means "A intersect B," or the elements that are common to both sets. "A intersect B" represents "A and B," that is, an element is in the intersection of A and B if it is in A *and* it is in B. The elements 2, 5, and 8 are common to both sets.

36. C: To find the probability of an event, divide the number of favorable outcomes by the total number of outcomes. When there are two events in which the first depends on the second, multiply the first ratio by the second ratio. In the first part of the problem, the probability of choosing a licorice jelly bean is two out of twenty possible outcomes, or $\frac{2}{20}$. Then, because one jelly bean has already been chosen, there are four cinnamon beans out of a total of 19, or $\frac{4}{19}$. By multiplying the two ratios and dividing by a common denominator, one arrives at the final probability of $\frac{2}{95}$.

37. C: There are 36 months in 3 years. The following proportion may be written: $\frac{450}{3} = \frac{x}{36}$. The equation $3x = 16{,}200$, may be solved for x. Dividing both sides of the equation by 3 gives $x = 5{,}400$.

38. D: 75% of the data in a set is above the first quartile. Since the first quartile for this set is 73, there is a 75% chance that a student chosen at random from class 2 scored above a 73.

39. C: If x is a prime number and the greatest common factor of x and y is greater than 1, the greatest common factor of x and y must be x. The least common multiple of two numbers is equal to the product of those numbers divided by their greatest common factor. So, the least common multiple of x and y is $\frac{xy}{x} = y$. Therefore, the values in the two columns are the same.

40. C: If 1" represents 60 feet, 10" represents 600 ft, which is the same as 200 yards because there are 3 feet in a yard.

Social Studies

1. B: The Bluebonnet is the state flower of Texas. The Blue Lacy is the state dog and the Lone Star is the state symbol. The song Yellow Rose of Texas dates back to at least the 1850's though its true origins are unknown. In approximately the 1950's Emily West, a folk hero from the Texas revolution, came to be associated with the song.

2. A: The latest occurring decolonization event was the Eastern Bloc and Soviet Satellite states of Armenia, Azerbaijan, Estonia, Georgia, Kazakhstan, Kyrgyzstan, Latvia, Lithuania, Moldova, Russia, Tajikistan, Turkmenistan, Ukraine, and Uzbekistan, which all became independent from the Soviet Union in 1991. (Note: This was the last decolonization of the Cold War years, as the end of the Soviet Union marked the end of the Cold War.) Canada completed its independence from British Parliament via the Canada Act (B) in 1982. In the Caribbean, the Bahamas gained independence from the United Kingdom (C) in 1973. Algeria won its independence from France when the Algerian War of Independence, begun in 1954, ended in 1962 (D). In Africa, Libya gained independence from Italy and became an independent kingdom in 1951.

3. B: Historians have determined that the Yellow River Valley in China began to develop into a cultural center during the Neolithic Era between c. 12,000-10,000 BC. The Shang Dynasty occurred between c. 1700-1046 BC—still part of the Ancient Era, but very long after the Neolithic era. The Xia Dynasty ruled between circa 2100-1600 BC, preceding the Shang Dynasty but still long after the Neolithic Era. The Paleolithic Era came even before the Neolithic Era. Archaeological evidence exists of Homo erectus in China from more than a million years ago, during the Paleolithic Era, but the Yellow River Valley was not an emergent cultural center that long ago.

4. C: Article III judges are appointed for life and can retire at 65. They can only be removed from their posts by impeachment in the House and conviction in the Senate. Having judges serve life terms is meant to allow them to serve without being governed by the changing opinions of the public.

5. B: The philosophy of history is concerned with the ultimate significance of history as a field of study and asks questions concerning how history should be studied, including what social unit is correct to use when studying history—whether it is more important to look at the individual lives of ordinary people or to concentrate on the so-called big picture, looking at the overall trends in a society or culture; only giving personal treatment to people, such as George Washington, who had particular significance to the events surrounding them. The philosophy of history also looks for broad historical trends and progress.

6. D: It is not true that the Gilded Age is a term whose origins have not been identified clearly. In 1873, Mark Twain and Charles Dudley Warner co-authored a book entitled The Gilded Age: A Tale of Today. Twain and Warner first coined this term to describe the extravagance and excesses of America's wealthy upper class (B), who became richer than ever due to industrialization. Furthermore, the Gilded Age was the era of the "robber barons" (A) such as John D. Rockefeller, Cornelius Vanderbilt, J.P. Morgan, and others. Because they accumulated enormous wealth through extremely aggressive and occasionally unethical monetary manipulations, critics dubbed them "robber barons" because they seemed to be elite lords of robbery. While these business tycoons grasped huge fortunes, some of them—such as Andrew Carnegie and Andrew Mellon—were also philanthropists, using their wealth to support and further worthy causes such as literacy, education, health care, charities, and the arts. They donated millions of dollars to fund social improvements. Carnegie himself dubbed this large philanthropic movement the "Gospel of Wealth" (C). Another characteristic of the Gilded Age was the Beaux Arts architectural style, a neo-Renaissance style modeled after the great architectural designs of the European Renaissance. The Panic of 1893 ended the Gilded Age and began a severe four-year economic depression. The Progressive Era followed these events.

7. A: One example of the multiplier effect of large cities would be if the presence of specialized equipment for an industry attracted even more business. Large cities tend to grow even larger for a number of reasons: they have more skilled workers, they have greater concentrations of specialized equipment, and they have already-functioning markets. These factors all make it easier for a business to begin operations in a large city than elsewhere. Thus, the populations and economic productivity of large cities tend to grow quickly. Some governments have sought to mitigate this trend by clustering groups of similar industries in smaller cities.

8. A: Samuel Morse invented a code of dots and dashes that became known as Morse Code and in 1844 the first message was transmitted over a telegraph line. Morse code played an important role in communications during the Civil War.

9. C: The increasing popularity of Thai food in the United States is an example of cultural convergence, or the intersection of traits or customs from two distinct cultures. Thailand's cuisine has been introduced to the United States, but it has undergone subtle changes as a result of the desires and practices of the American consumer. The phenomenon of cultural convergence is credited with much of the innovation in any society. Cultural divergence, on the other hand, is the practice of shielding one culture from the influence of another. France, for instance, seeks to limit the influence of American culture on its citizens. Assimilation is the process by which a minority group gradually adopts the culture of the majority group. For example, many Native Americans assimilated into the European-style culture of the early American settlers. Acculturation is the process of obtaining the practices and ideas of a culture. A child undergoes acculturation, wherein he or she learns to think and act appropriately for his or her setting.

10. C: Mercantilism is the economic theory that nations advance the goal of accumulating capital by maintaining a balance of trade such that the value of exports exceeds that of imports. Great Britain maintained colonies to provide an inexpensive source of raw materials while creating markets for the goods manufactured in England. Under free trade, governments refrain from hindering the international exchange of goods and services. Nations that are granted most favored nation status are assured of enjoying equal advantages in international trade. A laissez-faire capitalist economy would theoretically be completely free of government regulation.

11. B: During the early Medieval period (or Middle Ages), Europe was characterized by widespread illiteracy, ignorance, and superstition once the unifying influence of the Roman Empire was lost. Few universities, like the university at Constantinople founded in 2 AD and those at Athens, Antioch, and Alexandria around the same time, existed then. Before the 5th and 6th centuries C.E., any education was conducted at cathedral or monastery schools or privately in the homes of wealthy families, which cannot be considered "main centers of literacy." More religious schools were created through Charlemagne's reforms in the 9th century, and early forms of universities began developing in the 11th and 12th centuries.

12. A: The Supreme Court interprets law and the Constitution. The inferior courts are bound to uphold the law as the Supreme Court interprets and rules on it.

13. B: Direct democracy is a system in which all members of a population vote directly on the issue at hand. A representative democracy refers to a system in which representatives vote on behalf of the population. The House of Representatives, the Senate, and the Electoral College are all representative democracies. The House of Representatives gives weight to population, whereas the Senate and the Electoral College do not. Members of the House of Representatives are elected in proportion to the population of each state. Representation by senators is not based on population and is therefore skewed in electoral weight. The Electoral College can and has contradicted the popular vote in the Presidential election.

14. D: Federalists who helped frame the Constitution believed the central government needed to be stronger than what was established under the Articles of Confederation. Anti-federalists were against this and feared a strong federal government. A system of checks and balances was established to prevent the central government from taking too much power.

15. B: Reification is the act of treating an abstraction as a real, concrete thing. For example, the concept of society might be useful, but it is not an actual, concrete thing separate from the components (such as people and infrastructure) that make up society. Options A, C, and D can all be rejected because none accurately capture the concept of reification. Social scientists might indeed be concerned with relative appropriateness of qualitative data and quantitative data, but using one over the other is not reification. Social scientists might use heuristic devices, but this is not simply reification (not all cases of reification are cases of using heuristic devices). Reification is not mistaking subjectivity for objectivity.

16. C: When a nation follows the theory of comparative advantage, it specializes in producing the goods and services it can make at a lower opportunity cost and then engages in trade to obtain other goods.

17. A: Presidents may veto legislation passed by both houses of Congress, and in turn, Congress can override a presidential veto with a 2/3 majority. These governmental practices are a further manifestation that each branch of government is watched by the other branches and, when necessary, can undo a decision it deems ill-advised or unconstitutional.

18. D: One key to an opinion statement is the use of superlatives. This sentence states apartheid was the worst political system, an opinion that could be challenged, given Nazism and fascism during World War II. All other statements can be verified as fact.

19. C: The President must be a natural citizen, be at least 35 years old, and have lived in the U.S. for 14 years. There is no education requirement for becoming President. Truman did not have a college education, but most Presidents have degrees.

20. C: A person who has taken out a fixed-rate loan can benefit from inflation by paying back the loan with dollars that are less valuable than they were when the loan was taken out. In the other examples, inflation harms the individual or entity.

21. B: Growth of industry was concentrated in urban areas, which cyclically drew laborers into cities, growing the population of cities and increasing efficiency and quality in industry.

22. A: The production possibilities frontier shows the different possible combinations of goods (and/or services) a society can produce. If all other factors are even, producing more of Good A leads to a decreased production of Good B. If the PPF moves outward, that means a change in the factors of production that allows the economy to produce more goods—economic growth—has occurred. Something like innovation is an example of a cause of economic growth.

23. B: The Trail of Tears was the forcible removal of Native American tribes from their homes in the Southeastern US to Oklahoma. The name came due to the high number of Native Americans who died on the journey.

24. B: Tropical regions near the Equator tend to experience relatively constant temperatures year-round because the angle at which sunlight hits them remains relatively constant throughout the year. In regions that are farther north or south, the angle at which sunlight hits them changes much more drastically due to the changing angle of the Earth's axis relative to the Sun. This results in greater variations in the length of daylight and in temperatures. Tropical regions do have seasons (usually a "wet" season and a "dry" season), but temperature fluctuations are less pronounced than those in regions farther from the Equator.

25. B: In order to prosper, a nation should not try to increase its imports. Mercantilism is an economic theory including the idea that prosperity comes from a positive balance of international trade. For any one nation to prosper, that nation should increase its exports (C) but decrease its imports. Exporting more to other countries while importing less from them will give a country a positive trade balance. This theory assumes that money and wealth are identical (A) assets of a nation. In addition, this theory also assumes that the volume of global trade is an unchangeable quantity. Mercantilism dictates that a nation's government should apply a policy of economic protectionism (D) by stimulating more exports and suppressing imports. Some ways to accomplish this task have included granting subsidies for exports and imposing tariffs on imports. Mercantilism can be regarded as essentially the opposite of the free trade policies that have been encouraged in more recent years.

26. A: The input and output data illustrates the Law of Diminishing Marginal Returns, which states that as inputs are added during production, there eventually comes a time when increased inputs coincide with a decrease in marginal return.

27. B: Members of the House are elected for two-year terms. Senators serve six-year terms, but the elections are staggered so roughly one-third of the Senate is elected every two years.

28. A: A city located at 6,000 feet above sea level is likely to have a cooler climate, all other things being equal. Since air is less dense at higher altitudes, it holds heat less effectively and temperatures tend to be lower as a result. Precipitation is not as strong an indicator of temperature. Some areas that receive moderate or large amounts of precipitation are cooler (temperate and continental climates), while some areas that receive lots of precipitation, like the tropics, are warmer.

29. B: The Erie Canal opened in 1825 and created a water route between the Hudson River and Lake Erie. Water routes have historically been cheaper and easier than overland ones and the Erie Canal was originally proposed in the 1700s as a means of providing a shipping route to assist in settling the areas west of the Appalachian Mountains. The Mississippi River is to the west of the Great Lakes, its source is in Minnesota and it discharges into the Gulf of Mexico approximately 100 miles downstream of New Orleans, Louisiana. The Susquehanna River runs through New York, Pennsylvania and Maryland and is the home of Three Mile Island, the site of the United States' largest nuclear disaster. The Lehigh River is located in eastern Pennsylvania.

30. B: Latitudes are lines that run east and west on geographical maps, and are also called parallels. Longitudes (A) are lines that run north and south, so longitude is not a synonym for latitude. Longitudes are also called meridians (C), so meridian is a synonym for longitude, not latitude. Coordinates (D) are the numbers of degrees assigned to various latitudes and latitudes.

31. C: A caucus is a private event run by political parties, and a primary is an indirect election run by state and local governments. Voters may award delegates to candidates for the national conventions, depending on state laws.

32. D: Most people were literate, due to well-financed public education programs.. Despite the growing amount of literacy in the 1500s, due principally to the invention of the printing press and the availability of texts, the majority of Europeans remained illiterate.

33. C: Hernando Cortes conquered the Mexican Aztecs in 1519. He had several advantages over the indigenous peoples, including horses, armor for his soldiers, and guns. In addition, Cortes' troops unknowingly transmitted smallpox to the Aztecs, which devastated their population as they had no immunity to this foreign illness. Vasco Nunez de Balboa (A) was the first European explorer to view the Pacific Ocean when he crossed the Isthmus of Panama in 1513. Juan Ponce de Leon (B) also visited and claimed Florida in Spain's name in 1513. Cabeza de Vaca (D) was one of only four men out of 400 to return from an expedition led by Panfilio de Narvaez in 1528 and was responsible for spreading the story of the Seven Cities of Cibola (the "cities of gold"). Hernando de Soto led an expedition from 1539-1541 to the southeastern part of America.

34. B: Economists understand the true cost of an action as not only its monetary cost but the cost of other opportunities missed as a result of pursuing that action. For example, if a person chooses to go to school rather than working, the cost of the action involves not only tuition and other associated fees and expenses, but the money one would have earned working, as well as the time one could have spent pursuing other activities. The concept of opportunity cost is not described by options A, C, or D, each of which is concerned only with monetary costs. Each of these answers can be rejected on that basis.

35. B: The rate of incarceration for juveniles did decrease after 1995. Answer A is a correct statement. Fewer women than men are incarcerated in each year sampled, even though the number of females incarcerated is growing. Response C is also accurate; in the years specified, more whites were incarcerated in jails than any other race. The chart clearly shows an increase in the number of Hispanics being jailed, making response D an accurate statement. Sadly, the fifth response, likewise, is true; the number of black inmates jumps by nearly half a million every five years.

36. C: Data collected from 2003 show that more than 15% of African-American families had violent conflicts; over 11% of Latino families did; and fewer than 9% of White families did. While researchers concede that cultural and demographic variables can influence styles of disagreement in families, they find parental stress the strongest influence on whether family conflicts become violent (A). The National Survey of Child and Adolescent Well-Being found that children of socioeconomically disadvantaged families have more developmental and behavioral problems than in other groups (B). However, these children were also less likely to receive help with their problems (D). For example, more than 40% of toddlers and more than 68% of preschoolers in contact with the child welfare system had high levels of developmental and behavioral needs; yet fewer than 23% of these children were receiving services to address those needs.

37. B: Determining methods of carrying babies and studying the toddlers in several countries would be the best method for gathering data for this study.

38. B: Diversity is not one of the demographic variables. Demographers, or those who study population, rely on fertility, mortality, and migration to determine the number of people in a region. The general equation is *Total Population = Original Population + Births – Deaths + Immigration – Emigration*. The natural increase, on the other hand, is calculated only with the number of births and deaths. The diversity of a population may be relevant to subsequent research performed by the demographer, but it is not considered one of the essential three demographic variables.

39. A: The Nile River flooded regularly and reliably, irrigating the crops of the ancient Egyptians. This best explains the stability of Egyptian culture. Answer B can be rejected because though the Nile River is expansive; its size did not prevent the Egyptian people from settling elsewhere. Answer C can be rejected because the Valley of the Kings, an ancient Egyptian city, did not separate Upper and Lower Egypt. Answer D can be rejected because, even if true, interaction with other cultures is more likely to lead to a dynamic, changing culture than a stable, unchanging culture.

40. C: The possibility of British interference aimed towards outlawing slavery in the territory, which the British has done throughout its empire three years before Texas gained its independence from Mexico, and the possibility that Texas emancipation might undermine American slavery was a key factor in the choice by President John Tyler to seek the annexation of Texas. Fears of both unrest over the issue of slavery and a possible Mexican conflict had to be addressed before annexation was brought before congress. At the time of annexation, the border issues remained unsettled. The southern Texas border was not set until the 1848 Treaty of Guadalupe-Hidalgo. The western border was not settled until the Compromise of 1850.

Science

1. A: A good hypothesis is testable and logical, and can be used to predict future events. A good hypothesis is also simple, not complex.

2. A: They will be refracted and converge. When light waves hit a convex lens they are refracted and converge. A convex lens curves or bulges with the middle being thicker and the edges thinner. A magnifying glass is an example. Light rays are refracted by different amounts as they pass through the lens. After light rays pass through, they converge at a point called the focus. An object viewed with a magnifying glass looks bigger because the lens bends the rays inwards. Choice B would indicate a concave lens as it would cause the light to be refracted and diverge. Light is not reflected in this case, so neither choice C nor D would be applicable.

3. D: Circulatory System – exchanges gasses with the environment by delivering oxygen to the bloodstream and releasing carbon dioxide, is not paired correctly. It is the respiratory system that exchanges gasses with the environment by delivering oxygen to the bloodstream and releasing carbon dioxide. The circulatory system transports nutrients, gasses, hormones, and blood to and away from cells. The muscle system controls movement through three types of muscle tissue. The nervous system controls sensory responses by carrying impulses away from and toward the cell body. The digestive system breaks down food for absorption into the blood stream where it is delivered to cells for respiration.

4. C: The benefits to people and the economy must outweigh the risks to determine whether their decision to build is fair. This is why governments would conduct a risk-benefit analysis in making decisions about city planning and development. Answer A, Governments must know what the benefits of a new development are for people and the economy in order to persuade opponents and the public who are against it, would be incorrect because the intention would be to build regardless of risk. Answer D, The benefits to people and the economy can be used to ignore the risks associated with any new development, would also be incorrect as it would be unethical to ignore the risks.

5. A: Dispose of the solutions according to local disposal procedures. Solutions and compounds used in labs may be hazardous according to state and local regulatory agencies and should be treated with such precaution. Emptying the solutions into the sink and rinsing with warm water and soap does not take into account the hazards associated with a specific solution in terms of vapors or interactions with water, soap, and waste piping systems. Ensuring the solutions are secured in closed containers and throwing them away may allow toxic chemicals into landfills and subsequently into fresh water systems. Storing the solutions in a secured, dry place for later use is incorrect as chemicals should not be re-used due to the possibility of contamination.

6. C: 4/16. The fraction of offspring that that have the genotype BbSs is 4/16. A dihybrid cross considers two traits at a time, in this case, eye color and hair color. In the parent (P) generation, a parent with the genotype BBSS would be crossed with a parent with the genotype bbss. The offspring are considered the F1 generation and all would have the genotype BbSs. This question asks about the F2 generation, which is the offspring between a cross of the F1 generation. Therefore, the parent genotypes in this question would be BbSs. To solve, develop a Punnet square of 16 cells. Each parent will produce the following gametes: BS, Bs, bS, bs. Place these across the top and the side. After completing the square, the resulting offspring show that four would have the genotype BbSs.

P → F1

	BS
bs	BbSs

F1 → F2

	BS	**Bs**	**bS**	**bs**
BS	BBSS	BBSs	BbSS	BbSs
Bs	BBSs	BBss	BbSs	Bbss
bS	BbSS	BbSs	bbSS	bbSs
bs	BbSs	Bbss	bbSs	bbss

7. C: Sources of renewable energy include geothermal power, solar energy, and wind power. Sources of nonrenewable energy include nuclear power, natural gas, and fossil fuels like coal, natural gas, and crude oil.

8. A: Repeating a measurement several times can increase the accuracy of the measurement. Calibrating the equipment (B) will increase the precision of the measurement. None of the other choices are useful strategies to increase the accuracy of a measurement.

9. C: The chaparral biome features scrubby plants and small evergreen trees and also has a hot, dry summer followed by a wetter winter. This biome is mainly found around the Mediterranean Sea, though there are also chaparrals in Australia, South Africa, and the American Southwest. The taiga is a colder biome found primarily in northern Europe and Asia. The vegetation of the taiga is mainly scattered stands of coniferous trees. A coniferous forest, meanwhile, is a warmer forest composed of trees that have needles and cones rather than leaves. These trees are better suited for a cold climate than are deciduous trees. A savanna is a tropical grassland with only a few trees. Savannas are clustered around the equator.

10. C: The pressure decreases to one-third. A gas in a closed container at constant temperature will decrease in pressure to one-third when the volume of the container is tripled. The ideal gas law is $PV = nRT$ where P is pressure, V is volume, n is the moles of the gas, R is the gas constant and T is temperature. A variation to solve for pressure is: $P = nRT/V$. Boyle's Law indicates that pressure and volume are inversely proportional. The pressure cannot be increased because that would imply that pressure and volume are directly proportional.

11. C: Laccolith. A laccolith is formed when an intrusion of magma injected between two layers of sedimentary rock forces the overlying strata upward to create a dome-like form. Eventually, the magma cools, the sedimentary rock wears away and the formation is exposed. Sills and dikes are both examples of sheet intrusions, where magma has inserted itself into other rock. Sills are horizontal and dikes are vertical. A caldera is a crater-like feature that was formed from the collapse of a volcano after erupting.

12. C: For an experiment to be considered successful, it must yield data that others can reproduce. Choice A may be considered part of a well-designed experiment. Choices B and D may be considered part of an experiment that is reported on by individuals with expertise.

13. C: Heat transfer can never occur from a cooler object to a warmer object. While the second law of thermodynamics implies that heat never spontaneously transfers from a cooler object to a warmer object, it is possible for heat to be transferred to a warmer object, given the proper input of work to the system. This is the principle by which a refrigerator operates. Work is done to the system to transfer heat from the objects inside the refrigerator to the air surrounding the refrigerator. All other answer choices are true.

14. A: It is the only way to prove that an experiment is valid. If an experiment can't be successfully repeated with the same outcome, one cannot determine that the experimental results are valid. Repetition is the key to scientific progress.

15. C: The closer the data points are to each other, the more precise the data. This does not mean the data is accurate, but that the results are very reproducible.

16. D: The most recently formed parts of the Earth's crust can be found at mid-ocean ridges. New crust forms here when magma erupts from these ridges and pushes pre-existing crust horizontally towards the continental plates. Such ridges include the Mid-Atlantic Ridge and the East Pacific Rise.

17. A: Fission. Fission is a nuclear process where atomic nuclei split apart to form smaller nuclei. Nuclear fission can release large amounts of energy, emit gamma rays and form daughter products. It is used in nuclear power plants and bombs. Choice B, Fusion, refers to a nuclear process whereby atomic nuclei join to form a heavier nucleus, such as with stars. This can release or absorb energy depending upon the original elements. Choice C, Decay, refers to an atomic nucleus spontaneously losing energy and emitting ionizing particles and radiation. Choice D, Ionization, refers to a process by which atoms obtain a positive or negative charge because the number of electrons does not equal that of protons.

18. C: The best control group would be women with wrinkles around their eyes using a harmless cream that has no effect. A scientific control group is used to minimize the unintended influence of other variables on a scientific study. Such extraneous variables include researcher bias, environmental changes, and biological variation. Scientific controls ensure that data are valid, and are a vital part of the scientific method.

19. A: The prevailing westerlies. The prevailing westerlies drive weather systems to move west to east in the mid-latitudes. The direction refers to that which the wind is coming from. The polar easterlies that travel from the northeast occur between 90-60 degrees north latitude. The ones from the southeast are between 90-60 degrees south latitude. The trade winds refer to those occurring near the equator in the tropics moving east. The doldrums are also in the tropics but refer to an area of low-pressure where frequently the winds are light and unpredictable.

20. A: Many organisms, especially organisms that live in harsh conditions such as deserts or frozen icy areas, have developed specific adaptations that allow them to survive. For example, cacti are able to expand to store large amounts of water, coyotes absorb some water from their food, and snakes can escape the heat by hiding within rocks.

21. D: Mario balances a book on his head. In this example, work is not applied to the book because the book is not moving. One definition of work is a force acting on an object to cause displacement. In this case, the book was not displaced by the force applied to it. Mario's head applied a vertical force to the book to keep it in the same position.

22. A: Should the packaging of meat products that come from cloned animals be labeled? This is an issue that would be regulated by the Food and Drug Administration (FDA) as it regulates the packaging of meat products, among many other types of food. Answer B, Should nitrate or sulfate fertilizers be added to oil spills to assist the decomposition of crude oil by bacteria, would not be an issue for the FDA. The Environmental Protection Agency (EPA) regulates issues regarding the environment as well as superfund clean ups. Neither Answer C, about genetic engineering of humans, nor Answer D, about cell use in industry, relate to food and drugs and would not fall under the jurisdiction of the FDA.

23. A: Glass is manufactured and can be recycled, but is considered a non-renewable resource. Wood is considered a renewable resource because with proper management, an equilibrium can be reached between harvesting trees and planting new ones. Cattle are managed in herds and a balance can be achieved between those consumed and those born. Soil is the result of long-term erosion and includes organic matter and minerals needed by plants. Soil found naturally in the environment is renewed. Crops can be rotated to help maintain a healthy soil composition for farming.

24. A: The stream of charged particles that escape the Sun's gravitational pull is called solar wind. Solar wind is comprised primarily of protons and electrons, and these particles are deflected away from the Earth by its magnetic field. When stray particles do manage to enter the atmosphere, they cause the aurorae (Northern and Southern Lights) and geomagnetic storms that can affect power grids.

25. B: Voltage and current are directly proportional to one another. Ohm's Law states that voltage and current in an electrical circuit are directly proportional to one another. Ohm's Law can be expressed as $V = IR$, where V is voltage, I is current and R is resistance. Voltage is also known as electrical potential difference and is the force that moves electrons through a circuit. For a given amount of resistance, an increase in voltage will result in an increase in current. Resistance and current are inversely proportional to each other. For a given voltage, an increase in resistance will result in a decrease in current.

26. C: Flowers. Flowers are the reproductive organs of a plant. Flowering plants reproduce by sexual reproduction where the gametes join to form seeds. Pollen is sperm. Pollinators help transfer the sperm to the ovule, the egg. The style is the part of the female reproduction system that transports the sperm between the stigma and the ovary, which are all parts of the pistil. The stigma is the sticky tip of the style on which the pollen lands. Sepals are usually small leaves between or underneath the petals and are not as obvious or as large and colorful as the petals.

27. B: Work is defined as the force used to move a mass over a distance. Choice A may be a secular (non-scientific) definition of work. Choice C is the definition of power. Choice D is the definition of potential energy.

28. D: In a homogeneous solution, the substance that is dissolved is the solute. A mixture of sugar and water is a homogenous solution in which the sugar is the solute, and the water is the solvent. A mixture of salt and water is a homogeneous solution in which the salt is the solute, and the water is the solvent. A mixture of ash in air is a description of smoke which is a colloid. A mixture of salt and pepper is a heterogeneous mixture.

29. A: Glaciers move because they are incredibly heavy, and the force of gravity slowly pulls them lower. Erosion is a result rather than a cause of glacier movement. Although large glaciers may only move a few inches a year or may not move at all, some valley glaciers in Europe move as much as 600 feet annually. The result is a rounded valley and a trail of rock and soil debris known as a moraine. The Great Lakes in the United States were formed by the passage of glaciers long ago.

30. D: Exhaust fumes are an ever-present concern, while the others are incidents that might or might not occur. A combustion engine of any kind produces fumes which can rapidly cause health damage, brain damage or death if allowed to fill an inadequately ventilated space. Therefore activities of this kind are usually conducted near an open garage door or loading dock if not out-of-doors. A situation guaranteed to happen--the production of fumes--is of higher priority than incidental dangers.

31. B: A stoma (plural: stomata) is the part of a plant system that responds to stimuli by releasing water via transpiration. It can also close during adverse conditions like a drought to prevent the plant from dehydration. Stomata closure can also be triggered by the presence of bacteria. Pith refers to the central, spongy part of the stem in vascular plants. Guard cells flank stomata and regulate the opening. Sepals are modified leaves that protect the flower bud before it opens.

32. B: The electrolysis of water is a chemical change that transforms water into hydrogen and oxygen gases. Synthesis reactions are those that combine reactants to form a product, which is the opposite of what happens when electrolyzing water. Reverse osmosis is a technique often used to purify water by forcing impure water through a semi-permeable membrane using a pressure differential.

33. A: By multiplying the ocular lens power times the objective being used. When using a light microscope, total magnification is determined by multiplying the ocular lens power times the objective being used. The ocular lens refers to the eyepiece, which has one magnification strength, typically 10x. The objective lens also has a magnification strength, often 4x, 10x, 40x, or 100x. Using a 10x eyepiece with the 4x objective lens will give a magnification strength of 40x. Using a 10x eyepiece with the 100x objective lens will give a magnification strength of 1,000x. The shorter lens is the lesser magnification; the longer lens is the greater magnification.

34. B: Technology often results from scientific discoveries. The relationship between science and technology is evident when scientific discoveries prompt technologic advances.

35. A: Testing, observing, and recording data. Before drawing a conclusion about a hypothesis, one should test and observe it and record data about the test results.

36. C: All typical living organisms need food, water, sunlight, and air. Shelter, space, and nurturing are essential for most organisms, but are technically indirect needs and not directly crucial to sustaining life.

37. D: Temperature. The amount of potential energy an object has depends on mass, height above ground and gravitational attraction, but not temperature. The formula for potential energy is $PE = mgh$, or potential energy equals mass times gravity times height. Answers A, B, and C are all valid answers as they are all contained in the formula for potential energy. Potential energy is the amount of energy stored in a system particularly because of its position.

38. B: Some RNA molecules in extant organisms have enzymatic activity; for example, the formation of peptide bonds on ribosomes is catalyzed by an RNA molecule. This and other information have led scientists to believe that the most likely molecules to first demonstrate enzymatic activity were RNA molecules.

39. D: After a secondary consumer dies, such as a wolf, its body is partially consumed by decomposers, such as bacteria and fungi. Bacteria and fungi live in soil and digest body tissues of dead organisms converting them into basic nutrients that plants need to grow. Therefore, after secondary consumers die, their energy is consumed by decomposers, who make nutrients available in the soil for producers to use. *Do not confuse nutrients in the soil with energy that producers get from the Sun to make their own food.*

40. A: Heat between objects in contact with each other is transferred by conduction, choice A. Convection is transfer by currents within a body of fluid, and radiation is the transfer of heat between objects *not* in contact, through light rays emitted by the hotter object and absorbed by the cooler one.

41. B: A long nail or other type of metal, substance or matter that is heated at one end and then the other end becomes equally hot is an example of conduction. Conduction is energy transferred by neighboring molecules from an area of hotter temperature to cooler temperature. Radiation, or thermal radiation, refers to heat being transferred without the need for a medium by electromagnetic radiation. An example of radiation is sunlight heating the earth. Convection refers to heat being transferred by molecules moving from one location in the substance to another creating a heat current, usually in a gas or a liquid. Entropy relates to the second law of thermodynamics and refers to how much heat or energy is no longer available to do work in a system. It can also be stated as the amount of disorder in a system.

42. B: Venus. Venus experiences a greenhouse effect similar to that observed on Earth as its dense atmosphere traps the solar radiation and creates a greenhouse effect. The greenhouse gasses, including ozone, carbon dioxide, water vapor and methane, trap infrared radiation that is reflected back toward the atmosphere. Human activity generates more of the greenhouse gasses than necessary. Some practices that increase the amount of greenhouse gasses are burning natural gas and oil, farming, which leads to more methane and nitrous oxide, deforestation, which decreases the amount of offset oxygen, and population growth in general, which increases the volume of greenhouse gasses. Increased gasses mean more infrared radiation is trapped and the overall temperature at the Earth's surface rises.

43. B: A trace fossil shows evidence of existence but is not an organism itself. A trace fossil can be contrasted with a body fossil, which has been formed from an organism. Other examples of trace fossils include eggs, nests, burrows, borings, and coprolites (fossilized feces). A mouse jaw and a shark tooth are examples of body fossils. A cast of a skull is a replica and neither a body nor a trace fossil.

44. A: When two tectonic plates are moving laterally in opposing directions, this is called a transform boundary. When there is friction at transform boundaries and pressure builds up, it can result in shallow earthquakes (usually at a depth of less than 25 meters). California's San Andreas Fault is an example of a transform boundary.

45. B: The energy radiated by stars is produced by nuclear fusion. This is the process whereby the nuclei of individual atoms bind together to form heavier elements and release energy outward. By the time this energy, which is created in the star's core, reaches the outer walls of the star, it exists in the form of light.

Fine Arts, Health and Physical Education

1. B: Line is the artistic element most commonly used to create the illusion of depth in a painting. For instance, an artist could use line to convey depth by incorporating an object, such as a road, that stretches from the foreground to the background of a painting. Balance is a principle of art that involves creating an impression of stability in a work; contrast and symmetry would not function to create the illusion of depth.

2. A: A rubric would not be an appropriate evaluation tool for a summative assessment with multiple-choice questions. Rubrics are tools for grading student work with multiple facets and dimensions that may be more or less independent of one another. For example, a rubric would be an appropriate evaluation tool for a project in which students write a report and deliver a presentation about a famous work of art, because this project has many different aspects that should be assessed independently. A teacher might want to assign separate grades for the content of the report, the organization and writing of the report, the content of the presentation, and the student's confidence and poise in delivering the presentation.

3. C: Allegro, which uses a tempo between 120 and 168 beats per minute (bpm). While Allegro can be thought of as a "quick" tempo, it is not as fast as Presto, played between 168 and 200 bpm. Therefore, Choice A is incorrect. Moderato and Largo—played between 108-120 and 40-60, respectively—are slower tempos, proving Choices B and D incorrect.

4. A: The most appropriate activity for students at this grade level would be making pinch pots and coil pots. Pinch pots are formed by creating a depression in the center of a ball of clay and smoothing the sides. Coil pots are formed by creating a long, thin length of clay and coiling it to form a pot. Unlike making and attaching handles to pots or throwing pots using a pottery wheel, creating this type of object with clay is appropriate given the fine motor skills and technical sophistication of second graders. The art teacher could model glazing pots using a kiln, but this activity would be too dangerous for young students to attempt on their own.

5. B: A stone plate would be used to produce a lithograph. In printmaking, the original surface, or matrix, that is used varies based upon the type of print. Linoleum plates are used to produce linocuts, fabric matrices are used to produce screen prints, and etchings are produced using metal plates.

6. D: A photograph of a small child standing alone in an empty room would have lots of negative space. Positive space in a painting or photograph is the space occupied by the subject (in this case, the child); negative space is the "empty" part of the composition. The description given of this photograph does not indicate whether the composition is symmetrical or asymmetrical, nor does it indicate whether or not the photograph achieves artistic unity.

7. C: Value refers to the relative lightness or darkness of the colors in a painting. Intensity relates the vibrancy of colors in a painting; high-intensity colors are pure, while low-intensity colors are mixed with other colors to suggest a somber mood. A color's hue refers to the actual pigmentation (red, blue, green, or yellow). Texture is a tactile quality of an artwork's surface, rather than a property of color.

8. D: Johannes Brahms, who composed music in the middle to late 19th century. Therefore, Brahms is most strongly associated with the Romantic Period in classical music, which ran from about 1815 to about 1910. Bach is most strongly associated with the Baroque Period (1600-1760), and Ravel is most closely associated with the Impressionist Period (1890-1940). Choice D, Aaron Copland, often is considered "the dean of American composers" and composed music in the mid to late 20th century; he would not fit into any of the above listed periods.

9. A: Cajun music of Louisiana traces its roots back to French musical traditions. Early French settlers on the North American continent migrated from New Brunswick and Nova Scotia to southern Louisiana, and brought with them traditional French ballads that, over time, developed into present-day Cajun music.

10. B: Plenty of third-grade-level scripts *do* contain lessons at the end of the story. Typically, though, only fables are supposed to include a moral lesson. Therefore, answer choice A is incorrect. If a script called for expensive props or contained offensive language, it would not be suitable to be performed by third-graders or to be viewed by an audience. Therefore, while both answer choices C and D are correct, B is the better choice because it is broader and encompasses both C and d.

11. A: Analyzing and studying characters are important aspects of script analysis, but script analysis is much too broad to be the correct choice here. Plot development focuses on the storyline and occurs during the developmental stages before the script is complete. Psychological dissection is not a term that is used in theatre. The question is clearly asking for a choice that is related to better understanding a work's characters and their relationships with one another.

12. B: In aerobic exercise, slow twitch muscles take oxygen from the blood and use it to produce ATP (adenosine triphosphate) energy. Without this energy, a person could not engage in aerobic exercise. Fast twitch muscles are not the kind of muscles mainly used in aerobic exercise; rather, fast twitch muscles are used in physical activity that requires faster movement for shorter periods time (fast twitch muscles are used in a sprint, but slow twitch muscles are used in running for a long time). Therefore, Choice D can be rejected. Regarding Choices A and C, it is the circulatory system as a whole that distributes oxygen throughout the body, not fast or slow twitch muscles.

13. A: An arpeggio is defined as a chord that is played note-by-note, successively, instead of simultaneously. Also termed as a broken chord, the arpeggio can be played from the highest note to the lowest note, but is more commonly played from the lowest note to the highest note.

14. A: Visual literacy can best be described as the ability to communicate through images and comprehend the messages contained in images. In visual literacy education, students are taught not only to create images that appropriately communicate information, but also to interpret and derive meaning from both artistic and informational images.

15. A: It is important to first recognize that "slug line" is another term for "scene heading." The term should not be confused with the term "header." The question is asking about a script element that appears in all capital letters and describes the current setting. The only two script elements that are written in all capital letters are character names and slug lines. Since the question does not reference character names, answer choice A is correct.

16. A: Cardiovascular endurance is the ability to engage in activities that require oxygen, and to do so for significant periods of time. Activities that involve sustained, aerobic exercise are the best activities to develop cardiovascular endurance, and of the activities named in the choices, cross-country running is the activity that involves the most sustained, aerobic exercise. Volleyball (Choice B) involves periods of standing and waiting, or moving just a little – for example, waiting for a serve, or hovering nearby as teammates handle the ball in play. Rock climbing (Choice D) typically involves methodical, precise action, but not constant aerobic exercise; weight training (Choice C) also does not involve sustained, aerobic exercise. All these choices can be rejected.

17. C: A high-fiber diet supplies the body with many essential vitamins and minerals and may help lower cholesterol levels.

18. A: The body's main fuel is the simple sugar glucose. Complex carbohydrates provide the body with sustained energy by slowly breaking down into glucose.

19. D: Blind reading is not used in the theatre industry, so answer choice A can be eliminated. While a cold read is indeed preliminary in nature, answer choice B is incorrect because the technical term is *cold.* Sight reading is when a performer runs through a piece of sheet music for the first time. It is not related to script reading, so answer choice C is incorrect.

20. D: While playing sports is excellent for cardiovascular fitness, weight training builds muscle strength and endurance. Resistance training for young people should be limited to three times a week. It builds strength most efficiently when less weight is lifted many times.

21. A: Here is an easy way to remember stage directions: There is an old wives' tale about stage construction that claims that stages used to be built on a slope (the back end was higher than the front). When a director wanted an actor to stand at the back of the stage, he literally meant, "Go *up* the stage." If the director wanted an actor positioned toward the front of the stage, he would say, "Go *down* the stage." Eventually, these directions were shortened to "upstage" and "downstage."

22. B: While strenuous exercise is likely to trigger an asthma attack, moderate exercise is essential to good health and rarely represents a danger to asthma sufferers. Choices A, C, and D are common triggers for asthma.

23. C: One of the main ways people catch colds is by touching their eyes, nose, or mouth after coming in contact with an infected person or object. Thorough hand washing can prevent the spread of colds and other illnesses. Most scientists dispute the value of vitamin C in preventing or treating the common cold.

24. A: Saturated fat is found primarily in beef, pork, lamb, cheese, and egg yolks. It tends to raise the level of LDL, or "bad cholesterol," in the blood. Nuts and beans are generally a good source of monounsaturated fat, which tend to lower harmful cholesterol levels.

25. A: Contusions are often characterized by ruptured blood vessels and discoloration. Choice B describes a strain; Choice C describes a sprain; Choice D describes a concussion.

26. A: The situation clearly shows two different viewpoints. This difference creates conflict between the two friends. If the scenario described a situation where the two friends were working toward a resolution, but the reader was still unaware of the consequences of their decision, answer choice B would be appropriate. Foreshadowing would have given hints as to where the story was headed, and role reversal is clearly not involved in this situation. Therefore, answer choices C and D are incorrect.

27. B: Process-centered drama is the correct answer because this method of teaching is focused on a child's ability to play and act out what they see in actual life. It is more perception based, whereas product-centered drama focuses on teaching acting skills. It is more structured. Method acting is when a performer uses his thoughts and emotions to convey a message to the audience. A child cannot fully understand product-centered drama or method acting until he understands process-centered drama. Natural-state drama does not exist.

28. B: While aerobic exercise primarily benefits the cardiorespiratory system, anaerobic exercise, such as weight lifting or rope jumping, builds strength by using muscles at high intensity for a short period of time.

29. C: When encountering a difficult passage, musicians most effectively practice that passage slowly and thoughtfully. Playing through a challenging passage quickly can be detrimental to the learning process. Studying away from the instrument and practicing the sections before and after can be helpful, but will not address the difficult passage in the most effective manner.

30. B: Girls are twice as likely as boys to experience depression during adolescence. Some depressed adolescents do not act sad at all and are consequently misdiagnosed as having ADHD or a learning disorder.

31. B: A fresco is actually a painting style that involves applying paint or pigment directly to plaster. In order to give pigment the desired consistency for fluid painting, several things can be mixed with the pigment: A tempera such as oil, egg, or water; turpentine, which is used as a cleaner and thinner; and an oil medium, which has opposite effects as turpentine, making the paint fatter.

32. B: Dimension, texture, and space are all *elements* of art, while unity is one of the *principles* of art. Unity in artwork is achieved when an artist's use of the elements produces a sense of wholeness or completeness in the finished product.

33. C: Although each of the other choices correctly identifies a factor in motor development, self-confidence is the factor that is most likely to be affected by motor development itself. A person might be reluctant to engage in physical activities (either in group settings or independently) because of low confidence in his or her own abilities and talents. However, engaging in physical activity and thereby actually developing one's motor skills is likely to increase one's confidence, making it more likely that the person will engage in, or not mind engaging in, such activities. Therefore, although self-confidence can negatively affect motor development, motor development can positively affect self-confidence. This is true of some other psychological factors in motor development as well.

34. D: Blues music was heavily influenced by the black church through improvisation, storytelling, call and response, vocal inflections, and the blues progression. Many of these musical features are now representative of the blues genre of music.

35. A: There are many possible activities to teach students motor skills. Activities should vary to keep the students interested; using the same activity over and over again to teach the same basic skill is likely to get boring. Choice B can be rejected because it wrongly suggests using the same activity repeatedly to teach a basic skill. Choice C can be rejected because students should learn motor skills sequentially, mastering simpler skills before moving on to more sophisticated skills; this means that teaching should be structured, rather than allowing students to play as they please. Choice D should be rejected because students should master certain skills before having to use those skills in actual games.

36. D: Antibodies are a component of the specific immune response: unlike the components of the non-specific immune mechanism, antibodies (a kind of protein) are tailored to respond to a specific kind of foreign particle, not to foreign particles generally speaking. The non-specific immune mechanism in the human body includes skin (Choice A), mucus membranes, the inflammatory response (such as swelling in response to injury) (Choice B), and white blood cells, such as neutrophils (Choice C). White blood cells consume particles that do not belong in the body and that may cause harm.

37. C: In 3/4 time, the quarter note is selected as the one beat unit, while in 6/8 time the eighth note is used. Essentially, 6/8 time is the same as the six-note form of 3/4. The only difference is that the eighth note is used as the one-beat unit.

38. B: Physical exercise improves a person's circulation. This, in turn, leads to greater blood flow to the brain, helping to improve a person's mental abilities. Choice A is false: physical exercise does affect mental functioning. Although physical exercise does lower cholesterol, there is no clear link between this and improved mental abilities; this eliminates Choice C. Regarding Choice D, it is true that physical exercise does cause the brain to release endorphins, which make a person feel good and can put a person in a good mood. But improved mood and feelings are not the same as improved mental abilities; therefore, Choice B is clearly the better option, and Choice D can be rejected.

39. B: 2:1. Both notes are G, separated by one octave. An octave is the interval between two notes, where the higher note's frequency is exactly twice that of the lower. Choice A, 1:1, is incorrect, because obviously the notes are not the same. One is higher than the other and therefore has a higher frequency. Choices C and D are both incorrect, since a frequency ratio of 4:1 or 8:1 refers to differences of two and three octaves, respectively.

40. B: To develop cardiovascular endurance, one should engage in exercise that uses major muscle groups for at least 20 minutes a day at least three days a week. Choices A and C understate the correct minimum amount of time for an exercise session to develop cardiovascular endurance. Choices B and D both correctly describe the minimum number of times one should exercise in this way each week, as well as the minimum amount of time each exercise session should be. However, Choice B is better than Choice D because Choice B involves racquetball rather than baseball, and racquetball involves more ongoing, repeated use of major muscle groups than baseball. Racquetball is, therefore, better suited for developing cardiovascular endurance.

How to Overcome Test Anxiety

Just the thought of taking a test is enough to make most people a little nervous. A test is an important event that can have a long-term impact on your future, so it's important to take it seriously and it's natural to feel anxious about performing well. But just because anxiety is normal, that doesn't mean that it's helpful in test taking, or that you should simply accept it as part of your life. Anxiety can have a variety of effects. These effects can be mild, like making you feel slightly nervous, or severe, like blocking your ability to focus or remember even a simple detail.

If you experience test anxiety—whether severe or mild—it's important to know how to beat it. To discover this, first you need to understand what causes test anxiety.

Causes of Test Anxiety

While we often think of anxiety as an uncontrollable emotional state, it can actually be caused by simple, practical things. One of the most common causes of test anxiety is that a person does not feel adequately prepared for their test. This feeling can be the result of many different issues such as poor study habits or lack of organization, but the most common culprit is time management. Starting to study too late, failing to organize your study time to cover all of the material, or being distracted while you study will mean that you're not well prepared for the test. This may lead to cramming the night before, which will cause you to be physically and mentally exhausted for the test. Poor time management also contributes to feelings of stress, fear, and hopelessness as you realize you are not well prepared but don't know what to do about it.

Other times, test anxiety is not related to your preparation for the test but comes from unresolved fear. This may be a past failure on a test, or poor performance on tests in general. It may come from comparing yourself to others who seem to be performing better or from the stress of living up to expectations. Anxiety may be driven by fears of the future—how failure on this test would affect your educational and career goals. These fears are often completely irrational, but they can still negatively impact your test performance.

Review Video: 3 Reasons You Have Test Anxiety
Visit mometrix.com/academy and enter code: 428468

Elements of Test Anxiety

As mentioned earlier, test anxiety is considered to be an emotional state, but it has physical and mental components as well. Sometimes you may not even realize that you are suffering from test anxiety until you notice the physical symptoms. These can include trembling hands, rapid heartbeat, sweating, nausea, and tense muscles. Extreme anxiety may lead to fainting or vomiting. Obviously, any of these symptoms can have a negative impact on testing. It is important to recognize them as soon as they begin to occur so that you can address the problem before it damages your performance.

Review Video: 3 Ways to Tell You Have Test Anxiety
Visit mometrix.com/academy and enter code: 927847

The mental components of test anxiety include trouble focusing and inability to remember learned information. During a test, your mind is on high alert, which can help you recall information and stay focused for an extended period of time. However, anxiety interferes with your mind's natural processes, causing you to blank out, even on the questions you know well. The strain of testing during anxiety makes it difficult to stay focused, especially on a test that may take several hours. Extreme anxiety can take a huge mental toll, making it difficult not only to recall test information but even to understand the test questions or pull your thoughts together.

Review Video: How Test Anxiety Affects Memory
Visit mometrix.com/academy and enter code: 609003

Effects of Test Anxiety

Test anxiety is like a disease—if left untreated, it will get progressively worse. Anxiety leads to poor performance, and this reinforces the feelings of fear and failure, which in turn lead to poor performances on subsequent tests. It can grow from a mild nervousness to a crippling condition. If allowed to progress, test anxiety can have a big impact on your schooling, and consequently on your future.

Test anxiety can spread to other parts of your life. Anxiety on tests can become anxiety in any stressful situation, and blanking on a test can turn into panicking in a job situation. But fortunately, you don't have to let anxiety rule your testing and determine your grades. There are a number of relatively simple steps you can take to move past anxiety and function normally on a test and in the rest of life.

Review Video: How Test Anxiety Impacts Your Grades
Visit mometrix.com/academy and enter code: 939819

Physical Steps for Beating Test Anxiety

While test anxiety is a serious problem, the good news is that it can be overcome. It doesn't have to control your ability to think and remember information. While it may take time, you can begin taking steps today to beat anxiety.

Just as your first hint that you may be struggling with anxiety comes from the physical symptoms, the first step to treating it is also physical. Rest is crucial for having a clear, strong mind. If you are tired, it is much easier to give in to anxiety. But if you establish good sleep habits, your body and mind will be ready to perform optimally, without the strain of exhaustion. Additionally, sleeping well helps you to retain information better, so you're more likely to recall the answers when you see the test questions.

Getting good sleep means more than going to bed on time. It's important to allow your brain time to relax. Take study breaks from time to time so it doesn't get overworked, and don't study right before bed. Take time to rest your mind before trying to rest your body, or you may find it difficult to fall asleep.

Review Video: The Importance of Sleep for Your Brain
Visit mometrix.com/academy and enter code: 319338

Along with sleep, other aspects of physical health are important in preparing for a test. Good nutrition is vital for good brain function. Sugary foods and drinks may give a burst of energy but this burst is followed by a crash, both physically and emotionally. Instead, fuel your body with protein and vitamin-rich foods.

Also, drink plenty of water. Dehydration can lead to headaches and exhaustion, especially if your brain is already under stress from the rigors of the test. Particularly if your test is a long one, drink water during the breaks. And if possible, take an energy-boosting snack to eat between sections.

Review Video: How Diet Can Affect your Mood
Visit mometrix.com/academy and enter code: 624317

Along with sleep and diet, a third important part of physical health is exercise. Maintaining a steady workout schedule is helpful, but even taking 5-minute study breaks to walk can help get your blood pumping faster and clear your head. Exercise also releases endorphins, which contribute to a positive feeling and can help combat test anxiety.

When you nurture your physical health, you are also contributing to your mental health. If your body is healthy, your mind is much more likely to be healthy as well. So take time to rest, nourish your body with healthy food and water, and get moving as much as possible. Taking these physical steps will make you stronger and more able to take the mental steps necessary to overcome test anxiety.

Mental Steps for Beating Test Anxiety

Working on the mental side of test anxiety can be more challenging, but as with the physical side, there are clear steps you can take to overcome it. As mentioned earlier, test anxiety often stems from lack of preparation, so the obvious solution is to prepare for the test. Effective studying may be the most important weapon you have for beating test anxiety, but you can and should employ several other mental tools to combat fear.

First, boost your confidence by reminding yourself of past success—tests or projects that you aced. If you're putting as much effort into preparing for this test as you did for those, there's no reason you should expect to fail here. Work hard to prepare; then trust your preparation.

Second, surround yourself with encouraging people. It can be helpful to find a study group, but be sure that the people you're around will encourage a positive attitude. If you spend time with others who are anxious or cynical, this will only contribute to your own anxiety. Look for others who are motivated to study hard from a desire to succeed, not from a fear of failure.

Third, reward yourself. A test is physically and mentally tiring, even without anxiety, and it can be helpful to have something to look forward to. Plan an activity following the test, regardless of the outcome, such as going to a movie or getting ice cream.

When you are taking the test, if you find yourself beginning to feel anxious, remind yourself that you know the material. Visualize successfully completing the test. Then take a few deep, relaxing breaths and return to it. Work through the questions carefully but with confidence, knowing that you are capable of succeeding.

Developing a healthy mental approach to test taking will also aid in other areas of life. Test anxiety affects more than just the actual test—it can be damaging to your mental health and even contribute to depression. It's important to beat test anxiety before it becomes a problem for more than testing.

Review Video: Test Anxiety and Depression
Visit mometrix.com/academy and enter code: 904704

Study Strategy

Being prepared for the test is necessary to combat anxiety, but what does being prepared look like? You may study for hours on end and still not feel prepared. What you need is a strategy for test prep. The next few pages outline our recommended steps to help you plan out and conquer the challenge of preparation.

Step 1: Scope Out the Test

Learn everything you can about the format (multiple choice, essay, etc.) and what will be on the test. Gather any study materials, course outlines, or sample exams that may be available. Not only will this help you to prepare, but knowing what to expect can help to alleviate test anxiety.

Step 2: Map Out the Material

Look through the textbook or study guide and make note of how many chapters or sections it has. Then divide these over the time you have. For example, if a book has 15 chapters and you have five days to study, you need to cover three chapters each day. Even better, if you have the time, leave an extra day at the end for overall review after you have gone through the material in depth.

If time is limited, you may need to prioritize the material. Look through it and make note of which sections you think you already have a good grasp on, and which need review. While you are studying, skim quickly through the familiar sections and take more time on the challenging parts. Write out your plan so you don't get lost as you go. Having a written plan also helps you feel more in control of the study, so anxiety is less likely to arise from feeling overwhelmed at the amount to cover.

Step 3: Gather Your Tools

Decide what study method works best for you. Do you prefer to highlight in the book as you study and then go back over the highlighted portions? Or do you type out notes of the important information? Or is it helpful to make flashcards that you can carry with you? Assemble the pens, index cards, highlighters, post-it notes, and any other materials you may need so you won't be distracted by getting up to find things while you study.

If you're having a hard time retaining the information or organizing your notes, experiment with different methods. For example, try color-coding by subject with colored pens, highlighters, or post-it notes. If you learn better by hearing, try recording yourself reading your notes so you can listen while in the car, working out, or simply sitting at your desk. Ask a friend to quiz you from your flashcards, or try teaching someone the material to solidify it in your mind.

Step 4: Create Your Environment

It's important to avoid distractions while you study. This includes both the obvious distractions like visitors and the subtle distractions like an uncomfortable chair (or a too-comfortable couch that makes you want to fall asleep). Set up the best study environment possible: good lighting and a comfortable work area. If background music helps you focus, you may want to turn it on, but otherwise keep the room quiet. If you are using a computer to take notes, be sure you don't have any other windows open, especially applications like social media, games, or anything else that could distract you. Silence your phone and turn off notifications. Be sure to keep water close by so you stay hydrated while you study (but avoid unhealthy drinks and snacks).

Also, take into account the best time of day to study. Are you freshest first thing in the morning? Try to set aside some time then to work through the material. Is your mind clearer in the afternoon or evening? Schedule your study session then. Another method is to study at the same time of day that you will take the test, so that your brain gets used to working on the material at that time and will be ready to focus at test time.

Step 5: Study!

Once you have done all the study preparation, it's time to settle into the actual studying. Sit down, take a few moments to settle your mind so you can focus, and begin to follow your study plan. Don't give in to distractions or let yourself procrastinate. This is your time to prepare so you'll be ready to fearlessly approach the test. Make the most of the time and stay focused.

Of course, you don't want to burn out. If you study too long you may find that you're not retaining the information very well. Take regular study breaks. For example, taking five minutes out of every hour to walk briskly, breathing deeply and swinging your arms, can help your mind stay fresh.

As you get to the end of each chapter or section, it's a good idea to do a quick review. Remind yourself of what you learned and work on any difficult parts. When you feel that you've mastered the material, move on to the next part. At the end of your study session, briefly skim through your notes again.

But while review is helpful, cramming last minute is NOT. If at all possible, work ahead so that you won't need to fit all your study into the last day. Cramming overloads your brain with more information than it can process and retain, and your tired mind may struggle to recall even previously learned information when it is overwhelmed with last-minute study. Also, the urgent nature of cramming and the stress placed on your brain contribute to anxiety. You'll be more likely to go to the test feeling unprepared and having trouble thinking clearly.

So don't cram, and don't stay up late before the test, even just to review your notes at a leisurely pace. Your brain needs rest more than it needs to go over the information again. In fact, plan to finish your studies by noon or early afternoon the day before the test. Give your brain the rest of the day to relax or focus on other things, and get a good night's sleep. Then you will be fresh for the test and better able to recall what you've studied.

Step 6: Take a Practice Test

Many courses offer sample tests, either online or in the study materials. This is an excellent resource to check whether you have mastered the material, as well as to prepare for the test format and environment.

Check the test format ahead of time: the number of questions, the type (multiple choice, free response, etc.), and the time limit. Then create a plan for working through them. For example, if you have 30 minutes to take a 60-question test, your limit is 30 seconds per question. Spend less time on the questions you know well so that you can take more time on the difficult ones.

If you have time to take several practice tests, take the first one open book, with no time limit. Work through the questions at your own pace and make sure you fully understand them. Gradually work up to taking a test under test conditions: sit at a desk with all study materials put away and set a timer. Pace yourself to make sure you finish the test with time to spare and go back to check your answers if you have time.

After each test, check your answers. On the questions you missed, be sure you understand why you missed them. Did you misread the question (tests can use tricky wording)? Did you forget the information? Or was it something you hadn't learned? Go back and study any shaky areas that the practice tests reveal.

Taking these tests not only helps with your grade, but also aids in combating test anxiety. If you're already used to the test conditions, you're less likely to worry about it, and working through tests until you're scoring well gives you a confidence boost. Go through the practice tests until you feel comfortable, and then you can go into the test knowing that you're ready for it.

Test Tips

On test day, you should be confident, knowing that you've prepared well and are ready to answer the questions. But aside from preparation, there are several test day strategies you can employ to maximize your performance.

First, as stated before, get a good night's sleep the night before the test (and for several nights before that, if possible). Go into the test with a fresh, alert mind rather than staying up late to study.

Try not to change too much about your normal routine on the day of the test. It's important to eat a nutritious breakfast, but if you normally don't eat breakfast at all, consider eating just a protein bar. If you're a coffee drinker, go ahead and have your normal coffee. Just make sure you time it so that the caffeine doesn't wear off right in the middle of your test. Avoid sugary beverages, and drink enough water to stay hydrated but not so much that you need a restroom break 10 minutes into the test. If your test isn't first thing in the morning, consider going for a walk or doing a light workout before the test to get your blood flowing.

Allow yourself enough time to get ready, and leave for the test with plenty of time to spare so you won't have the anxiety of scrambling to arrive in time. Another reason to be early is to select a good seat. It's helpful to sit away from doors and windows, which can be distracting. Find a good seat, get out your supplies, and settle your mind before the test begins.

When the test begins, start by going over the instructions carefully, even if you already know what to expect. Make sure you avoid any careless mistakes by following the directions.

Then begin working through the questions, pacing yourself as you've practiced. If you're not sure on an answer, don't spend too much time on it, and don't let it shake your confidence. Either skip it and come back later, or eliminate as many wrong answers as possible and guess among the remaining ones. Don't dwell on these questions as you continue—put them out of your mind and focus on what lies ahead.

Be sure to read all of the answer choices, even if you're sure the first one is the right answer. Sometimes you'll find a better one if you keep reading. But don't second-guess yourself if you do immediately know the answer. Your gut instinct is usually right. Don't let test anxiety rob you of the information you know.

If you have time at the end of the test (and if the test format allows), go back and review your answers. Be cautious about changing any, since your first instinct tends to be correct, but make sure you didn't misread any of the questions or accidentally mark the wrong answer choice. Look over any you skipped and make an educated guess.

At the end, leave the test feeling confident. You've done your best, so don't waste time worrying about your performance or wishing you could change anything. Instead, celebrate the successful completion of this test. And finally, use this test to learn how to deal with anxiety even better next time.

Review Video: 5 Tips to Beat Test Anxiety
Visit mometrix.com/academy and enter code: 570656

Important Qualification

Not all anxiety is created equal. If your test anxiety is causing major issues in your life beyond the classroom or testing center, or if you are experiencing troubling physical symptoms related to your anxiety, it may be a sign of a serious physiological or psychological condition. If this sounds like your situation, we strongly encourage you to seek professional help.

Thank You

We at Mometrix would like to extend our heartfelt thanks to you, our friend and patron, for allowing us to play a part in your journey. It is a privilege to serve people from all walks of life who are unified in their commitment to building the best future they can for themselves.

The preparation you devote to these important testing milestones may be the most valuable educational opportunity you have for making a real difference in your life. We encourage you to put your heart into it—that feeling of succeeding, overcoming, and yes, conquering will be well worth the hours you've invested.

We want to hear your story, your struggles and your successes, and if you see any opportunities for us to improve our materials so we can help others even more effectively in the future, please share that with us as well. **The team at Mometrix would be absolutely thrilled to hear from you!** So please, send us an email (support@mometrix.com) and let's stay in touch.

If you'd like some additional help, check out these other resources we offer for your exam:
http://mometrixflashcards.com/TExES